geog.3

geography for key stage 3

< rosemarie gallagher > < richard parish >

OXFORD
UNIVERSITY PRESS

Great Clarendon Street, Oxford OX2 6DP

Oxford University Press is a department of the University of Oxford.
It furthers the University's objective of excellence in research,
scholarship, and education by publishing worldwide in

Oxford New York

Auckland Bangkok Buenos Aires Cape Town Chennai
Dar es Salaam Delhi Hong Kong Istanbul Karachi Kolkata
Kuala Lumpur Madrid Melbourne Mexico City Mumbai
Nairobi São Paulo Shanghai Taipei Tokyo Toronto

Oxford is a registered trade mark of Oxford University Press
in the UK and in certain other countries

© RoseMarie Gallagher, Richard Parish 2002

The moral rights of the authors have been asserted

Database right Oxford University Press (maker)

First published 2002

All rights reserved. No part of this publication may be reproduced,
stored in a retrieval system, or transmitted, in any form or by any means,
without the prior permission in writing of Oxford University Press, or as
expressly permitted by law, or under terms agreed with the appropriate
reprographics rights organization. Enquiries concerning reproduction
outside the scope of the above should be sent to the Rights Department,
Oxford University Press, at the address above

You must not circulate this book in any other binding or cover and you
must impose this same condition on any acquirer

British Library Cataloguing in Publication Data

Data available

ISBN 0 19 913415 4

10 9 8

Acknowledgements

The Publisher would like to thank the following for permission to reproduce copyright material:

Chapter 1 p.4 Jeremy Horner/Corbis UK Ltd; p.6 Charles O'Rear/Corbis UK Ltd (top), Maurice Harvey/Hutchison Library (bottom); p.7 NikWheeler/Corbis UK Ltd.; **Chapter 2** p.8 Jorgen Schytte/Still Pictures (top left), John Isaac/Still Pictures (centre left), Michael MacIntyre/Hutchison Library (bottom left), Chris Caldicott/Still Pictures (top centre), Sarah Murray/Hutchison Library (bottom centre), Ron Giling/Still Pictures (top right), Michael MacIntyre/Hutchison Library (centre right), Ron Gilling/Still Pictures (bottom right); p.9 Jorgen Schytte/Still Pictures (left), Ron Giling/Still Pictures (centre), S. Carmona/Corbis UK Ltd (right); p.10 Jorgen Schytte/Still Pictures; p.11 Jorgen Schytte/Still Pictures; p.12 Corel (all); p.13 Crispin Hughes/Hutchison Library; p.15 B. Apicella/Photofusion Picture Library (centre left); p.15 E. Guigenan-Christian Aid/Still Pictures (left), Ed Eckstein/Corbis UK Ltd (centre right), Harmut Schwarzbach/Still Pictures (right); p.17 Anna Tully/Panos Pictures; p.20 Nick Haslam/Hutchison Library (bottom left), Corbis UK Ltd (bottom right), p.20 Ron Giling/Still Pictures (top); p.21 Liba Taylor/Panos Pictures; p.22 Liba Taylor/Corbis UK Ltd (left), Jean-Leo Dugast/Panos Pictures (centre); p.23 J.C. Tordai/Hutchison Library; p.24 Ron Giling/Still Pictures; p.25 Heine Pedersen/Still Pictures; p.26 Water Aid (top), Peter Turnley/Corbis UK Ltd (centre), Jorgen Schytte/Still Pictures (bottom); p.27 Water Aid; p.28 Mark Edwards/Still Pictures; p.29 Crispin Hughes/Photofusion Picture Library (top), Janis Austin/Photofusion Picture Library (bottom); p.30 Amy Broadstock/Groundwork Methyrn & Rhondda Cynon Taff (all); p.31 Amy Broadstock/Groundwork Methyrn & Rhondda Cynon Taff (all); **Chapter 3** p.32 Tony Lees/Oxford University Press (top left), BMW Oxford Plant (top centre), Peter Olive/Photofusion Picture Library (top right); p.33 Karen Huntt H Mason/Corbis UK Ltd (top left), BMW (bottom left), Michael St. Maur Sheil/Corbis UK Ltd (top), Tony Lees/Oxford University Press (bottom); p.35 Private Collection/Bridgeman Art Library; p.36 Panos Pictures (top), Philip Wolmuth/Panos Pictures (bottom); p.38 Albert Walker Collection/National Coal Mining Museum for England (top), Andrew Hall/Ashfield District Council (bottom); p.39 Kirkby Cyber Centre (left), Andrew Hall/Ashfield District Council (right); p.40 Bohemian Nomad Picturemakers/Corbis UK Ltd (top left), Ken Naylor/Capricorn MCS (bottom left), Christa Stadtler/Photofusion Picture Library (top centre), Rex Features (bottom centre), Ed Kashi/Corbis UK Ltd (top right), Jeremy Sutton Herbert/Rex Features (bottom right); **Chapter 4** p.42 Dave G. Houser/Corbis UK Ltd (top left), Charles O'Rear/Corbis UK Ltd (centre left), Ray Roberts/Rex Features (bottom left), Larry Lee Photography/Corbis UK Ltd (top right), Owen Franken/Corbis UK Ltd (centre right), p.42 Owen Franken/Corbis UK Ltd (bottom right), Steve Wood/Rex Features (centre); p.43 Karl Weatherly/Corbis UK Ltd (top left), Edward Holub/Corbis UK Ltd (bottom left), GailMooney/Corbis UK Ltd (top centre), Philippe Schuller/Editing/Panos Pictures (bottom centre), Marc Garanger/Corbis UK Ltd (top right), Associated Press (bottom right); p.44 Annie Griffiths Belt/Corbis UK Ltd (left), Franz-MarcFrei/Corbis UK Ltd (right); p.48 Patrick Gripe/Editing/Panos Pictures (top left), Adam Woolfitt/Corbis UK Ltd (bottom left), Roger Ressmeyer/Corbis UK Ltd (top right), Owen Franken/Corbis UK Ltd (centre right), Stéphane Gautier/Editing/Panos Pictures (bottom right); p.52 Susan Anthony (all); p.54 CNES, 1993 Distribution Spot Image/Science Photo Library (A), Corel (B,C,D,J), Carlos Freire/Hutchison Library (G), Véronique Paul/Editing/Panos Pictures (K); p.55 Sarah Murray/Hutchison Library (centre left), Hutchison Library (left), Sarah Murray/Hutchison Library (centre right), Jacques Graf/Editing/Panos Pictures (right), Nigel Dickinson/Still Pictures; p.56 Owen Franken/Corbis UK Ltd (left), Photothèque Epamarne/EPAMarne / EPAFrance - Establissements Publics d'Aménagement de Marne-La-Vallée (right); p.57 Photothèque Epamarne/E.Morency, 1998/EPAMarne / EPAFrance - Etablissements Publics d'Aménagement de Marne-La-Vallée (all); p.58 David Turnley/Corbis UK Ltd (left), Drew Gardner/Rex Features (right); p.60 Andrew Hall, Ashfield District Council (top left), Philip Wolmuth/Panos Pictures (bottom left), Peter Turnley/Corbis UK Ltd (top right), Enzo & Paolo Ragazzini/Corbis UK Ltd (bottom right); **Chapter 5** p.62 Mark Mason/Oxford University Press; p.64 Don Ryan/Associated Press (top left), George Hall/Corbis UK Ltd (centre left), Daniel O'Leary/Panos Pictures (bottom left), Getty Images (top centre), Duomo/Corbis UK Ltd (bottom centre), Getty Images (top right), Panos Pictures (bottom right), Irene Siegt/Panos Pictures (centre), Mark Mason/Oxford University Press p.66 Corel; p.67 Toby Adamson/Still Pictures; p.68 Chris Stowers/Panos Pictures (top), Paul A. Souders/Corbis UK Ltd (bottom); p.69 Martin Sookias/Oxford University Press; p.70 Anna Clopet/Corbis UK Ltd (top), David Gibson/Photofusion Picture Library (bottom); p.72 Paul A. Souders/Corbis UK Ltd (top left), Bettmann/Corbis UK Ltd (centre left), Lito C. Uyan/Corbis UK Ltd (bottom left), Charles O'Rear/Corbis UK Ltd (top right), Paul A. Souders/Corbis UK Ltd (centre right), Paul A. Souders/Corbis UK Ltd (bottom right); p.73 Donald Stampfli/Associated Press (top), Joerg Boethling/Still Pictures (bottom); p.74 Anders Gunnartz/Panos Pictures (top left), Harmut Schwarzbach/Still Pictures (centre left), David Reed/Panos Pictures (bottom left), Ron Giling/Still Pictures (top right), Mike Williams/Peak Pictures (centre right), Catherine Karnow/Corbis UK Ltd (bottom right); p.75 Paul A. Souders/Corbis UK Ltd (top), David Turnley/Corbis UK Ltd (centre), Robert Maass/Corbis UK Ltd (bottom); **Chapter 6** p.76 Kennan Ward/Corbis UK Ltd (bottom left), Mark Henley/Panos Pictures (left), Stephanie Maze/Corbis UK Ltd (top centre), Jeremy Horner/Hutchison Library (bottom centre), Jeremy Horner/Corbis UK Ltd (bottom right), Henryk T. Kaiser/Rex Features (top), John Isaac/Still Pictures (centre); p.78 Martin Rogers/Corbis UK Ltd (top left), Paul A.Souders/Corbis UK Ltd (top right), Paul Harrison/Still Pictures (bottom); p.80 Henryk T. Kaiser/Rex Features (top), Mark Mason/Oxford University Press (bottom); p.81 Mark Mason/Oxford University Press; **Chapter 7** p.82 Jim Zuckerman/Corbis UK Ltd; p.83 Michael T. Sedam/Corbis UK Ltd; p.85 Thomas Raupach/Still Pictures (top left), Getty Images (bottom left), Getty Images (top right), Bob Krist/Corbis UK Ltd (centre right), Sean Holmes/Eye Ubiquitous/Corbis UK Ltd (bottom right), Deutsche Presse Agentur (bottom); p.86 Bob Edwards/Science Photo Library; p.88 Stumpf/Sipa/Rex Features (bottom left), Deutsche Presse Agentur (bottom centre), Natalie Fobes/Corbis UK Ltd (bottom right), Reuters/Popperfoto (top); p.89 Deutsche Presse Agentur; p.90 Peak Pictures (top), Peter James Millar/Science Photo Library (bottom); p.92 Mike Williams/Peak Pictures (left), Peak Pictures (right); p.94 Peak Pictures; p.95 Mike Williams/Peak Pictures; p.96 Peak Pictures; p.97 Peak Pictures; p.98 Roland Seitre/Still Pictures; p.99 Bettmann/Corbis UK Ltd; p.100 Roland Seitre/Still Pictures (bottom left), Leonard de Selva/Corbis UK Ltd (bottom right), Michael Nicholson/Corbis UK Ltd (top); p.101 Galen Rowell/Corbis UK Ltd; p.102 M. Sewell/Peter Arnold Inc./Still Pictures (centre left), NASA (centre), Roland Seitre (top), Norbert Wu/Still Pictures (centre right), Godard Space Flight center Scientific Visualization Studio/NASA (bottom); p.103 Vincent Bretagnolle/Still Pictures (top), Fred Hoogervorst/Panos Pictures (centre), Chris Sattleberger/Panos Pictures (bottom); **Chapter 8** p.104 Reinhard Janke/Still Pictures; p.108 Rex Features; p.110 Paisajes Españoles (top left), Paisajes Españoles (top right), David Cumming/Eye Ubiquitous (bottom); p.112 Rex Features, James Davis Worldwide; p.114 Jan Butchofsky-Houser/Corbis UK Ltd (top), RoseMarie Gallagher (bottom); p.115 Kevin Schafer/Corbis UK Ltd (top), Kevin Schafer/Corbis UK Ltd (centre), Michael S. Yamashita/Corbis UK Ltd (bottom); **Chapter 9** p.116 Mark Mason/Oxford University Press (top, bottom left & centre,), Dave Caulkin/Associated Press (bottom right/background); p.119 Chaumussy/Sipa-Press/Rex Features (top left), Corel (bottom left), Lawrence Migdale/Science Photo Library (top centre), JohnHulme; Eye Ubiquitous/Corbis UK Ltd (bottom centre), Mike Jackson/Still Pictures (top right), Liba Taylor/Panos Pictures (bottom right), Mark Mason/Oxford University Press (top).

The Ordnance Survey map extracts on pages 32, 95 and 108 are reproduced with the permission of the Controller of Her Majesty's Stationery Office © Crown Copyright.

The map extract on page 53 is reproduced with the permission of Michelin Editions du Voyage. The population map on page 46, by Olivier Belbéoch, is reproduced with permission of Editions Magnard, Paris.

Illustrations are by Stefan Chabluk, Richard Deverell, Karen Donnelly, Roger Fereday, John Hallett, Richard Morris, David Mostyn, Mike Nesbitt, Colin Salmon, Mike Saunders.

The publisher and authors would like to thank all the individuals and organizations who have helped during research for this book. In particular, and in topic order:

Tamsin Maunder and other staff of WaterAid; Amy Broadstock of the Taff Bargoed Community Park Project, Wales; Kate Kilpatrick, Oxfam; Michael Busby; The Coal Authority; Andrew Hall, Economic Development Officer for Ashfield District Council, Nottinghamshire; Mary Gill, Centre Manager of Learn@ Kirkby Cyber Centre, West Nottinghamshire College; Susan Anthony; EPAMARNE (the Development Agency for Marne-la-Vallée); Alex 'Walter' Middleton; Michael Gallagher; the International Coffee Organization; Eric Sprokkereef and the International Commission for the Hydrology of the Rhine basin (CHR); Andrew Ashe; Omar Farooque; Mick Nisbet of Penwith District Council, Cornwall; Natty Bayo of the Spanish Embassy Education Office; Patricia Barnett and Tourism Concern, London.

We would like to thank our excellent reviewers who have provided thoughtful and constructive comments: Anna King, Phyl Gallagher and John Edwards.

We would also like to thank Janet Williamson for both general and specific contributions to the *geog.123* course.

Information has been drawn from many sources. We would like to acknowledge in particular: the Peak District National Park website, the British Antarctic Survey *Antarctic* schools pack, and an article about jeans in the Guardian of 29th May 2001.

Every effort has been made to contact copyright holders of material reproduced in this book. Any omissions will be rectified in subsequent printings if notice is given to the publisher.

Printed in Italy by Rotolito Lombarda.

Contents

1 Get the picture!

1.1 Still nosy? 4
1.2 Picture practice 6

2 Development

2.1 A glimpse of Ghana 8
2.2 This is poverty … 10
2.3 What exactly is development? 12
2.4 How developed is Ghana? 14
2.5 Mapping development around the world 16
2.6 How did the development gap grow? 18
2.7 So what are Ghana's problems? 20
2.8 The problem of Third World debt 22
2.9 Akosombo: Ghana's big dam 24
2.10 Small is beautiful 26
2.11 Poverty in the UK 28
2.12 Development on your doorstep 30

3 Earning a living

3.1 Economic activity 32
3.2 The changing pattern of economic activity 34
3.3 The rise and fall of the coal industry 36
3.4 When an industry declines 38
3.5 The growth of new industries 40

4 Focus on France

4.1 Bienvenues en France 42
4.2 What's France like? 44
4.3 So where is everyone? 46
4.4 The economic geography of France: part 1 48
4.5 The economic geography of France: part 2 50
4.6 Letter from Langy 52
4.7 The Paris problem 54
4.8 The new towns around Paris 56
4.9 France in the world 58
4.10 More about the European Union 60

5 Global fashion

5.1 Walter's global jeans 62
5.2 Behind the swoosh 64
5.3 Why go global? 66
5.4 A fashion victim? 68
5.5 Global actions, local effects 70
5.6 Is globalisation a good thing? 72
5.7 Against globalisation 74

6 Coffee break!

6.1 Coffee break! 76
6.2 Bitter coffee 78
6.3 Fair trade for coffee growers 80

7 Local actions, global effects

7.1 Planet Earth, your home … 82
7.2 Case study 1: The Rhine 84
7.3 Case study 1: The Rhine is dead … 86
7.4 Case study 1: Long live the Rhine! 88
7.5 Case study 2: Britain's National Parks 90
7.6 Case study 2: The Peak District 92
7.7 Case study 2: Castleton calling 94
7.8 Case study 2: Conflicts in the Peak District 96
7.9 Case study 3: Antarctica 98
7.10 Case study 3: The history of Antarctica 100
7.11 Case study 3: Antarctica today 102

8 Tourism – good or bad?

8.1 Introducing tourism 104
8.2 The UK on holiday 106
8.3 Holiday at home: St Ives 108
8.4 Beautiful Benidorm? 110
8.5 Gambling with Gambia? 112
8.6 Towards sustainable tourism 114

9 Your passport to the world

9.1 You, citizen of the world 116
9.2 Going places with geography 118

Key for OS maps 120

Map of the British Isles 121
Map of Europe 122
Map of Ghana 123
Map of the world (political) 124

Glossary 126
Index 128

Still nosy?

A good geographer must be nosy. Just like a good detective!
Remember the kinds of questions you can ask …

And here are some of the answers, for this photo …

- The place is just off the coast of Weligama, a fishing village in Sri Lanka, in the Indian Ocean.
- These are the stilt fishermen of Weligama, who perch sitting or standing for hours on their wooden poles, catching fish to sell.
- Men have fished like this, in this beautiful place, for generations.
- But when *these* men look back at the shore, they may see a line of cameras – because now they're a tourist attraction!

Stuck for questions?

A detective must ask *smart* questions, to find out what's going on.
So must you, in geography. But sometimes it is hard to think of them.
The **development compass rose** will help.

What is the development compass rose?

It is a question framework to help you find out about people and their lives. It is based on the compass:

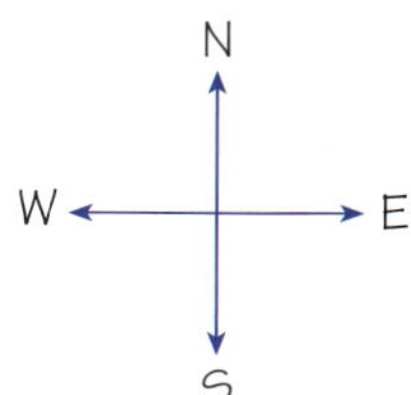

▲ *The normal compass points.*

N for Natural

Questions about the environment (air, soil, water, climate, wildlife) and how people are affecting it.

For example, for the photo opposite:

◆ *Does this sea get stormy?*

W for Who decides?

Questions about who's in charge, who makes decisions, who gains, who loses. Like these:

◆ *Do the fishermen need permission to fish here?*

◆ *Do they work together as a group?*

E for Economic

Questions about money, earning a living, poverty, pay, and where the profits go.
Like these:

◆ *How much can the stilt fishermen earn a day?*

◆ *Is it enough for their families to live on?*

S for Social

Questions about how people live, and how their society behaves. Like these:

◆ *Why do they fish this way around here (but nowhere else in Sri Lanka)?*

◆ *Is it bad for the fishermen's health?*

Asking questions for each compass point will help you get the full picture.

Your turn

1 a   **The stilt fishermen of Weligama**

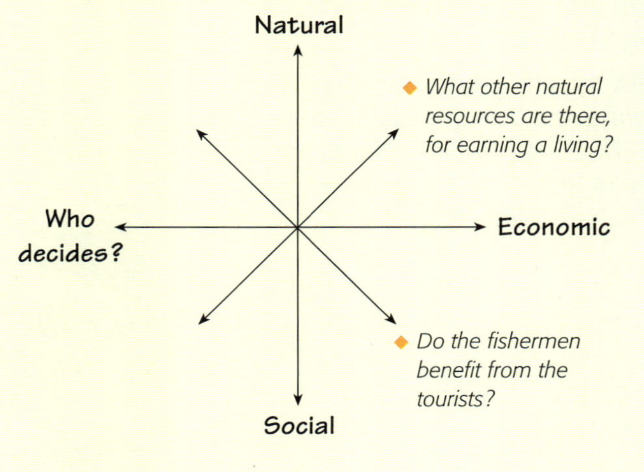

Make a *large* copy of this simple development compass rose (DCR) above. Don't forget the title.

b Write in *four* questions for each compass point, for the fishermen. (Okay, you can copy some of ours.)

2 A challenge! The DCR on the right has 'in-between' questions to explore links between areas. Write *at least one* 'in-between' question of your own, for each section of your DCR for **1**. (In a different colour?)

Picture practice

Homes come in all shapes and sizes, from caves to castles.

The three photos in this unit all show homes. We give some information for each photo. Then you have to think up questions about the people. So get ready to get nosy!

This shows a young woman of the Ndebele tribe (*In-dib-elly*) outside an Ndebele painted home in South Africa.

The homes are always painted by the women, and the patterns give clues about the family, its history and its wealth.

This tradition began around 1883, when the Boers (Dutch immigrants) seized the land from the Ndebele and made servants of them. House painting was a kind of protest, and a way for the tribe to assert itself.

▶ *An Ndebele woman and her home.*

Like to live life on a boat?
Like the thousands of Chinese on these **junks** (houseboats) in a harbour in Hong Kong.

They belong to the Tanka and Hoklo tribes, who've lived on these waters for thousands of years.

Some rear pigs and ducks and chickens on their boats. Many of the older people have *never* set foot on land.

But the Hong Kong government wants the boat people to move to housing estates on land, and there are big plans to develop the harbour for tourism.

▶ *Junks in Aberdeen harbour, Hong Kong.*

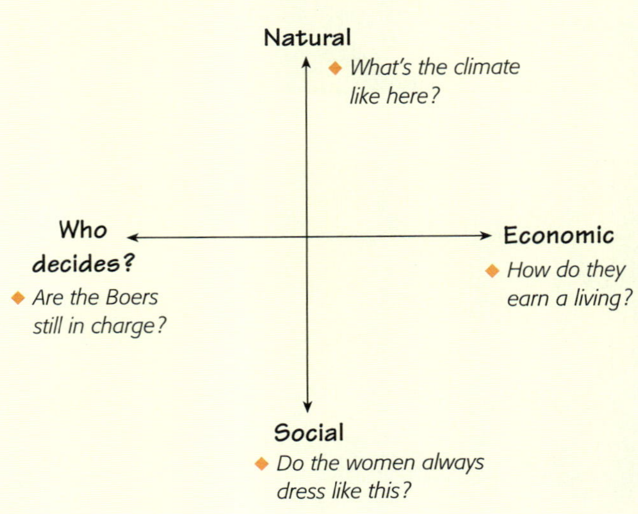

▲ *Marsh Arabs and their reed homes.*

In the wetlands of southern Iraq, these Marsh Arabs live in homes of plaited reeds, on islands built from reeds, like their people have done for more than 5000 years.

But now the Marsh Arabs face a grim future, for the wetlands are drying out and turning to desert. This is partly because some are being drained for farming. And partly because of all the dams (over 30 of them) that have been built on the two big rivers that feed the wetlands.

Your turn

1 a A development compass rose (DCR) for photo **1** is shown on the right. Make a larger copy.
  b Now think of other questions you could ask about the Ndebele and write them on your rose.
  Try for *at least two* questions each for N, S, E and W. Write answers where you can, in a different colour.

2 Now do the same for the Chinese people living in the junks in photo **2**. (Please don't just repeat your questions from **1**.)

3 You are a leader of the Marsh Arabs (photo **3**), and you are worried about their future. On a DCR, write questions you'd try to answer, to help your people.

4 You can use a DCR about changes in your own area.

LOCAL SCHOOL TO CLOSE!

The council plans to close your school and turn it into luxury homes. Draw a DCR and use it to write down as many questions as you can about the proposal.

The Ndebele and their lives

5 Now choose one of your DCRs and try to make up a question for each in-between direction.

A glimpse of Ghana

Welcome to Ghana, the tropical country joined to the UK by history and the prime meridian. Where you'll find …

▲ … *a warm welcome for visitors …*

▲ … *some great wealth …*

▲ … *a great sense of style …*

▲ … *tropical rainforest to explore …*

▲ … *gold and diamond mines …*

▲ … *outdoor markets everywhere …*

▲ … *traditional ceremonies and rituals …*

▲ … *music, dancing, laughter …*

▲ … *hundreds of small rural villages …*

▲ … *millions living in poverty …*

▲ … *and a passion for football.*

It's an LEDC

Almost 20 million people live in Ghana. About 6 million of them live in great poverty. Compared with many countries, Ghana is poor. It is a **less economically developed country** or **LEDC** for short.

▲ *Ghana's flag.*

Your turn

1 Where is Ghana? Use these words and terms in your answer: ocean, meridian, West Africa, tropic, equator.

2 Name the countries that border Ghana. (Page 123.)

3 Using the map on page 123, write a paragraph about Ghana's *physical* features. (For example is it mountainous? What about lakes? Rivers? The coast?)

4 Ghana has three main climate zones. They are shown on this map – but the key is not complete!
   a Make a larger copy of the map and key.
   b Using the information in the map, shade in the climate zones to match the shading in the key.
   c The vegetation depends on the climate. Now colour in the three empty boxes and the map to show the three types of vegetation.

5

Some statistics	Ghana	UK
Area (thousands of sq km)	245	240
Population (millions)	20	60
% in rural areas	62	10
Life expectancy (years)	58	77

Using this table to help you, write a paragraph comparing Ghana and the UK. Give the *population density* for each country in your answer. (Glossary?)

6 a Ghana is an *LEDC*. What do the letters stand for?
   b What evidence can you see in the photos, that Ghana is an LEDC? (Give the photo numbers.)

This is poverty …

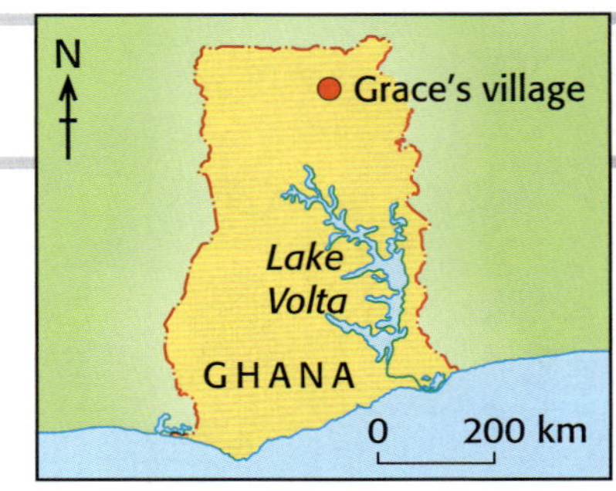

Like other LEDCs, Ghana has some very wealthy people. And millions of very poor people. Poverty is greatest in rural areas.

A day in the life of Grace

So you want to know what it's like to be poor?

I lie here on my straw mat, staring up into the darkness. My baby lies beside me, snuffling in her sleep. And over there on the mud floor my four other living children, all curled up together. Out in the yard, in their graves, the two dead ones. My firstborn died when she was three, and the youngest boy last year. How I cried when I buried them.

I lie here thinking about my problems. First, my husband. A good man. He works hard, and is always thinking of ways to make our lives better. Two months ago he went to Kumasi to find work. 'We will buy a goat with the money' he said, 'and send the eldest boy to primary school.' But I have had no message from him. He could be ill, or in trouble.

And the farm. The rains were poor last season. Out in our tiny field the millet is dry and stunted. Enough to feed us for two months, perhaps. What then? In the darkness I can feel my savings, tied in the corner of my cloth. Nineteen thousand cedis. If any of the children fall ill, that won't even be enough for medicine.

I could sell something – but what? You could count our possessions in seconds. Three enamel bowls. Two metal plates. The cooking pot. The water bucket. The kerosene lamp made from a bottle. The wooden pestle for pounding the millet. One machete. One hoe. Two small knives. A fork. A torch with no bulb. Two mats. And a few bundles of worn clothing.

But today is a new day. Soon I will rise and slip out to the clump of bushes behind the huts, which is the village toilet. Like the other women I go while it is still dark, for privacy. And at daybreak I will set off to get water. The river is nearly dry now, so the water will be very muddy and dangerous. It killed my children. But what can I do?

It takes me over an hour to get to the river, and longer to get back with my heavy bucket. I will give the children a little water to drink. I will breastfeed the baby. Then I will go to the farm to tend the millet and pick what's ready. And all day long I will hope that someone from the village will come running with a message from my husband.

While I am away my eldest daughter will pound millet. The eldest boy will go looking for firewood – every day a little further. Towards dusk we will eat our one meal for the day: millet porridge. At 6 it will get dark, as usual. I want to save the little kerosene that's left. So we will go to bed early, as usual – and, as usual, still hungry.

So, this is poverty. It takes all my energy to cope with it. But we will survive, and I will find a way to create a better future for my children.

▲ *Grace with two of her children.*

Did you know?

◆ A child dies every 10 seconds, somewhere in the world, from a disease carried by dirty water.

Did you know?

◆ Ghana's currency is the cedi.
◆ 10 000 cedis = £1 in 2001.

▲ *Grace's village. All her friends are poor, like her, but working hard to create a better future.*

Your turn

1 a List the items Grace has for her kitchen.

b Now list the things in your kitchen.

2

Time spent on tasks in Grace's household	
Task	**Minutes**
A preparing dinner (pounding and boiling millet, making a sauce)	200
B getting water (from the river)	170
C sweeping the compound (yard) and hut	45
D washing clothes (at the river)	200
E washing up (one meal a day)	20
F obtaining fuel (firewood)	120

a Make a table like this for these tasks in *your* household. (Change what's in the brackets.)

b Now draw a suitable graph to compare the times for these tasks in your household and Grace's.

c For which task is the time difference greatest? Why?

d For which is it least? Why?

e In total, how much longer is spent on these six tasks in Grace's household than in yours? How might this affect Grace and her family?

3 Grace lives in great poverty. Draw a spider map to show what poverty means, for her. You could start like this.

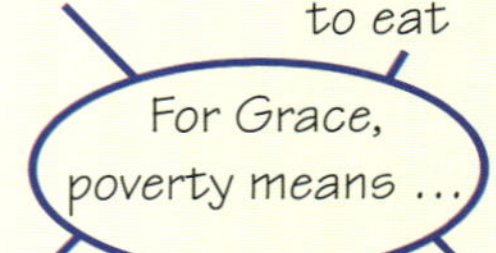

4 Like Grace, 40% of the people in Ghana do not have access to clean safe water. Why not? Draw a development compass rose like the one on the right, and add more questions you could ask, to find out.

5 You'd like to help the people of Grace's village. You can provide money and equipment to help them to:

A install a village pump, giving clean safe water

B read and write (so Grace can write to her husband)

C fit solar cells to the hut roofs, so they can have electric lighting

D build a latrine (a concrete toilet where the waste drains away into the ground)

a Which do you think Grace would like first? Why? Write down all the benefits it would bring.

b Arrange the four projects in order of priority, from Grace's point of view.

c Who should have most say in deciding about the projects, you or the villagers? Give your reasons.

Many in Ghana don't have access to clean safe water

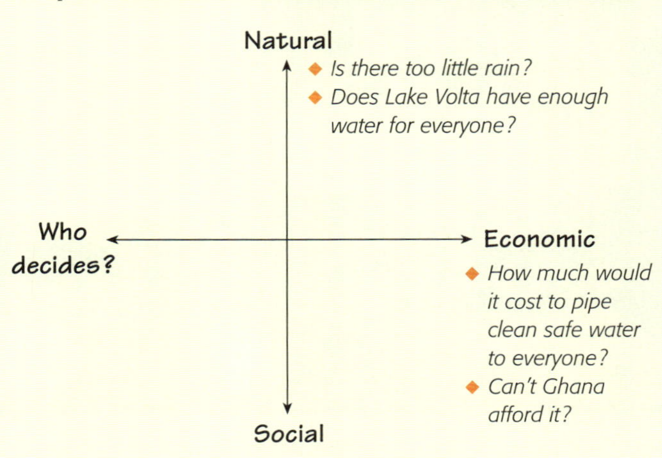

What exactly is development?

Development is a process of change and growth. But it is not just about getting richer, or having more things. It is about **improving the quality of life for people**. So it has many different aspects.

Some changes get called development but are *not* for the better! They may benefit a few people, but make life worse for many others.

Everybody's doing it

All countries strive to develop. But some are further along than others.
Some are developing very slowly – or even going backwards.

Your turn

1 To develop a country takes money. For example it costs a lot to provide a clean water supply for everyone. From page 12, write down:
   a four other changes you think would cost a lot
   b two that may need people to change their attitudes
   c two that may need a government to pass new laws

2 The aspects of development on page 12 are not all equally important to everyone. Arrange these in what you think is their order of importance for Grace:
   A the chance to live a long and healthy life
   B freedom from poverty
   C finding ways to live more sustainably

3 From Grace's point of view, which of these might not be 'good' developments for Ghana?
   a a stunning new palace for the president
   b ten new hi-tech war planes
   c a solar-powered public phone in every village

4 This photo shows Saravejo in Bosnia, during the Balkans war in the 1990s. War can halt the development of a country, or even reverse it. Explain why. You can give your answer as a spider map.

5 What aspects of development do you think the UK needs to work at? Write a letter to the Prime Minister giving your list, and your reasons.

How developed is Ghana?

To find out how developed Ghana is, you need to ask questions like these:

We use different **development indicators** to answer these questions. For example **life expectancy** is how long people can expect to live, in years.

GDP per capita

At first people thought about development in terms of money and wealth. So they used an **economic** indicator: GDP per capita.

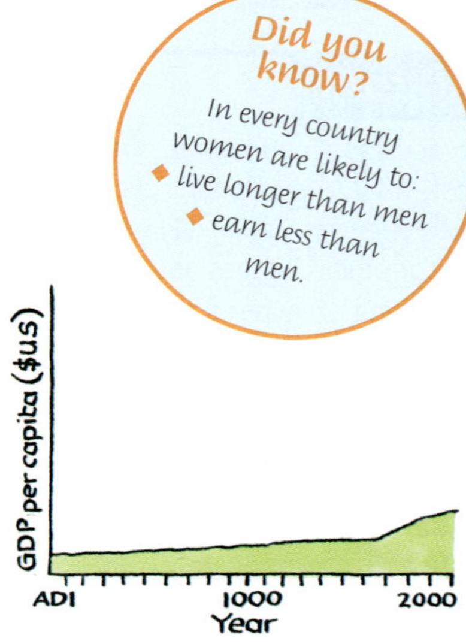

GDP or **gross domestic product** is the total value of the goods and services a country produces in a year. (It's given in US dollars.)

GDP per capita is what each person in the country would earn if this amount were shared out equally. (It never is!)

As a country develops it produces more goods and services. So the country's GDP per capita rises over the years.

But GDP per capita gives only part of the picture. It does not tell us whether a country provides clean safe water, or good health care, for example. So we need **social** indicators too, such as life expectancy.

Your turn

1 Page 14 shows questions you could ask, to find out how developed a country is. This box shows some development indicators.

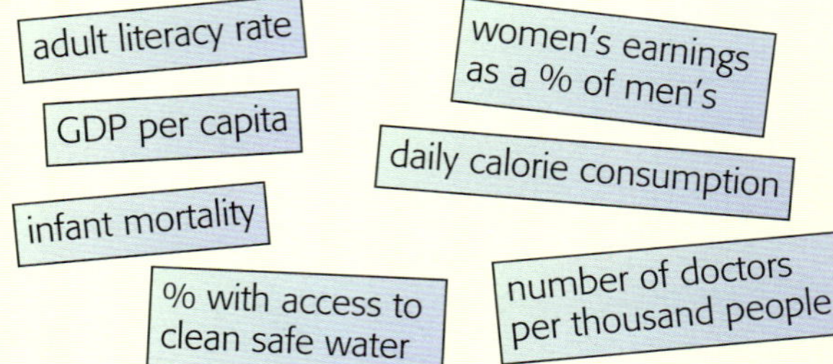

Write out each of the eight questions from page 14. After each question, write the matching development indicator. (If you need help, try the glossary!)

2 Now you will compare development in Ghana and three other countries.

a First make a table like this one.

	Ghana	UK	Brazil	India
		Score for ...		
Life expectancy	1	4		
Infant mortality				
Enrolment in primary school				
Access to safe water				
GDP per capita				
Total score				

b Now look at the data for the four baby girls below. Using this data, give each country a score 1–4 for each indicator. (This has been started for you.) The country with the *best* result each time gets 4.

c Find the total score for each country.

d Of the four countries, which appears to be: the most developed? the least developed?

3 The **human development index** or **HDI** gives a quick way to compare countries. It combines data for GDP per capita, life expectancy, adult literacy, and enrolment in education, to give each country a score between 0 and 1. The higher the better!

Human development index (HDI), 1998

Australia	0.929	Kenya	0.508
Bangladesh	0.461	Mali	0.380
Brazil	0.747	Nigeria	0.439
China	0.710	Pakistan	0.522
France	0.917	Saudi Arabia	0.747
Germany	0.911	Spain	0.899
Ghana	0.556	Trinidad	0.793
India	0.563	UK	0.918
Japan	0.924	USA	0.929

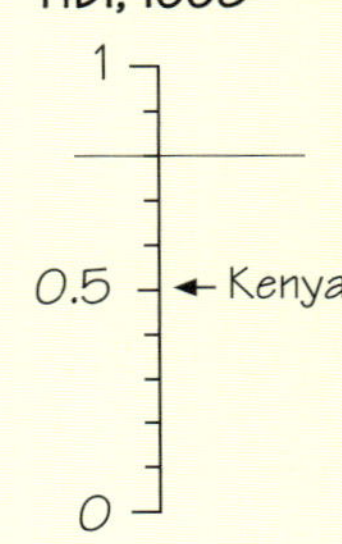

a Draw a vertical scale like this – but much longer. Use a full page. (Graph paper?)

b Mark in each country from the table above, on your scale.

c Now draw two horizontal lines, cutting the scale at 0.8 and 0.5 as started here.

d Above 0.8 = high human development. From 0.5 to 0.8 = medium human development. Below 0.5 = low human development.

 i Shade each group of countries (high, medium and low HDI) on your scale. Use a different colour for each and add a key for your shading.

 ii To which group does Ghana belong?

 iii To which group does the UK belong?

4 So how developed is Ghana? Write down your conclusions, and evidence to support them.

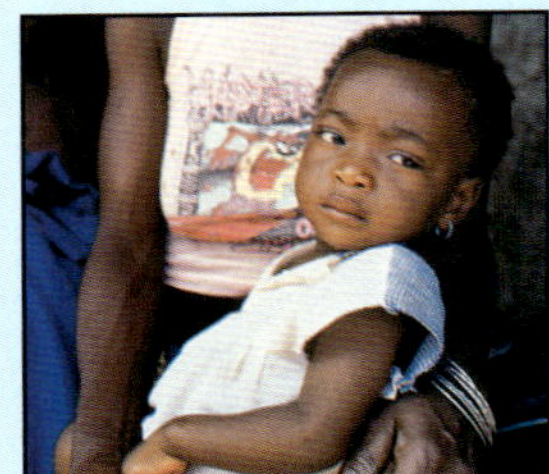
Akosua, Ghana
Life expectancy: 62
Chances of –
 dying before age 5: 6.7%
 going to primary school: 68%
 a safe water supply: 65%
GDP per capita: $1980

Molly, UK
Life expectancy: 80
Chances of –
 dying before age 5: 0.6%
 going to primary school: 100%
 a safe water supply: 100%
GDP per capita: $25 580

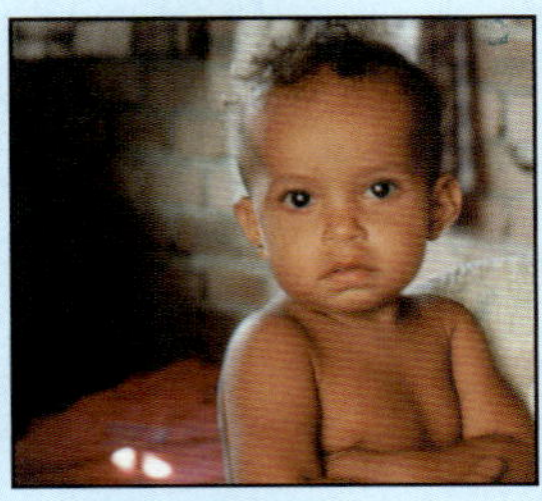
Maria Teresa, Brazil
Life expectancy: 71
Chances of –
 dying before age 5: 3.6 %
 going to primary school: 93%
 a safe water supply: 76%
GDP per capita: $9480

Prema, India
Life expectancy: 63
Chances of –
 dying before age 5: 6.9%
 going to primary school: 76%
 a safe water supply: 81%
GDP per capita: $2990

Mapping development around the world

The world is an unequal place. This map shows just how unequal!
It shows the **real GDP per capita** for different countries.
Real means it takes into account the different prices of things in
different countries. So it gives a truer picture of how much money
people have to live on, on average.

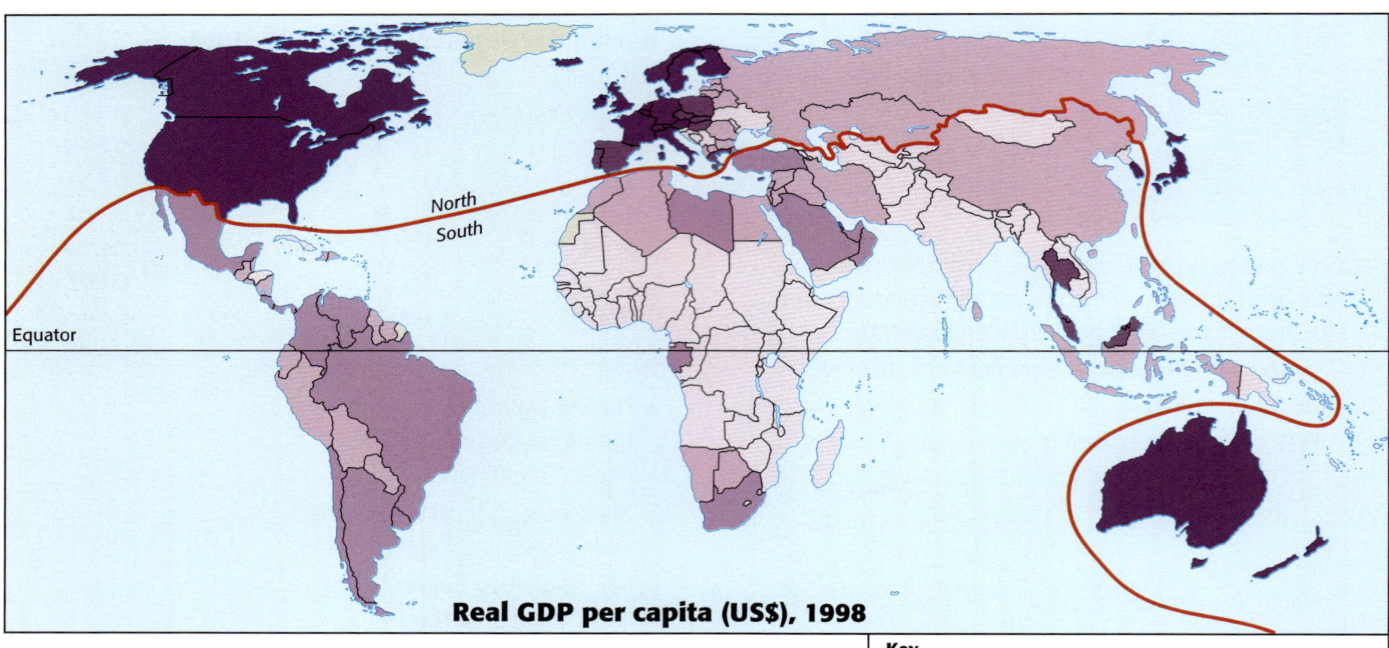

As you can see, there is a big difference in wealth
around the world. Note how the richest countries are
clustered together. So are the poorest countries.

Many different labels are used for the richer and
poorer groups of countries. Here are the main ones.

Rich North, poor South

Look at the red line on the map
above. The richest countries in
the world are above the line.
The poorest are mostly below it.

- So the richer countries are
  often referred to as the
  rich North (though some are
  south of the equator).

- The poorer countries are
  often referred to as the **poor
  South** (though some are in
  the northern hemisphere).

MEDC / LEDC

- The poorer countries are also
  called **less economically
  developed countries** or
  LEDCs. (You met this earlier.)

- The richer countries are called
  MEDCs. (What does that
  stand for?)

The Third World

- The poorer countries are
  sometimes called the **Third
  World**.

- At the start, this term meant
  poor countries that were not
  Communist.

Did you know?

- In the past, most of the
  Third World was colonised
  by other countries.
- That's one reason why it
  is still poor – and
  they're rich!

What were the other two worlds?

- The Second World meant
  the Communist countries.
  (China is the main one left.)

- The First World meant the
  richer nations.

Those terms are not used now.

More about the LEDCs

Some LEDCs are very large, like India. Some are very small, like Trinidad. But they tend to have quite a lot in common.

But in some LEDCs, such as South Korea and Brazil, industry has been growing fast. These are called **newly industrialised countries** or **NICs**.

How did the development gap grow?

As you have seen, many countries are very poor. The gap between the rich and poor countries is one of the world's biggest problems. But how did it happen?

There are three kinds of reasons.

1 Historical reasons

Most of the world's poor countries were once taken over or **colonised** by European countries, who wanted raw materials.

It started with friendly trading for things like gold, tobacco, timber, spices – and even slaves. But as time went by the Europeans grew greedier …

… and took over their trading partners by force. They took raw materials from them, and sold them finished goods – and that made many Europeans very rich!

In time, they were forced out. But they left behind countries with little or no industry, education, or skills – and often with a great deal of unrest.

Many of these colonised countries are still recovering.

2 Environmental reasons

These are to do with the natural environment. For example:

Some countries have very few natural resources they can trade to earn money for development. (But some deserts do have oil!)

In some countries the climate makes life difficult. For example rainfall may be unreliable so it is hard to grow crops.

Some have the opposite problem – too much rain, and severe floods. Years of hard work just get washed away.

3 Socio-economic reasons

These are a combination of **social** and **economic** reasons. (Glossary?)

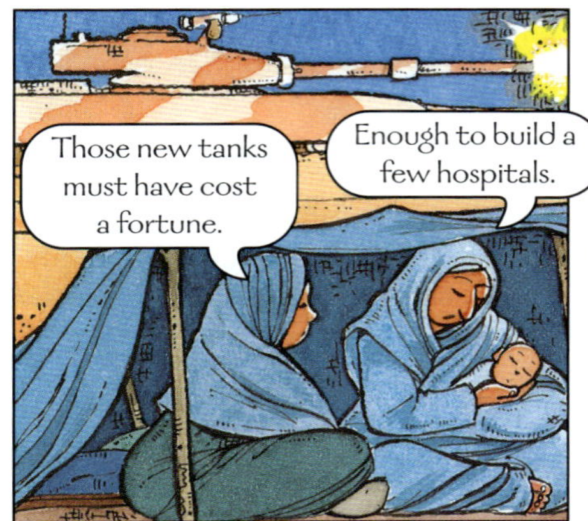

Many poor countries have wars going on, with much money and energy wasted in fighting.

Poor countries have few industries, so have to import most of the manufactured goods they need.

Most poor countries have borrowed a lot of money. Much of the money they make goes to pay back loans.

Most poor countries are striving hard to develop – but as you can see they face some enormous difficulties.

Your turn

1 a First, make a larger copy of this Venn diagram.

  b Now look at fact **A** below. Could it help to explain why a country is less developed? If *yes*, write the letter **A** in the correct place in your Venn diagram. (If you think it belongs to more than one loop, write it where they overlap.)

  c Repeat step **b** for each of the other facts **B – N**.

    A It is mostly stony desert.

    B It has plenty of copper to export but the price of copper has fallen sharply over the years.

    C It was a British colony for more than 50 years.

    D It is really mountainous and hard to reach.

    E A tribal war has been going on there for years.

    F The people who colonised it built no factories.

    G Millions of its people are suffering from AIDS.

    H There are few schools so people can't learn the skills the country needs.

    I It suffers serious flooding almost every year.

    J Bacteria and viruses that cause disease love its warm damp climate.

    K In the past, several million of its healthy adults were sold as slaves.

    L A small group of people owns most of its wealth.

    M Other countries refuse to trade with it, because of its politics.

    N It has to repay millions of dollars a year on loans.

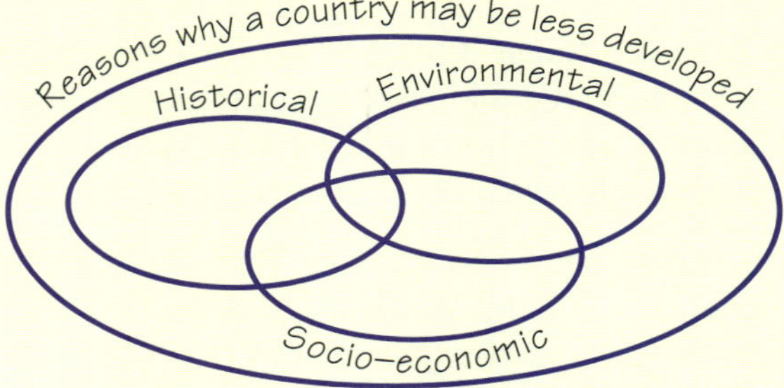

2 Now write down ten reasons why a country (like the UK) may be *more* developed. Label them 1 – 10. Then show them on a Venn diagram like the one above.

3 What do you think this cartoon is about? Write a paragraph explaining its message.

So what are Ghana's problems?

Ghana has many natural resources, including gold and diamonds. It's the world's second largest producer of cocoa (used in chocolate). Its people work hard. But 3 out of 10 of them live in deep poverty. Let's look at some reasons for this.

A little history

The first Europeans to arrive at the coast of Ghana are the Portuguese, in 1471. They find a group of kingdoms of different tribes. And gold in the soil! They quickly begin trading for it, in exchange for cloth, knives, beads, mirrors, rum and guns.

News spreads, and eventually Dutch, Danish, German and British traders arrive too. The British call the land the **Gold Coast**.

But by 1650, the **slave trade** has become more important than gold. The Europeans need workers for their plantations in the Americas. They buy over 100 000 people a year from the Gold Coast. The local tribes start fighting each other, to capture people to sell.

Bit by bit, Britain takes control of all the trade, and then the country. By 1901 all of the Gold Coast is a British colony. Its kingdoms and tribes are forced together to make a single unit.

The British ship gold, metal ores, diamonds, ivory, pepper, timber, corn and cocoa from the Gold Coast. They pay the local people very little for these valuable materials. They build railways to transport them to the coast. They build some roads, schools and hospitals too, but the people have to pay for these through taxes.

By 1945 the people have had enough. They are being exploited. They want their freedom. The British must go! At last, in 1957, the Gold Coast gains independence, and changes its name to Ghana. A free country – but with no factories, few services, and few people with the skills to run it. (And that wasn't even 50 years ago.)

▲ *Cocoa beans for chocolate. Ghana exports over 300 000 tonnes of cocoa beans a year.*

Did you know?
- West African tribes had slavery long before the Europeans arrived.
- They sold criminals and captured enemies to North African traders.

▲ *The fort at Elmina from which many slaves were shipped. It was owned in turn by the Portuguese, Dutch and British.*

▲ *These slaves were shipped to North America, and are being sold to plantation owners in an auction.*

Two environmental problems

In the south, much of Ghana's rainforest has been destroyed in the last 20 years – mostly by logging companies for timber, some by farmers for land to grow cocoa, and some for firewood. The exposed soil is soon useless.

And up in the north, parts of the savanna have turned into dusty desert. This is called **desertification**. The causes include drought, the chopping down of trees, heavy grazing, and erosion of bare soil by wind and rain.

Ghana depends mainly on farming. So soil is an important resource. Ruined soil means fewer crops, and fewer animals. And that means less food for poor farmers and their families.

Two economic problems

Cocoa is Ghana's most important export. But its price has fallen. By 2000 it was only a third of the 1980 price. So Ghana is earning less and less from cocoa, while its imports grow more and more expensive.

Ghana has also borrowed a lot of money. So it has to pay out a large amount of **interest** each year – which means less money for development.

Did you know?

◆ Only a quarter of Ghana's tropical rainforests are left.

▲ *A farm in the savanna in northern Ghana, at risk of desertification.*

Your turn

1 You have to draw a time line for Ghana.

a On a large sheet of paper draw a vertical time line from 1450 up to 2000. Make it 30 cm long if you can. (Use two pages?)

b On your line mark in events from the text **and** the event box below. (Small neat writing!) Add a title.

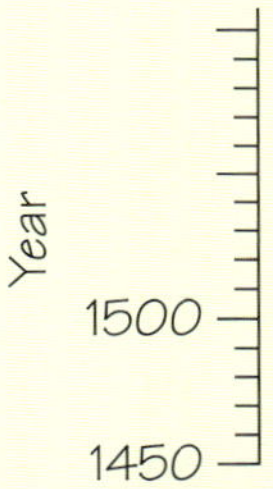

2 Beside your time line shade the period in which:

a West African slaves were bought by Europeans

b the Gold Coast was partly or wholly a British colony

3 Now underline the events that you think:

a *helped* Ghana to develop, in one colour

b *held back* its development, in another colour

c *did a mixture of both*, in a third colour.

4 Add a key for your colours and shading for **2** and **3**.

5 Choose *one* event you underlined for **3c** above, and explain why you underlined it.

6 'Since independence, Ghana's development has been completely under its own control.' Do you agree with this statement? Give your reasons, in 70–100 words.

EVENTS

- 1878: a Ghanaian brings back cocoa plants from Fernado Po, an island off Africa
- 1898–1927: railways built by the British
- 1928: a large harbour built at Takoradi
- 1980: economy almost collapses due to low cocoa price and other problems
- 1885: the first cocoa exported to Britain
- 1999: crisis in Asia and Russia causes world chocolate sales to fall
- 1830: the world's first chocolate bars made in England by J S Fry and Sons
- 1817: slavery abolished in Europe
- 1528: chocolate drink from the Aztecs introduced to Europe, by Spanish explorers
- 1502: first slave ship leaves West Africa
- 1807: Britain starts campaign to stop the slave trade
- 1618: first British trading settlement set up on the Gold Coast
- 1993: Ghana earns $222 million from selling rainforest timber
- 1657: London's first drinking chocolate café opens
- 1965: the Akosombo dam completed, to provide Ghana with hydroelectricity
- 1874: Britain takes control of the south of the Gold Coast
- 1949: campaign for independence starts
- 1983: Ghana has to pay back loans of $1.5 billion to other countries

The problem of Third World debt

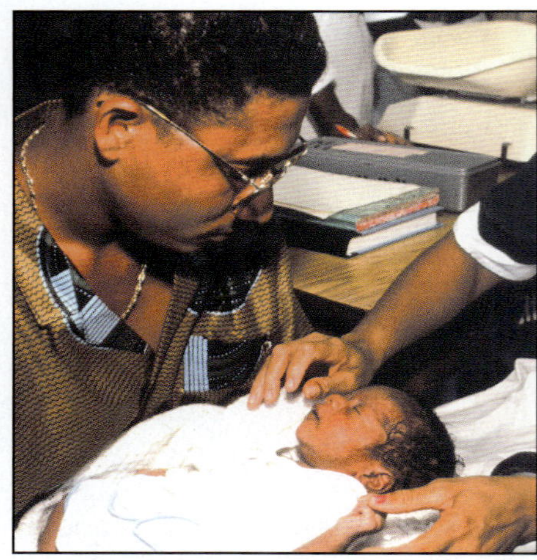

This is Patience from Ghana. She is just one week old. And like everyone in Ghana, she already owes $105 to other countries.

This is Tuan from Vietnam, 14 years old. He's got nothing. But like everyone else in Vietnam, he owes $92 to other countries.

This is Juana from Bolivia. She lives on less than $1 a day. But like everyone in Bolivia she owes $320 to other countries.

These three do not owe the money in person. Their governments owe it on their behalf. Such **debt** is a major problem for Third World countries.

How the debt arose

Poor countries want to develop fast – but that needs money, and they don't have much.

They do get some aid from richer countries. (Often 'tied' to promises.)

But aid is not enough. Over the years they have had to borrow. From **other governments** …

… or the **World Bank** (a joint bank set up by governments of over 180 countries) …

… or the **International Monetary Fund (IMF)**, a joint fund set up by governments for short term loans.

In the past they have even got loans from **High Street banks**, for projects.

The result

If you borrow a lot of money, but don't earn much, it means trouble!

The lenders want **interest** on the loan every year, and the loan paid back on time. Which means that …

… much of the money the country earns each year is used to pay its debts.

There's not enough left for schools and hospitals and all the other things the country badly needs.

Tackling the problem

It is clear that many countries will never be able to escape poverty, because of their debts.

So some groups in richer countries are putting pressure on their governments to **cancel** Third World debts. There is also pressure on the World Bank and IMF to reduce the interest they charge.

Ghana and some of the other **heavily indebted** countries have already had part of their debt cancelled. In return they have promised to use the money to help their poorest people.

▲ *The pressure is on …*

Your turn

1 When you take out a loan you have to pay *interest*. What does that mean? (Glossary?)

2 a Draw a circular flowchart with 6 large boxes. (Like the one on the right, but use a full page.)

b Write steps **A–F** in the boxes, *in the correct order*, to show how a country can slide further into debt.

c Give your flowchart a title.

  A So it borrows more money.

  B So it does not earn as much as it had hoped.

  C The next year the country sells crops and minerals to other countries, as usual.

  D And it has to pay a lot of interest on its loans …

  E But the prices for these have dropped again.

  F … which leaves it short of money for imports, and for development projects.

3 Ghana is *heavily indebted*. What does that mean?

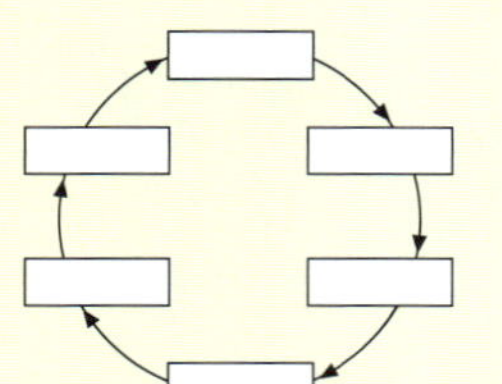

Did you know?

♦ In 1977 Mali (in Africa) paid out over $70 million for its debts.

♦ That's enough to have built it a good health service.

4 Look at these two people. Whose side are you on? Write a speech (at least a minute long) to try to change the *other* person's mind.

Akosombo: Ghana's big dam

When richer countries help poorer countries, it is not only out of kindness. Who has gained from Ghana's Akosombo dam?

The story behind the dam

When Ghana got its independence in 1957 it was in a hurry to develop. It wanted factories, schools, hospitals, roads, new homes. All this needs energy. And Ghana had the answer: the River Volta! A dam could be built on it to give **hydroelectricity**.

Dams cost a fortune. Ghana had no money. But it got loans from the World Bank and the UK, and a large loan from the USA. As part of this deal, an American company called Valco got the right to produce aluminium in Ghana, using electricity from the dam:

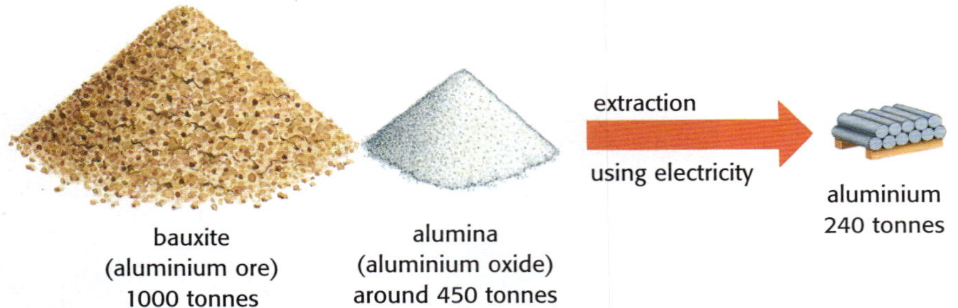

Ghana was happy because it has a lot of bauxite. It promised Valco cheap electricity for 50 years. This is what Ghana hoped would happen:

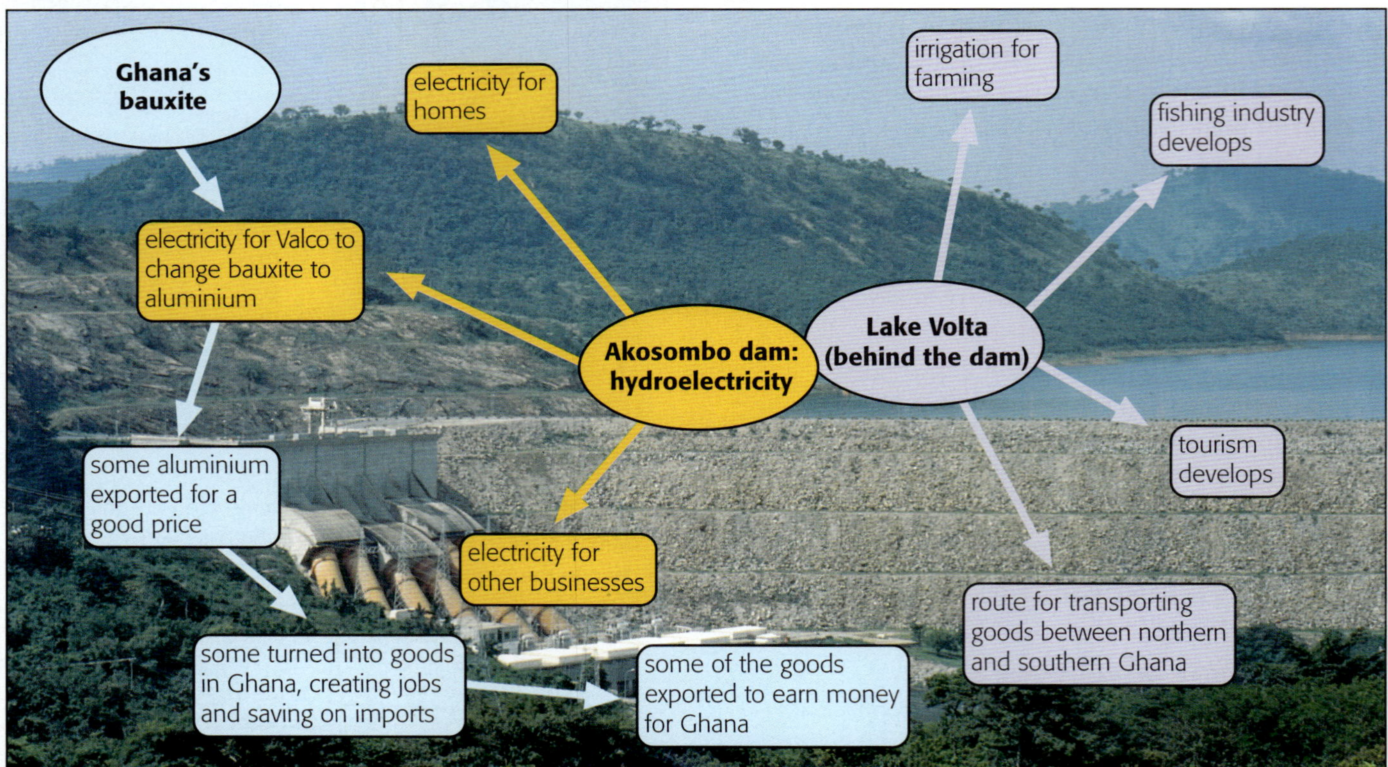

Over 80 000 people were moved from their farms and villages to make way for the Akosombo dam. Its giant lake drowned 4% of Ghana. (Look at the map on page 123.) It was completed in 1965.

The dam today

The electricity from the dam has helped Ghana to develop.
But many Ghanaians now feel they are being cheated.

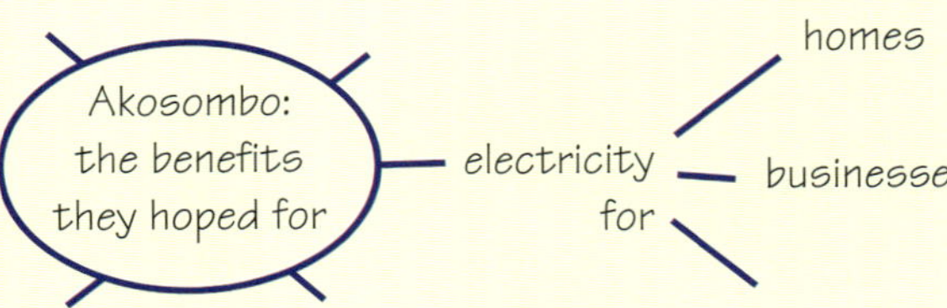

Your turn

1 What is *hydroelectricity*?

2 Draw a spider map to show how Ghana hoped to benefit from the Akosombo dam. Start like this:

> Akosombo: the benefits they hoped for — electricity for — homes / businesses

3 The diagram on page 24 shows what Ghana hoped would happen. Draw a diagram to show what actually *did* happen. (You *could* copy that one and cross bits out, and add notes in a different colour.)

4 'The Akosombo dam is an example of successful development.' Do you agree? Give your reasons.

5 Page 24 shows steps in making aluminium. This map shows Valco's aluminium route. Suggest reasons why:
   a it does not produce the aluminium in Jamaica
   b it changes the bauxite to alumina in Jamaica
   c It does not ship the bauxite to its USA plants.

6

> From: Form 3A, Accra High School
>
> To: The Chief Executive, Valco
>
> Valco, please go home. You are not helping Ghana to develop, in any way. In fact you are holding us back. We need all our own electricity.

Reply to this e-mail. Explain that if Valco had not promised to buy lots of electricity, Ghana could not have built the dam. You would use Ghana's bauxite if there was a railway to bring it from Kibi. (See the map on page 24.) Then come up with a fair proposal.

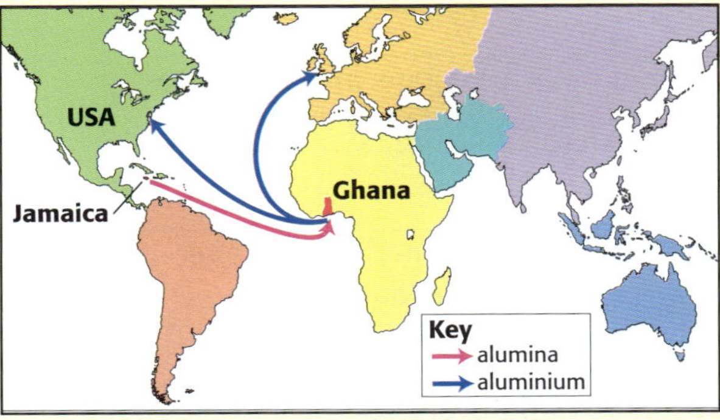

Small is beautiful

Development is not just about big expensive projects.

Ghana's water problem

◀ Like a drink of this?

This is Napoga. She thinks she is 12, but she does not know for sure. And this is her family's water supply, for drinking, cooking and washing. She has been here collecting water for over three hours already.

The water in the bucket looks very muddy. But far worse than the mud are the things you can't see: bacteria that cause diarrhoea, typhoid, and cholera; and tiny eggs that grow into worms inside you, leading to bilharzia and other diseases.

Development little by little

Napoga is not alone. Around 7 million Ghanaians have no access to clean safe water. One day everyone in Ghana will have piped water. But that could be years away. People can't wait. So, right now, many villages are digging wells for themselves with help from a UK charity called WaterAid. Everyone in the village gets involved:

WaterAid supplies the know-how, the materials for lining the well, and the pump.

⬇

Villagers form a committee to decide where the well will be, and organise the work.

⬇

Everyone in the village joins in to help clear the site, and dig, and carry soil away.

⬇

Some villagers are trained to look after the well and carry out repairs.

Cost of a hand-dug well: about £1200.
Cost of Akosombo dam: over £130 million (in 1960).

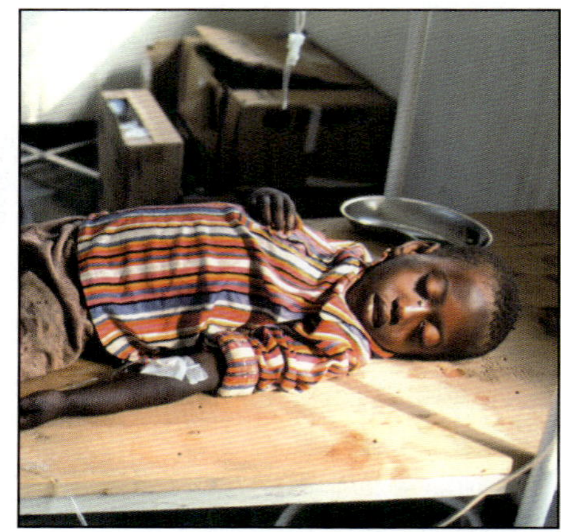

▲ This boy has cholera, one of the many diseases caught from dirty water.

▲ Everyone helped build the well, and everyone benefits.

The difference a well makes

Wells don't bring just clean water!
When Assibi (below) and other villagers were
asked how the wells had benefited them,
this list shows what they said.

The changes we noticed

- A more young people go to school
- B teachers happier to stay in the villages to teach
- C much less illness, so less spent on medicine
- D women potters can produce more pots
- E more people cooking food to sell
- F more people selling iced water
- G no more quarrels with neighbouring villages about water
- H people take more pride in the village
- I cooked foods look much better
- J visitors can be offered clean drinking water
- K clothing and homes kept cleaner
- L much less time taken to fetch water
- M less far to walk for water, so less tired

Your turn

1 This diagram shows a hand-dug well, and pump.
  a Draw a larger simpler version of it.
  b Then write the labels below in the correct places.
  (There are just *some* leader lines to help you.)

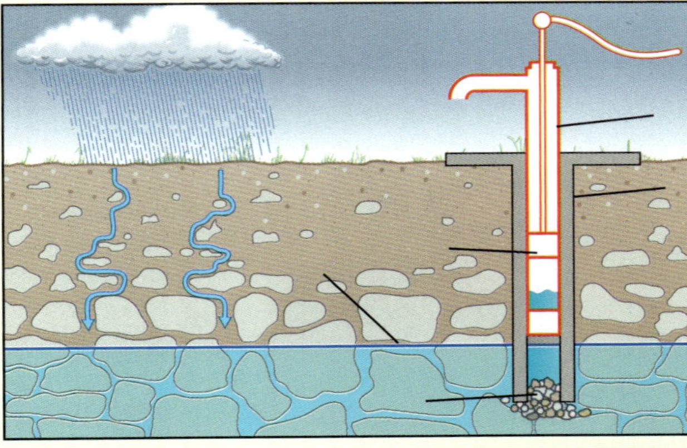

| rain soaks down to form groundwater | the pump | pushing the handle down draws water up the pipe |

| the water table (the top of the groundwater) | groundwater fills all the spaces in the rock | hand-dug well lined with concrete and steel |

| the water passes through valves in these plates | soil and rock filter the water, helping to keep it clean |

2 You are the chief of Napoga's village. You plan to get
a hand-dug well for your village.
  a Draw a large development compass rose and write
  in questions to help you think about your idea.
  For example two questions might be:
  How high is the water table here?
  Who decides where the well will go?
  b Write in any answers you can, below your questions,
  in a different colour.

3 Now look at the list of changes **A – M** above.
  a Draw a larger copy of this diagram.

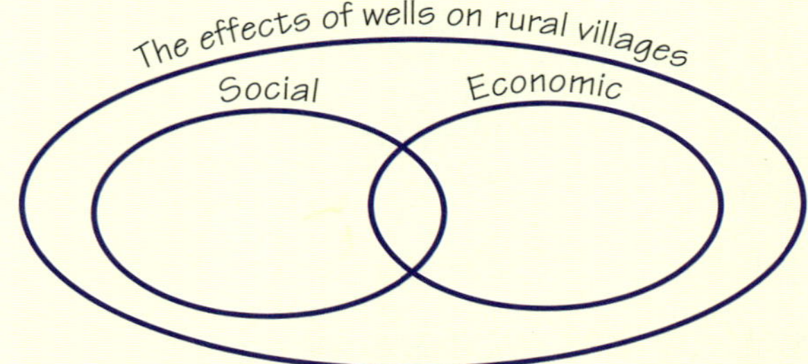

  b Write letters **A – M** where you think they should go.
  (Glossary?) At least one where the loops overlap!
  c Choose one change that you placed in the overlap
  and explain why it belongs there.

4 These are some of the signs of 'good' development:
  A Local people have a big say in the decisions.
  B It benefits local people.
  C It does not ruin the environment.
  Do you think the well in the photo on page 26 is an
  example of good development? Explain.

5

Dear Sir,

I am really fed up getting letters from charities, asking
for money for projects for less developed countries.

We should look after our own people and let other
countries look after theirs.

Yours

I M Seething

This appeared in today's paper. Think about it.
Then write a reply to fax for tomorrow's paper.
No more than 130 words, or the editor will cut!

Poverty in the UK

The UK is richer than most countries – but it has plenty of poverty.

Wealthy Britain – but for whom?

It's Saturday, and Julie is out shopping. But she is not enjoying it. After paying her bills, she has just £32 left to feed herself and her three children for the next week. She will go to the cheapest shops, and hunt for the cheapest food. She'd like to get a present for her son's birthday. But no – that would mean someone going hungry. And a birthday party? Out of the question.

Julie is not alone. According to a new survey, over a quarter of British households are poor. The researchers estimate that:

- about 9.5 million adults in the UK can't afford to keep their homes warm enough, or damp-free, or in good repair
- about 8 million can't afford at least one essential household item, such as a fridge or phone
- over 6.5 million adults can't afford essential clothing, for example a warm waterproof coat
- about 4 million adults can't afford to eat properly
- about 4 million children go without at least one essential item such as adequate clothing, or a healthy diet, or things needed for school.

(Adapted from newspaper articles, September 2000)

▲ *Nothing left for luxuries.*

Saved by the welfare system?

Julie has no job, so she earns nothing. But she gets payments from the government, because Britain is a **welfare state**.

That means it supports people to help them stay out of poverty. This is how the system works.

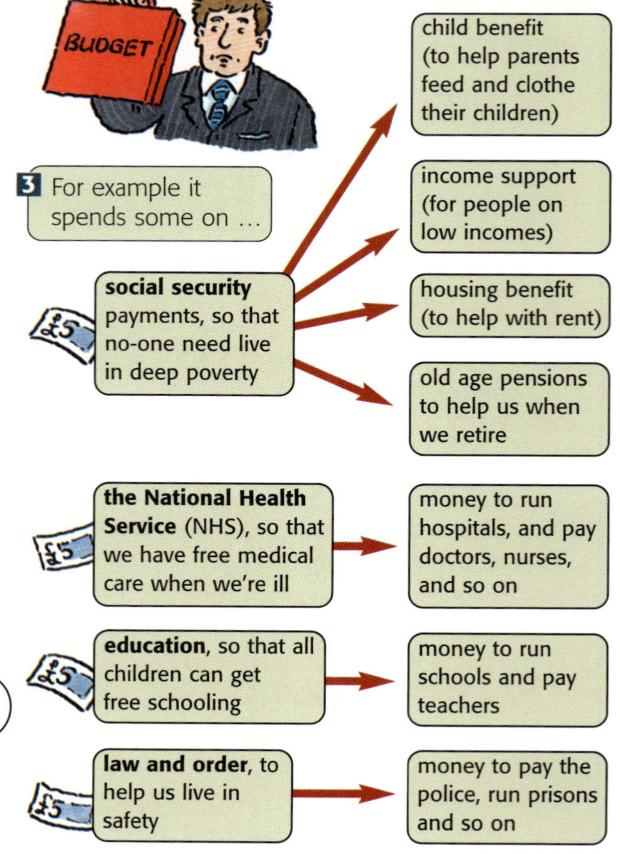

Poverty: relative or absolute?

Grace on page 10 lives in **absolute poverty**. She does not have basic resources such as clean water, a toilet, or enough food.

Julie lives in **relative poverty**. She is not nearly as poor as Grace, but she is poor relative to most people in the UK. She is too poor to take part properly in society. Without the welfare system, she and many other people in the UK could slide into absolute poverty.

▲ *Goody, pension day again.*

1 There is quite a lot of poverty in the UK. Think of some reasons for this. You could give your answer as a spider map or on a development compass rose.

2 The government gives Julie child benefit, income support and housing benefit.
   a Where does it get the money for this?
   b Suggest some reasons why it gives this kind of help to people.
   c The government of Ghana does not pay benefits to poor people. Give reasons.

3 **How our taxes were spent in 2000**

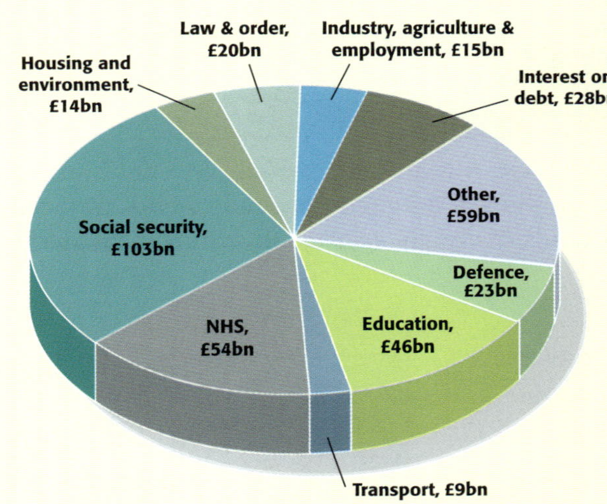

   a What was the total amount spent?
   b i What was the largest share spent on?
     ii About what % of the total was spent on this?
   c There was about ___ times as much spent on education as transport.
   d What % of the total was spent on the NHS?
   e Look at the other items. Does any of them surprise you? Explain why.

4 Now think about this suggestion.
Is it a good idea?
Explain your answer.

5
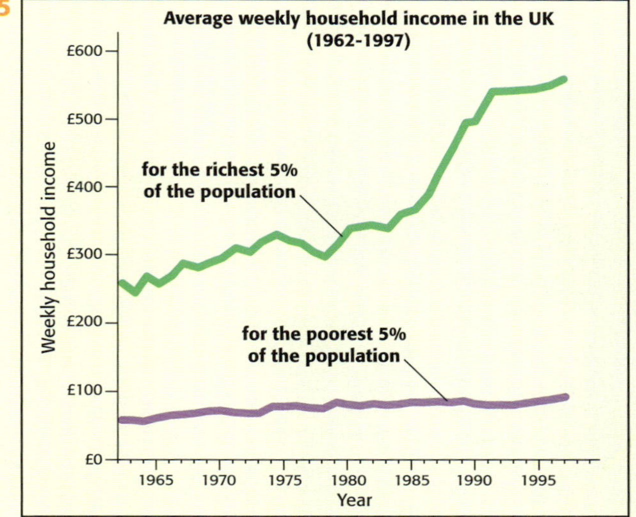

   a Look at the graph above. What data does it show?
   b About how much did the poorest 5% of households earn a week in 1997, on average?
   c About how much did the richest 5% earn?
   d What can you say about the income of the poorest 5%, from 1961 to 1997?
   e What happened to the gap between the richest and poorest households, as the years went by?
   f If this trend continues, it might cause problems. Suggest some problems it could cause.

6 Thousands of children in the UK don't have properly fitting shoes, or enough warm clothes, or a healthy diet. Many thousands don't get to go on holiday.

You are the Chancellor of the Exchequer, in charge of government spending. Write a memo to the Prime Minister with your plans for putting an end to child poverty.

Development on your doorstep

Development is about change for the better. Not just in poor countries, but right on your own doorstep.

Transforming the Taff Bargoed valley

In 1992 the future looked very bleak for the Taff Bargoed valley, home to ten thousand people in Wales. 'What can we do?' they asked. 'Our collieries have closed down. Our jobs have gone. Our shops have shut. And just look at the place – black with coal dust, and grime everywhere.'

The three collieries of the Taff Bargoed valley closed between 1989 and 1993. This was Deep Navigation, the second to close. Look at the scarred landscape.

By 2001, just 8 years later, the colliery sites had become the Taff Bargoed Community Park, attracting thousands of visitors. (*Bar-goed* rhymes with *void*.)

How did it happen?

A local branch of an organisation called Groundwork teamed up with the local people, to bring the area back to life. These were the aims:

◆ The area had to be developed in a **sustainable** way, helping both the local people and the environment.

◆ The development had to create **new jobs**.

◆ The local people (including young people like you) had to have a **say** in the decisions.

After lots of discussion, they decided on a short-break holiday centre, with a world-class climbing wall as the star attraction. But what about money? Groundwork managed to get £12.38 million in grants from the National Lottery (via the Millennium Commission), the Welsh Development Agency, the European Union, the Coal Authority, and other bodies.

The Taff Bargoed Community Park covers 50 hectares. It has already transformed the area, and there's more on the way. For example an ice wall where you can practice climbing on ice, and a youth shelter planned by young people for their own activities.

The park is expected to bring in over £1.2 million a year to the area. Training courses have been run for local young people (for example in catering) to help them get jobs in it.

▼ *The climbing wall.*

▲ *This is how the river used to look, because of mining. But now …*

▲ *… reeds clean the water by piping oxygen down to the 'cleaning' bacteria.*

▲ *Making picnic benches for the park.*

Your turn

1 Why were the people of Taff Bargoed fed up in 1992?

2 The Taff Bargoed Community Park is an example of *redevelopment* on a *brownfield* site. The site had been used for *collieries*. Explain each term in italics. (Glossary?)

3 The Taff Bargoed Community Park has something for everyone. Look at the map. Which *three* features do you think will appeal most to:
  a parents with toddlers?   **b** disabled people?
  c people who like keeping fit? **d** senior citizens?
  e serious climbers?   **f** teenagers like you?

4 Now draw a development compass rose for the project. At each compass point write a short paragraph. For example at E you could say who paid for the project, and how it can help local people earn a living. (Bed and breakfast for visitors? Campsites?)

5 Compare the Taff Bargoed project with a hand-dug well project in Ghana (page 26). In what ways are they similar? List these as bullet points. (Think about the role of the local people, where the money came from, the effects on the community …)

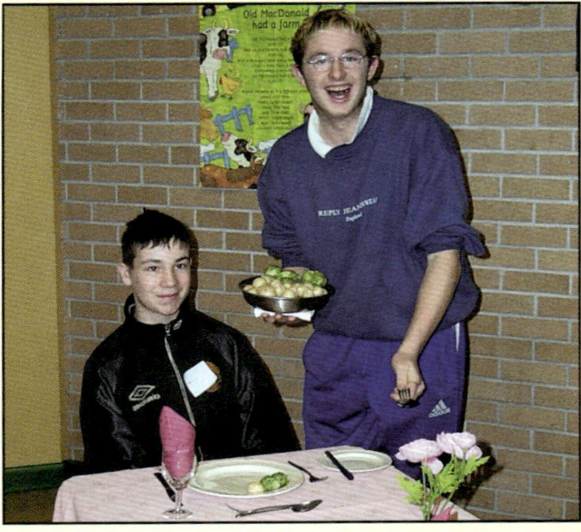

▲ *Practising service with a smile.*

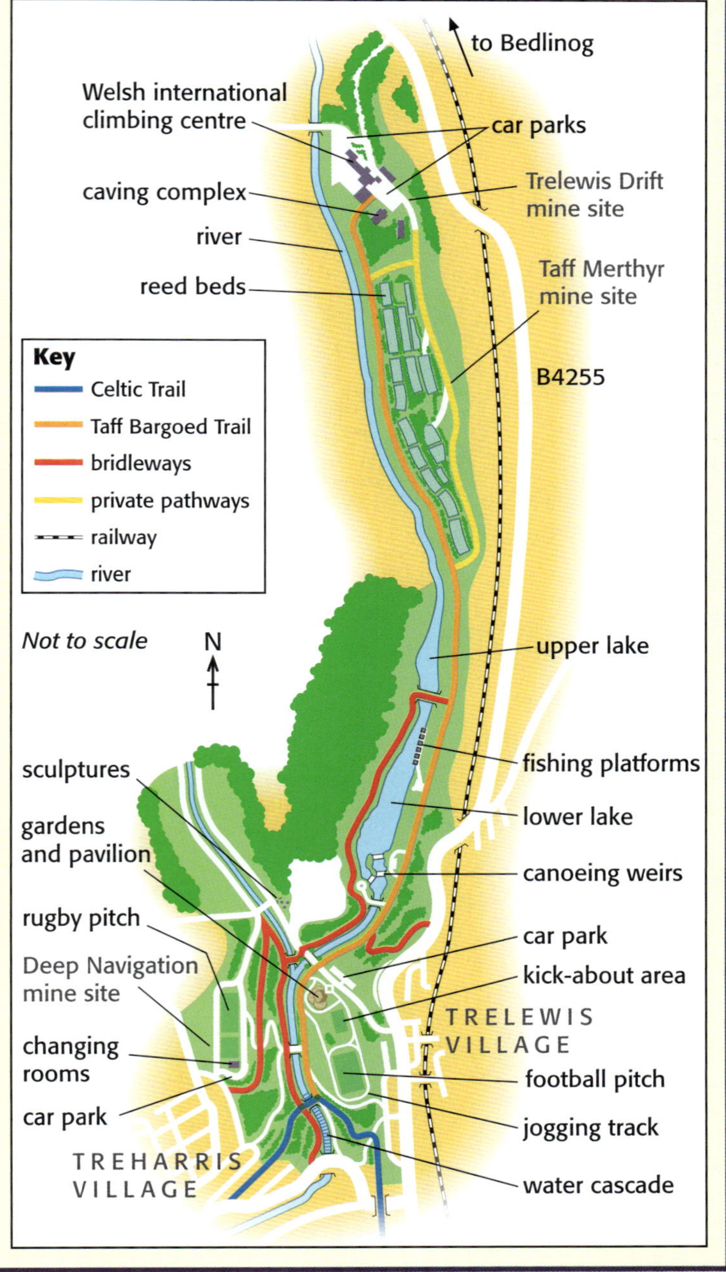

Economic activity

26 million people in the UK are engaged in **economic activity**. That means they are working for pay. Here are three of them:

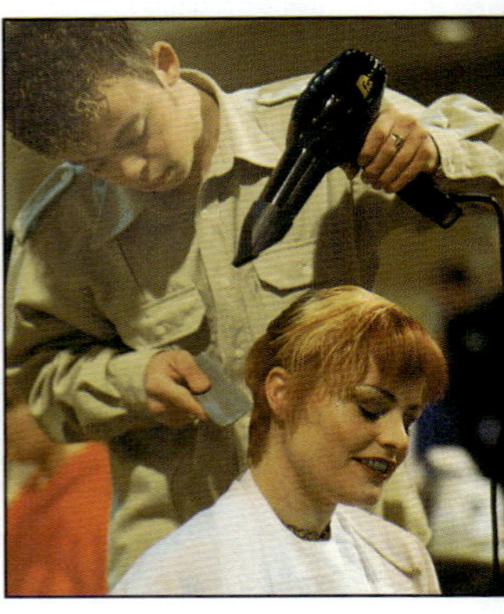

All three work on the edge of Oxford (along with several thousand other people) in the area shown below:

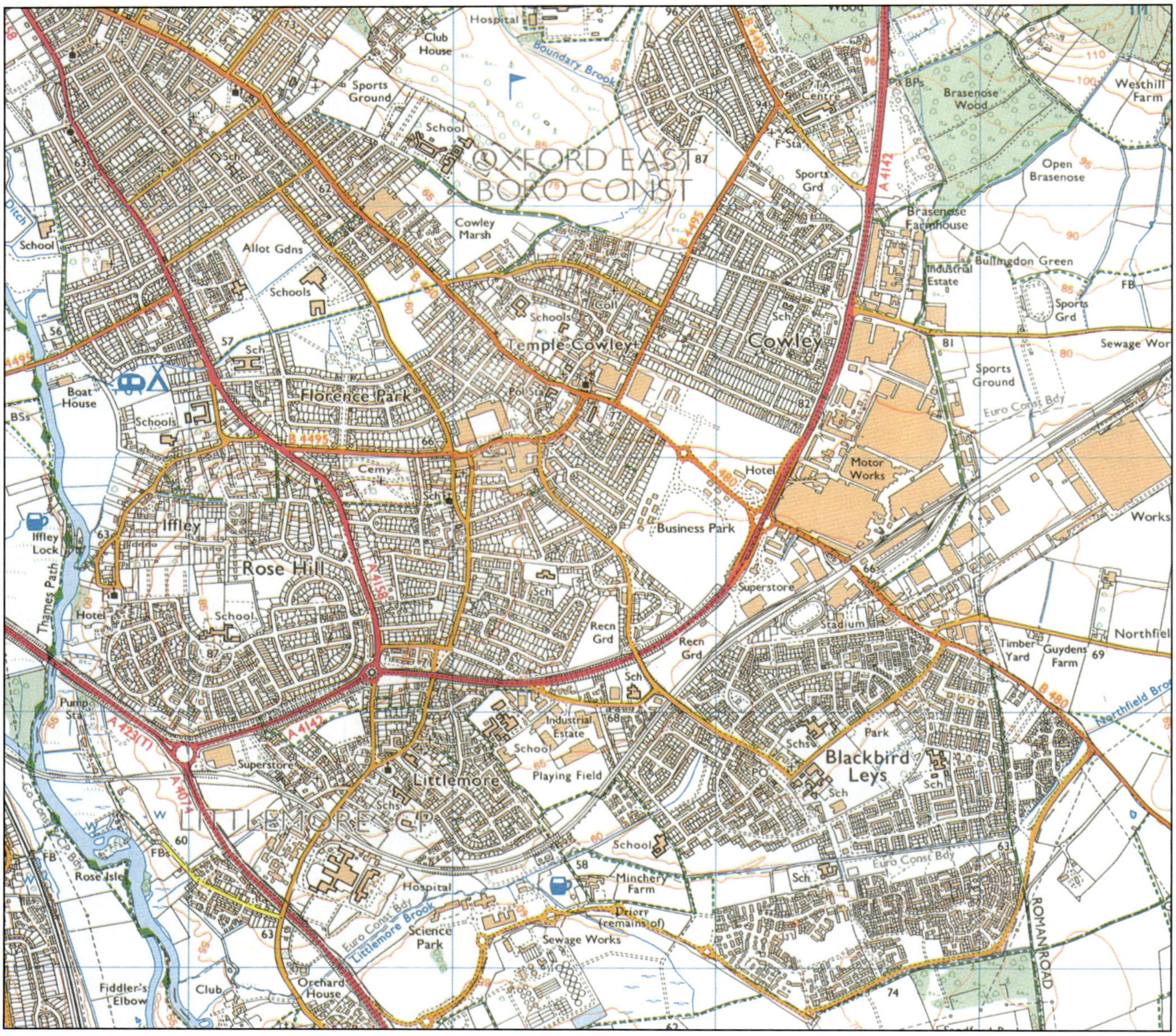

1 What is *economic activity*?

2 Decide whether this counts as economic activity:
   a being a radio DJ **b** having a baby
   c growing your own tomatoes **d** winning the lottery

3 The three people on page 32 are **economically active**.
   Match each to one of these grid references:
   a 543028 **b** 565055 **c** 543021
   d 543044 **e** 545058 **f** 555037

4 There are hundreds of different jobs. But they all fall into
   just four groups or **sectors** of economic activity:
   ◆ primary
   ◆ secondary or manufacturing
   ◆ tertiary or service
   ◆ quaternary
   a You met these four terms before. Try to write
   a definition for each, in your own words.
   Then use the glossary to check.
   b Now match each person on page 32 to a sector.

5 There are buildings at these grid references on the map.
   Match each to one of the four economic sectors:
   a 543043 **b** 539057 **c** 537027
   d 544057 **e** 543021 **f** 560033

6 

This photo shows a sign from the map area.
   a Match it to one of these three locations:
   i 551038 **ii** 546030 **iii** 542022
   b Does the shape on the sign's map match the
   shape on the OS map?
   c What kind of companies would you expect to find
   in a science park? In which economic sector?
   d Suggest some reasons why science parks get set up.
   e Why might Oxford be a good location for a science
   park? Think of as many reasons as you can.

7 A business chooses its location with care. Try to give
   three reasons why this business was set up here:
   a the superstore at 552035 **b** the hotel at 553039

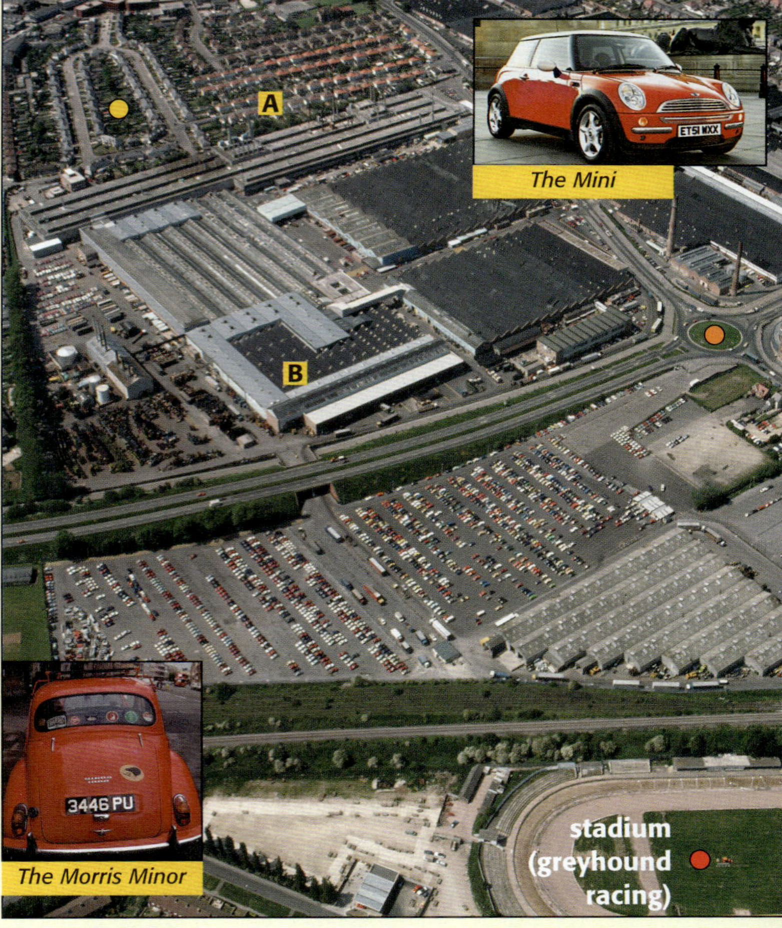

8 In 1912 William Morris started the motor works shown
   on the OS map. Morris Minors were made there.
   Today it belongs to BMW and Minis are made there.
   Above is a photo of the works taken around 1990.
   Since then it has gone through many changes.
   The OS map is from 1999.
   a The places marked with coloured dots are still there.
   Find the grid references to match the dots.
   b What kind of buildings are at A on the photo?
   Suggest reasons why they were built here.
   c In 1980 the motor works employed around 23 000
   people. Now it employs 5700 – but produces just as
   many cars. How is that possible? Try to explain.
   d i Look at area B on the photo. What was it used for?
   ii What is it used for today?
   iii Write a short snappy report about this change and
   the reasons for it, for the BMW staff magazine.

9 A high % of the people
   working in the map area
   are in manufacturing. Is this
   true for the UK overall?
   Look at the pie chart.
   a About what % of the
   workforce is in each of
   these three sectors?
   b Thousands of people work
   in the quaternary sector – but
   the pie chart does not show this. Give a reason.

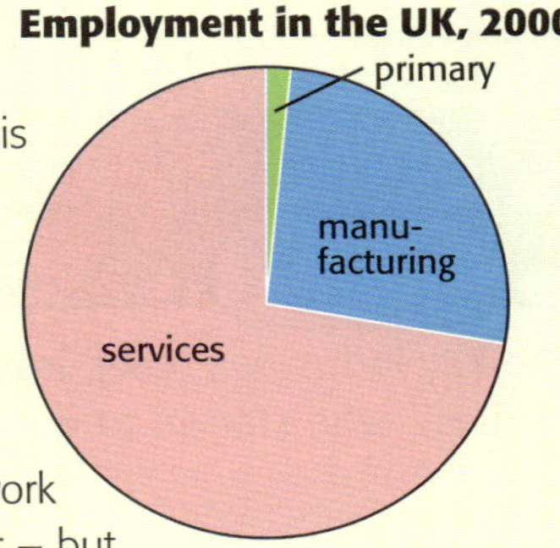
Employment in the UK, 2000

The changing pattern of economic activity

Today, most British workers provide services, rather than make things.
But it wasn't always like that!

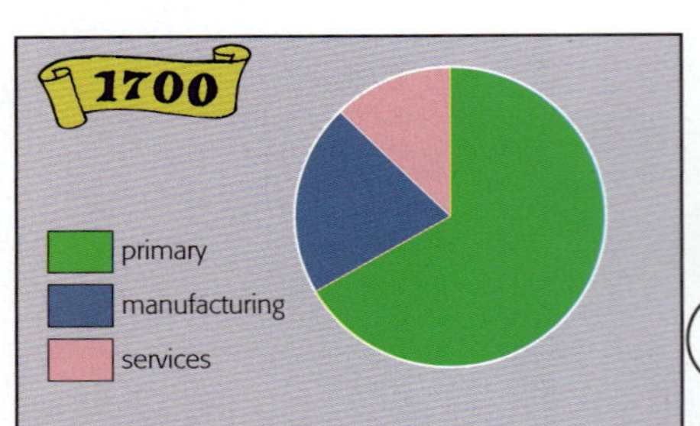

It's 1700 – and this shows where people are working.

Most work in the primary sector – mainly in farming.

The secondary sector is quite small by comparison …

… and the tertiary sector is the smallest.

Then the Industrial Revolution begins, and changes everything.

Britain produces huge amounts of iron and steel …

… and turns them into trains, railways, ships, new machinery.

People flock into towns to work in the new factories.

Now the pie chart looks like this. But not for much longer.

The key industries (coal, iron, steel, textiles) have started to decline …

… but the service sector keeps growing and growing …

… and that brings us to today's pattern.

But it is not just Britain. Most of the world's more developed countries have gone through similar changes.

Your turn

Page 34 will help you answer some of these questions.

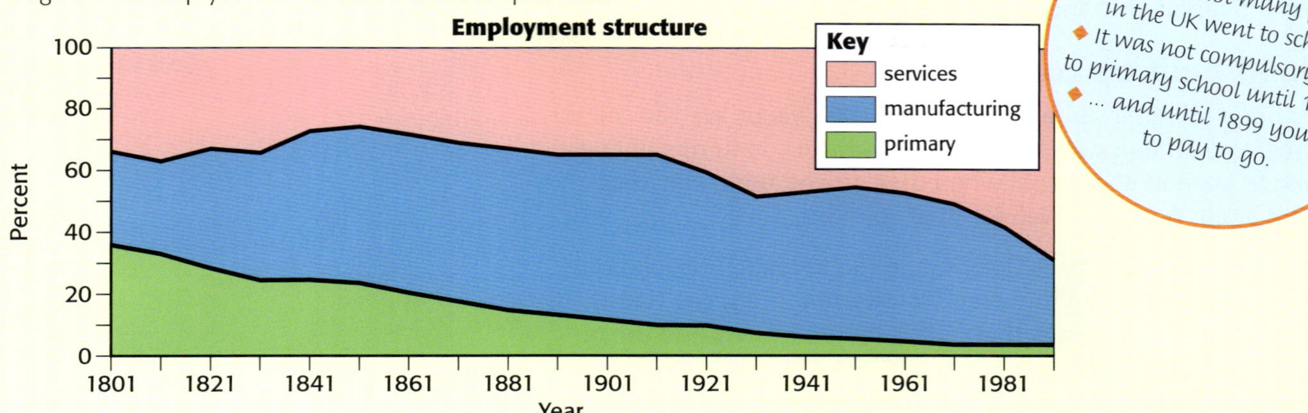

1 Look at the graph above. It is another way to show the changes described on page 34.
By 1821, about what % of people were working:
  a in the primary sector? What did most of them do?
  b in the secondary sector? (You need to subtract!) Name three jobs they could have done.
  c in the tertiary sector? Name three jobs these may have done.

2 Now look at the overall shape of the graph.
  a Which sector has declined steadily since 1801?
  b Since this sector has declined so much, why are we not all starving? Give as many reasons as you can.
  c Which sector has grown most, overall?

3 a In which sector did employment grow fastest between 1801 and 1850?
  b Suggest a reason for this.
  c Give reasons why this sector shrank overall, in the 20th century.
  d Since this sector has shrunk so much, why have we not run out of things to buy?

4 Now think about how life in Britain has changed.
  a This spider map sums up Britain in 1700. Make your own copy and add *at least three* more key facts. (Could be things you know from history.)

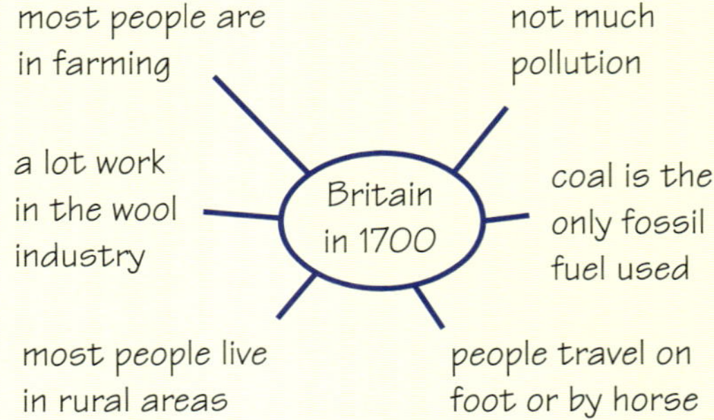

  b Now do a similar spider map for Britain in 1850.
  c And finally, do the same for Britain today.

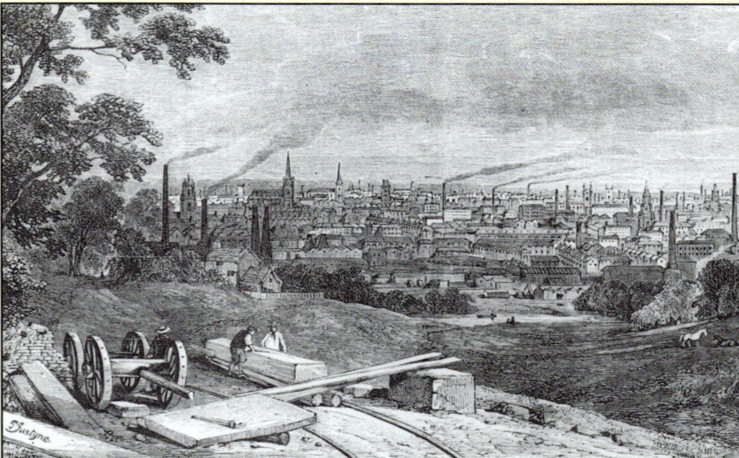

5 During the Industrial Revolution many towns grew fast. Manchester was one. This shows it around 1850. Look at all the tall factory chimneys.
The development compass rose (page 5) helps you think up questions about how and why places change, and the consequences of change.
  a Draw a *large* copy of the DCR below.

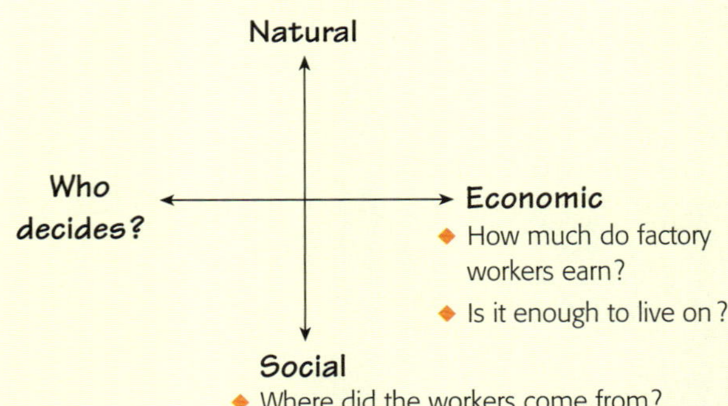

  b On your DCR, write in *at least* 8 more questions you could ask about Manchester in 1850, using the picture to help you.

The rise and fall of the coal industry

Industries can grow large and important – and then decline again. That's what happened to the British coal industry.

An island built on coal

Coal has been mined in Britain for at least 1000 years. We can tell this from some ancient flint axes that were found stuck in lumps of coal. The Romans learned about coal when they arrived here, and kept stores of it along Hadrian's Wall for their soldiers.

Britain has a lot of coal. That's what made the Industrial Revolution possible! Coal was needed to extract iron from iron ore (as coke), and to fuel the steam engines that pulled the iron trains and drove the new machinery in factories.

A map of Britain's coal deposits

This map shows Britain's coal deposits. Over the last 150 years there were around 1200 working **collieries**. Now there are less than 20.

At its peak, the coal industry employed over a million people. When a colliery closed there was often no other work in the area, so it was a disaster.

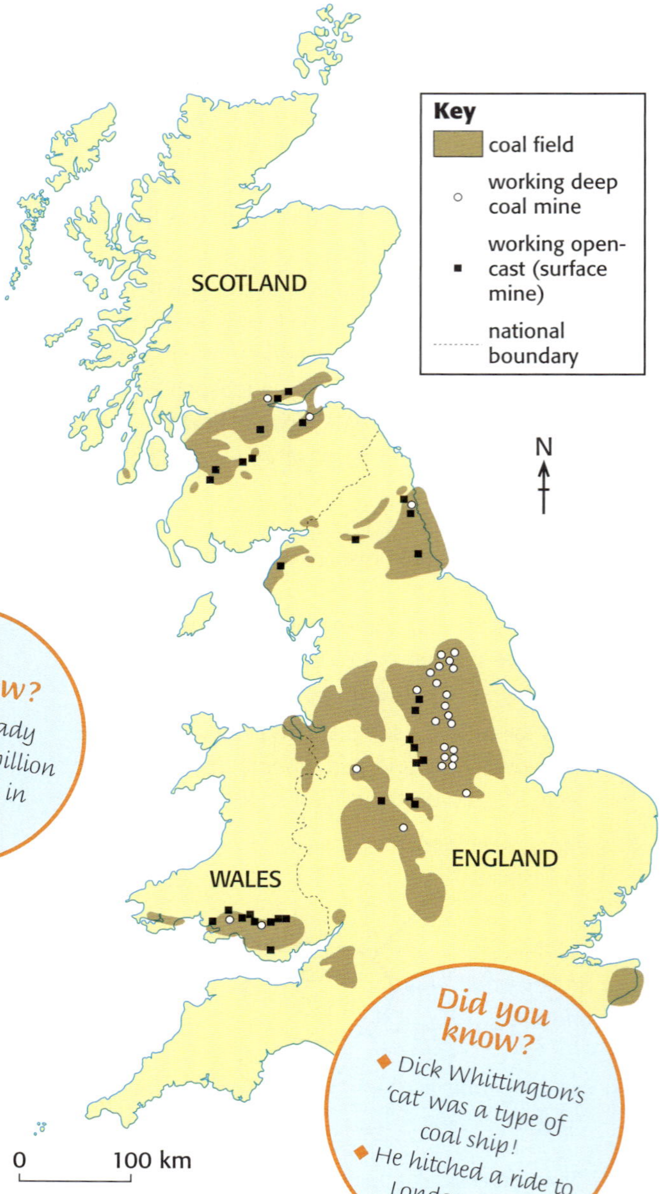

▲ A coal mine around 1700.

▲ At the coalface in Wales, 1977. Tough work …

▲ … but the miners don't want to lose it.

Did you know?
◆ We've already mined over 30 billion tonnes of coal in Britain.

Did you know?
◆ Dick Whittington's 'cat' was a type of coal ship!
◆ He hitched a ride to London on it.

Your turn

1 In which parts of Britain is coal found?
Imagine you are telling someone who has no map to look at. Make your answer very clear.

2 What is a *colliery*?

3 Look at the drawing and first photo on page 36.
Do you think miners had a tough job?
What problems might they have faced?
You could give your answer as a spider map.

4 Why did the coal industry decline? Time to find out!
You'll start by drawing a *large* graph using the data in the table on the right.
a First, draw axes like those on the far right.
Use your full page.
b Plot the data.
c Join the points with a smooth curve. No ruler!
d Give your graph a title.

5 Your next task is to **annotate** (add notes to) your graph using the fact box below. Use neat writing and keep your notes brief. Don't just copy the facts!

6 Look at your completed graph.
a Give three reasons why coal production increased so fast from 1750 to 1910.
b i About when did production reach its peak?
ii About how much coal was mined that year?
c Coal production fell sharply between 1910 and 1920. See if you can think of one reason.
d Give four reasons why it has fallen since 1950.

Coal production in Britain

Year	Coal production (millions of tons)
1750	5
1800	10
1830	31
1840	43
1850	63
1860	88
1870	116
1880	147
1890	182
1900	225
1910	265
1920	230
1930	244
1940	224
1950	204
1960	186
1970	135
1980	105
1990	88
1996	40
2000	22

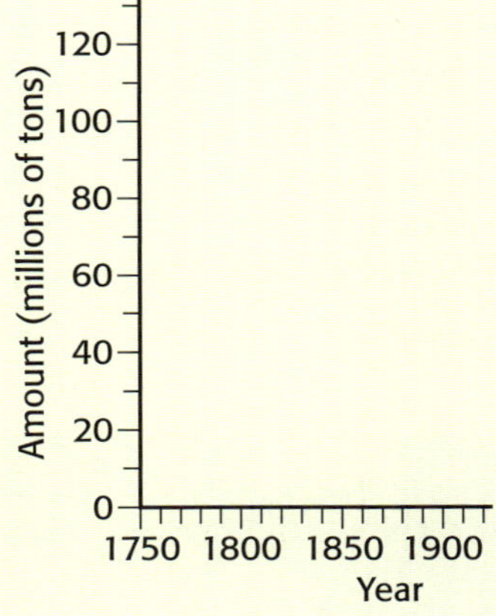

FACT BOX

1885 In Germany Mr Benz develops the first petrol-driven car.

1823 The first public railway (the Stockton and Darlington Railway) opens – with steam engines.

1782 James Watt develops a steam engine that can drive machinery. Coal is used to boil the water.

1813 The first gasworks built, in London, making **town gas** (from coal) to light homes.

1850 By now Britain is producing over half the world's iron.

1900 The UK's first power station opens, with coal as fuel. People rush to get electric lights in.

1859 The world's first oil well is drilled in America.

1913 1 128 000 men are employed in coal mining.

1965 Gas is discovered in the North Sea.

1967 The switch of homes from town gas to North Sea gas begins.

1956 The 'Clean Air Act' bans the burning of smoky coal in open fires in homes.

1992 There are now 58 000 miners.

1956 The UK's first **nuclear** power station opens.

2000 About 9000 miners left.

1896 The UK's first car factory is set up in Coventry. Cars use petrol, not coal – so oil is imported.

1969 Oil is discovered in the North Sea.

1965 By now many mines have closed down. (Some exhausted, others losing money.)

1970 By now imported coal is cheaper than UK coal!

1984 Miners go on strike for almost a year, to protest against pit closures.

1992 Power stations are switching from coal to gas – cleaner and cheaper.

1930 More and more oil is being imported – for cars *and* factories!

When an industry declines

The decline of an industry brings many problems.

Another blow for Ashfield

Friday 28 January 2000 was another tough day for Ashfield. 150 years after it opened, the Annesley Bentinck colliery closed its gates for the last time. 1000 miners went home with no jobs.

The Ashfield district is just north of Nottingham. It has a population of 109 000. 50 years ago it was a wealthy area. 12 coal pits and around 40 textile factories provided plenty of work for miners and their wives. Ashfield was famous not only for coal but for lace, tights, socks, and other knitted goods.

How times have changed. Of the 354 districts in the UK, Ashfield is now one of the poorest, 31 from the bottom. Its mines have closed one by one. And its textile factories have shrunk or closed, thanks to competition from other countries.

'Of course I'm sad', said Mick, one of the last miners to walk out Annesley gates. 'Mining is all I know. Like my father and his father, and his father before him. I have two kids, and we bought a new house two years ago, and my wife has no job. So life will be hard. Not just money, it's stress too. I've seen how it gets to people. This whole place has been going downhill for years. People fed up and going nowhere. No-one with money to spend. And now that includes me.'

▲ Annesley colliery - one industry ends …

▲ … but Ashfield is working hard to attract others.

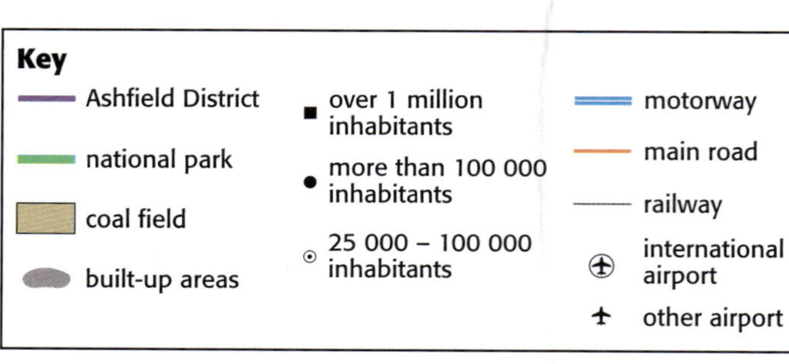

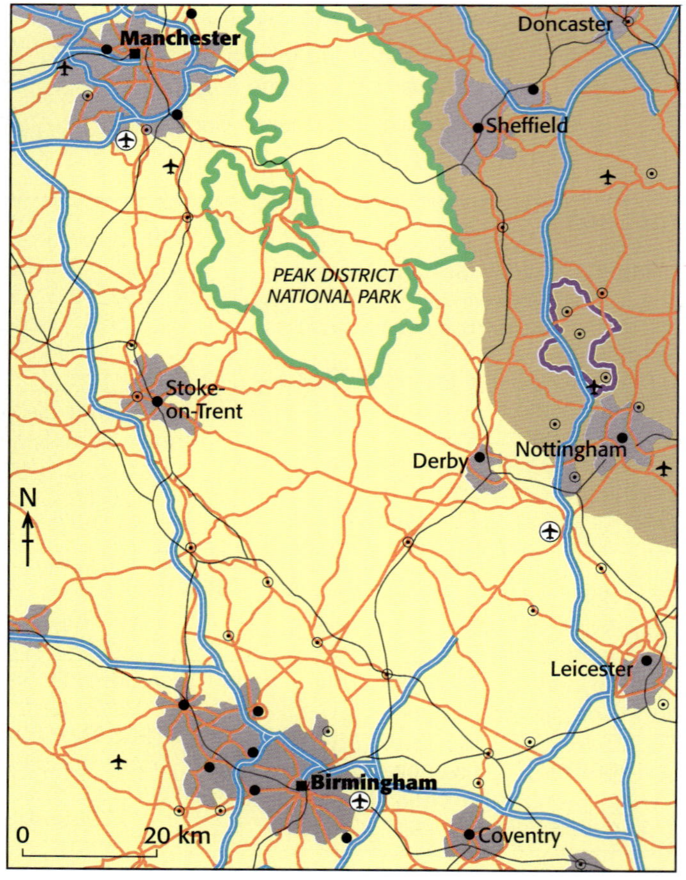

Ashfield fights back

Ashfield's two key industries have been in slow decline for over 40 years, leaving many big problems. But Ashfield is fighting back. It has formed the Ashfield Partnership to tackle the problems.

Ashfield: the problems in 2000

- unemployment
- great poverty in some areas
- above average levels of heart disease and infant mortality
- lots of crime in some areas
- many people in low-paid jobs
- poor exam pass rates
- few young people going on to higher education
- a shortage of skills
- land still scarred by mining

Money for the fight

Ashfield is getting grants from:
- the government
- the European Union
- the National Lottery
- the Coalfield Trust and other bodies.

Our aims

- to create a skilled workforce
- to attract new industries
- to make the community healthy and wealthy
- to provide a safe, clean, green environment.

A ▲ New skills: an ICT class for adults in Ashfield.

B ▲ A pleasant spot for Raleigh …

1 a 50 years ago, Ashfield was a wealthy area. Why?
b Why is it no longer wealthy?

2 a List all the groups who have joined up to form the Ashfield Partnership. (Look at the banners!)
b Do you think it's a good idea they have joined up? Or better if they worked separately? Give reasons.

3 In the past, Ashfield fell behind in education. But now it aims to give its people a high level of ICT skills. (Look at photo **A** above).
Draw a 'consequence map' like the one started here, to show why that's a good idea. (Add more boxes!)

4 The Ashfield Partnership wants to turn Ashfield into a safe, clean, green environment. (Look at photo **B**). Draw another consequence map to show why that's a good idea too.

5 Ashfield has already attracted new firms. Some have set up warehouses there to store goods for sending out to shops. Why is Ashfield is a good location for warehouses? (Hint: look at the map!)

6 You work for Ashfield District Council. Using the information in this unit to help you, write a short piece called
Ashfield: a great location for your business
to go on the Ashfield website.

Start by writing rough notes as a spider map. (You could give some distances. And mention the Peak District? You can read about it on page 92.)

The growth of new industries

Old industries decline, and new ones take their place. This has happened over and over again through the centuries.

The rise of Silicon Glen

Look at this map. Silicon Glen is the area between Glasgow, Edinburgh and Dundee.

Once it had lots of heavy industry: coal, steel, and shipbuilding. When these declined, many thousands of people were left without jobs.

Today the area has hundreds of new businesses. Many depend on computer chips, which are made of silicon. That's how the area got its new name.

Key

—— Silicon Glen	coal field
● university towns	----- national boundary
● other towns	

Silicon Glen's new industries

Here are some of them.

About 7% of the silicon chips that are made in Europe are made in Silicon Glen.

And over 10% of Europe's mobile phones. Do you have a Scottish mobile phone?

And almost 80% of Europe's workstations (computer terminals + keyboards).

Many new **call centres** have set up there. They handle phone calls for banks and other big organisations.

Over 500 companies in Silicon Glen produce software, including games. Ms Lara Croft started life here!

Biotechnology is booming too. Dolly, the first cloned sheep, was born here (just outside Edinburgh).

Where did they come from?

Most of the new businesses were started by people living in Scotland. But the largest were set up by **transnational corporations** or **TNCs** – big companies with branches all over the world.

A government body called **Locate in Scotland** works hard to attract companies from outside Scotland.

They offer good deals, to get companies to move into Scotland and provide jobs.

These are some of the TNCs from other countries that have set up branches in Silicon Glen.

But it is not always good news, as you'll see below.

Risky business?

Gloom hangs over Silicon Glen. Last week the American giant Motorola announced it would cut 3100 jobs at its Bathgate plant. The company blamed the fall in demand for mobile phones.

There is worse to come. Sun Microsystems, Panasonic, and Rosti (which makes cases for mobile phones) all plan to close factories. And the computer company Compaq plans to move 700 jobs from Scotland to the Czech Republic where labour costs less.

Bad news for Scotland, which depends heavily on these foreign companies. But there is some hope too. Scotland's own small software companies continue to grow.

(From a newspaper article, April 2001)

Did you know?

◆ In 2000, over 56 000 people in Scotland worked in the electronics industry (making computers, mobile phones and so on).

Your turn

1 Industry is shaped by new inventions. These spider maps compare the steam engine and silicon chip. Copy them, and see how many more links you can add.

steam ships   personal computers

the steam engine

the silicon chip

steam trains   mobile phones

2 Of the new industries in Silicon Glen, give an example:
 a from manufacturing
 b from the service sector
 c from the quaternary sector

3 **a** What is a *TNC*?
 b Name three TNCs whose products you use.
  (Think about clothes? drinks? music? games?)

4 These two events are linked – but how?

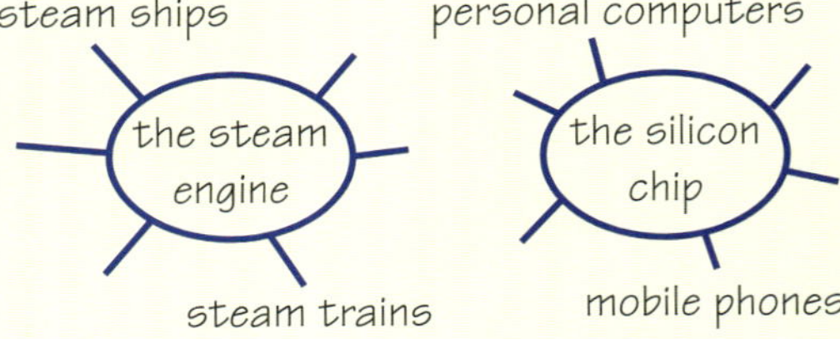

Draw a strip cartoon, with captions, to explain the link. (Do you need to check the glossary?)

5 You work for *Locate in Scotland*. You get this e-mail. Write a polite and serious reply.

Dear Locate in Scotland
You give away millions of pounds a year, of taxpayers' money, bribing companies to come here. And then they're up and off again, the minute the going gets tough. All that money down the drain! Why not just give it out to poor Scottish folk like me? I'd be very glad to start a wee corner shop. Regards, Donald.

Bienvenues en France

Welcome to France, the country you can travel to by tunnel.
Where you'll find…

▲ … *gleaming new developments* …

▲ … *famous monuments* …

▲ … *vineyards* …

▲ … *wonderful food* …

▲ … *hundreds of small rural villages* …

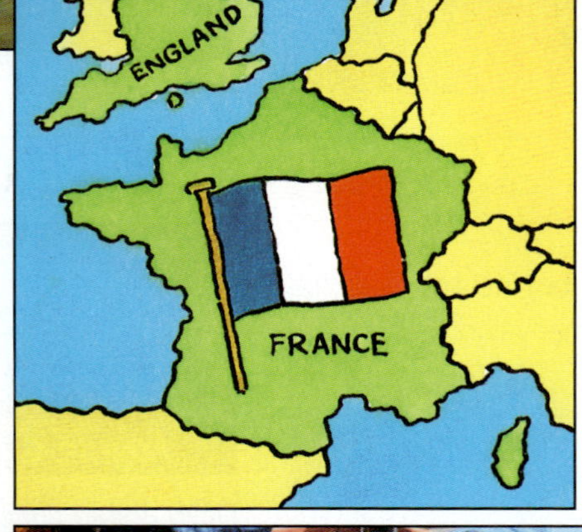

▲ … *lots of outdoor markets* …

▲ … *oodles of style and fashion* …

Did you know?

◆ 12 000 years ago, in the last Ice Age, you could walk from France to England.

▲ … great places to go skiing …

▲ … glamorous Mediterranean beaches …

▲ … miles of sleek motorway …

▲ … romance …

▲ … a rich culture …

▲ … and some quite good football.

Your turn

1 The maps on pages 44 and 122 will help you with this question.
  a Which strip of sea separates France and the UK?
  b About how close is France to England, by sea?
  c Name the other seas around France.
  d Which countries share a border with France?

2 You are thinking of a place to go on holiday.
  a Draw a scale like this, but twice as long:

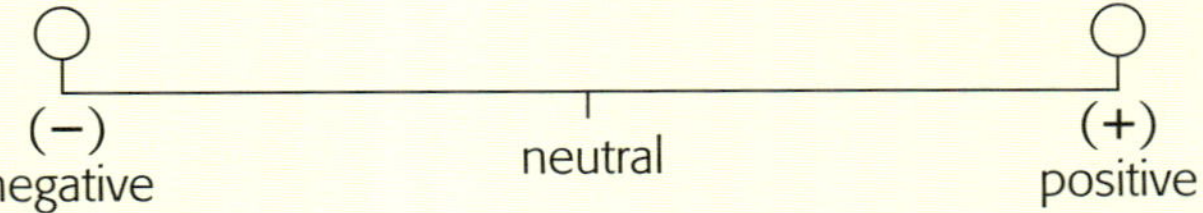

(−) negative   neutral   (+) positive

  b Now look at the images of France in this unit. Which one would attract you most to France? Write its number in the circle at (+) on the scale.
  c Which, if any, would put you off most? Write its number at (−) on the scale.
  d Now mark in the other images on the scale. If one has no effect on you, mark it at neutral.

3 **Stereotypes** are ideas about other races and cultures that we accept without thinking. *Welsh people love singing* is an example. Which images in this unit do you think show stereotypes about French people?

4 Look at these points of view:

Which do you agree *least* with? Write down what you would say to *that* person in reply.

5 Now draw a *large* spider map to summarise what you know about France already. Start like this?

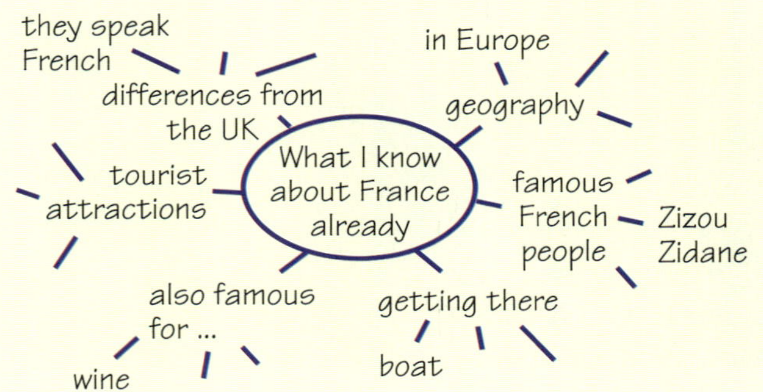

What's France like?

Detective time again. You are about to discover quite a lot about the geography of France. For yourself. With just a few maps for clues.

This is a relief map of France. Look at those mountains! It also shows the three longest rivers.

▲ Fishing on the River Cher, a tributary of the Loire.

▲ On the north coast of France. What landforms can you see?

Your turn

1 France is sometimes called *Le Hexagon*. Why?

2 This sketch map shows the main physical features of France, and its capital city.

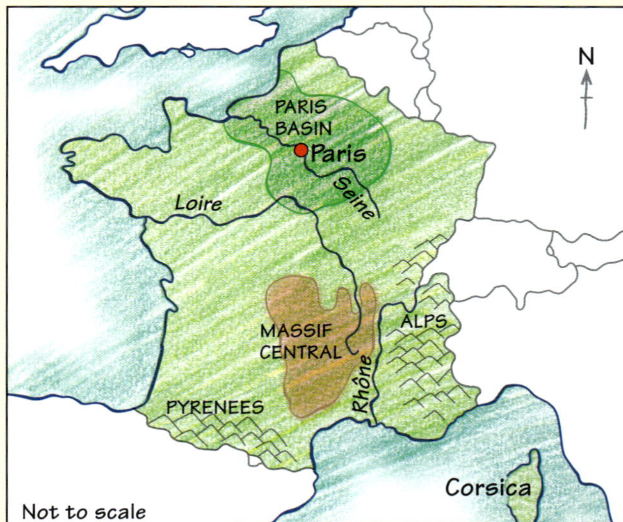

Your job is to copy and complete these sentences, using words and phrases from the boxes below. (You may need to use some more than once.) Use the maps on pages 44 and 122 for clues.

a The Paris basin is an area of _____ ____ around Paris.

b France has got _____ large mountain ranges. The Pyrenees separate France from ____. The _____ separate it from _____ and _____.

c The Massif Central is an _____ area, but not as high as the _____ or _____.

d The Rhône rises in the _____ in _____ and flows to the _____ ____.

e The _____ rises in the _____ _____ and flows to the _____ ____.

f The _____ is France's longest river.

g Paris is on the River _____.

h The _____ named Corsica is part of France. It is in the _____ ____.

i Overall, the ___ and ____ of France have low land.

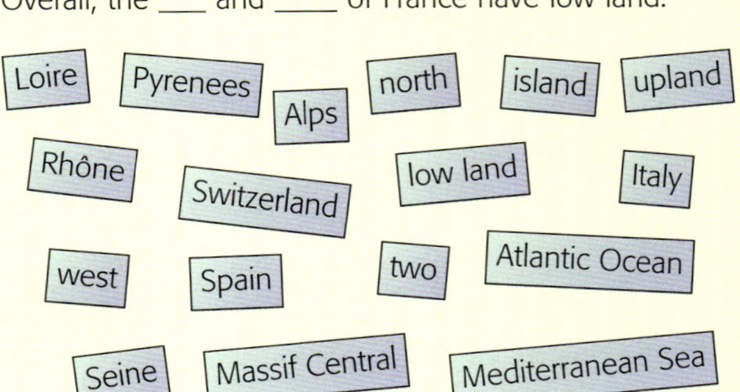

3 What does the word *climate* mean? (Glossary?)

4 France is a large country, with coast and mountains. So it has different **climate zones**. This map shows the climate zones – but something is missing!

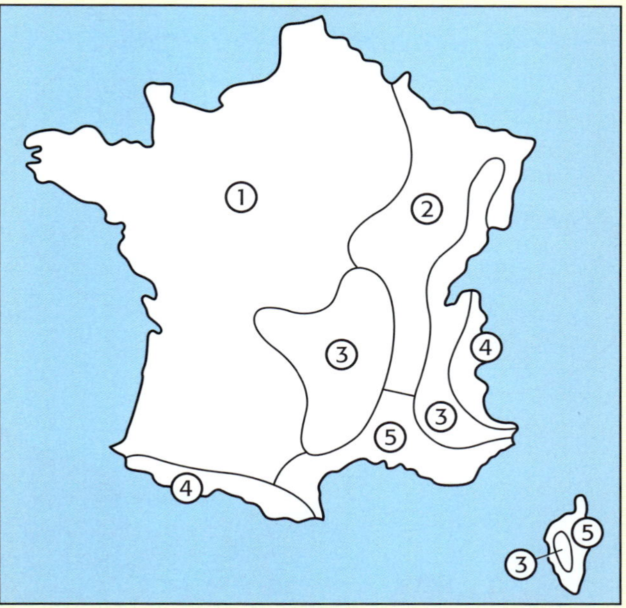

Key

☐ **A** Overall, much warmer than the UK; hot and very dry in summer; very mild winters with some rain.

☐ **B** Cold or very cold all year round; precipitation often in the form of snow.

☐ **C** Gets hot quickly in summer and cold quickly in winter; quite a bit of rain.

☐ **D** Overall, quite like much of the UK; quite mild in winter and warm in summer; quite a lot of rain all year, especially in the higher areas.

☐ **E** Quite cool all year, and cold in winter; a lot of rain in the higher areas.

a Make your own copy of the map and key.

b Shade in the key – a different colour for each box.

c Now colour in each zone on the map, to match the right box in the key. (The maps on pages 44 and 122 will give you clues. And use what you know about climate already.)

d Give your map a title.

5 Now give reasons for your choices in **4c**. Start like this: *I matched* ① *with* ___ *because* … (Put a letter A–E from the key in the 'missing' space.)

So where is everyone?

France has about the same population as the UK. And like the UK, it is divided into smaller regions.

This map shows the 22 regions and their French names. The map below shows population density.

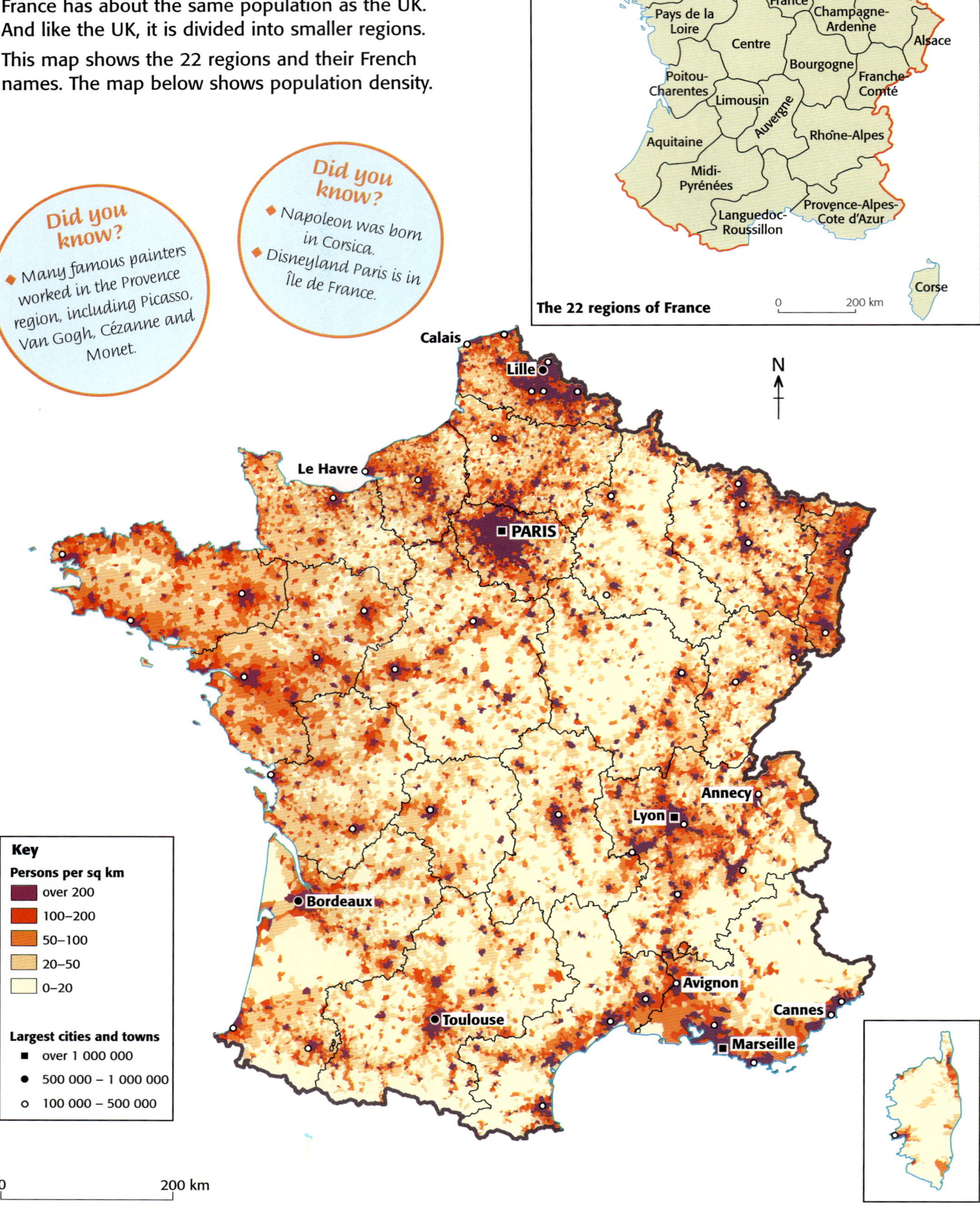

Your turn

1 First, compare France and the UK:

	France	**UK**
Population (million)	60	60
Area (sq km)	550 000	242 000

Using the table to help you, write out the paragraph below. Fill in the blanks from the list in italics.

France is over _____ the size of the UK. But their populations are _____. This means France is ____ crowded. The average number of people per square km is ____ for France and ___ for the UK.

equal   9166   248   half   2.27   very
109   three times   too   twice   less   4033

2 This is about the regions of France. You must give each answer as a full sentence. Name:

a the region that contains Paris

b the region nearest the UK

c a region in the Massif Central

d one where you could have a hot dry beach holiday in summer – and ski in winter

e a region bordering Spain *and* the Atlantic Ocean

f the one that juts out furthest into the Atlantic Ocean

g one that juts out into Germany (and used to be part of Germany!)

3 This is about population density in France. Write out each statement below, and after it write *True* or *False*.

A Île de France is the most crowded region of France.

B Alsace is much less crowded than Auvergne.

C Very few people live along the Mediterranean coast.

D Overall, the population density is highest in central France.

E The most mountainous regions of France have a low population density.

F Population density in France is highest around the largest cities.

4 This table shows the five largest French cities.

City	**Population in 2000 (millions)**
Lille	1.00
Lyon	1.35
Marseille	1.35
Paris	9.64
Toulouse	0.76

a Draw a *horizontal* bar chart to show this data. Beside each city, write its region in brackets.

b About how many times larger is Paris than the next city down?

c About what % of France's population lives in Paris?

5

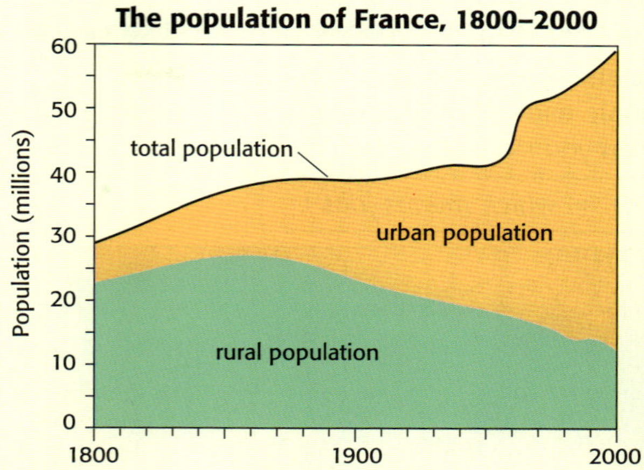

a Using this graph, describe how the *total* population of France changed between 1800 and 2000.

b Now look at the *rural* population. In 2000, did rural France have *more* people, or *fewer* people, than it had 200 years earlier?

c Try to suggest some reasons for the change in **b**.

6 **Population pyramid for France, for 2000**

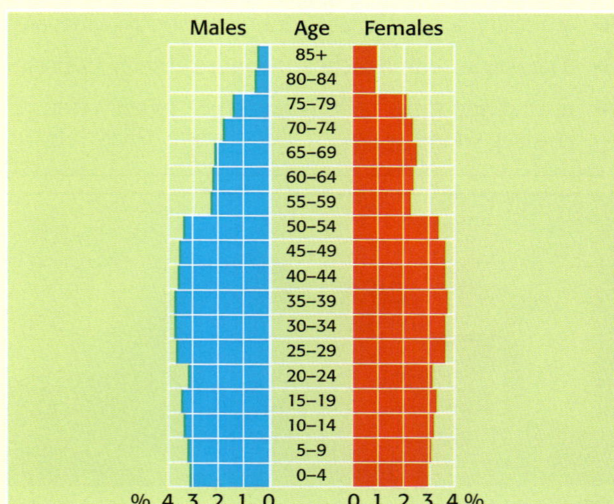

Now look at this population pyramid for France.

a It shows that girls aged 10–14 were about 3.2% of the population, in 2000. What was the % for:

i boys of 10–14?   **ii** women of 60–64?

b Overall, about what % of the population was:

i 19 or younger?   **ii** 45 or older?

(Think of a sensible way to count part squares.)

c Which statement is more correct?

A France has an ageing population.

B France is a country of young people.

d There's a 'bite' out of the pyramid at 55–59. Give a reason. (In which years was this group born?)

The economic geography of France: part 1

Economic geography is about *how* and *where* people earn their living. It depends on factors like 1 – 5 below.

Factors like these dictate how and where French people earn a living. And how *you* will earn a living when you start work! (Oh cruel day …)

$\longrightarrow$ = *which means jobs in*

1 Physical geography

This has a big influence on how people earn a living. For example France has:

- a lot of low flat fertile land $\longrightarrow$ farming
- a hot dry sunny climate zone $\longrightarrow$ tourism, vineyards
- a coastline, with beaches $\longrightarrow$ ports, fishing, tourism
- upland and mountainous areas $\longrightarrow$ forestry (for timber), winter sports

2 Other natural resources

Natural resources lead to jobs. France is *not* rich in natural resources, apart from its fertile soil. But it does have:

- some coal and iron ore $\longrightarrow$ making steel and steel products
- a little oil and natural gas $\longrightarrow$ producing fuel, chemicals and electricity
- some uranium ore $\longrightarrow$ making and using nuclear fuel
- fast-flowing rivers $\longrightarrow$ producing hydroelectricity
- plenty of stone and sand $\longrightarrow$ building, glass making, tile making

3 New technology

New technology brings new jobs. France is a leader in:

- flight technology $\longrightarrow$ making planes and rockets
- electronics $\longrightarrow$ making mobile phones, computers and so on

4 What people will buy

If people want something, and can afford to buy it, other people will work to provide it! For example:

- food $\longrightarrow$ processing and selling food
- transport $\longrightarrow$ making cars and trains

France earns lots from both of these.

5 Government policy

A government can have a big say in both how and where people earn a living. For example it might:

- decide that more nurses or police are needed
- give grants to encourage hi-tech research
- give grants to set up factories in poorer areas

More about the government's role

Many of France's key industries and services are owned fully or partly by the state. So the government can tell them what to do!

The government has chosen places in poorer regions to be **development centres**, where it helps new industries to set up.

It has helped farming by giving grants to older farmers to retire, and to young farmers for training courses, and to buy more land.

Key points about the French economy

◆ Agriculture has always been really important in France, and farmers have a lot of influence. But the number of farmers is falling.

◆ Like the UK, France went through an Industrial Revolution – but later, and much less dramatic. Industries like coal mining, steel and textiles flourished then.

◆ As in the UK, these traditional industries are in decline. Modern industries are taking their place.

◆ The government has taken steps to spread manufacturing around the country – but most is still in the north and east of France.

◆ As in the UK, the service sector is growing everywhere.

France's top 10 earners
Insurance
Foodstuffs (meat, crops, wine, …)
Construction and engineering
Cars
Chemicals
Telecoms and ICT
Making materials (steel, aluminium, glass, …)
Fashion and luxury goods (Dior, …)
Medical drugs
Tourism
Aerospace (planes, rockets)

Your turn

1 Give 5 factors that dictate what kinds of jobs there are, and where, in countries like France and the UK.

2 *web designer   farmer   teacher   disco manager*
Which of those four jobs:
  a depends most on physical geography?
  b depends most on being in an urban area?
  c depends most on technology?

3 Using maps and information from earlier pages, match each job to one place from the brackets:
  a a captain of an ocean-going container ship
  b running a beach café in summer
  c a politician in the French government
  d a coach driver taking people on day ski trips
  e a translator at meetings of the EU parliament
     (*Cannes   Annecy   Paris   Le Havre   Strasbourg*)

4 The French government has had a big influence on the economic geography of France. Explain how.

5 **% employed in each sector, in France**

Year	1970	1980	1990	2000
Primary	13	8	6	4
Secondary	38	35	29	25
Tertiary	49	57	66	71

As this table shows, the pattern of jobs is changing in France, just as in the UK.

a Give two examples of jobs in each sector, from page 48.

b Turn to the graph for the UK at the top of page 35, to see how it was drawn.

c Now draw a similar graph for France, using the table above. Join the points with a smooth curve.

d Compare the two graphs. In what ways are they similar? In what ways are they different?

e Suggest *three* jobs that *more* people in France do now than in 1970.

The economic geography of France: part 2

Detective time again! You have to answer questions about France from the information given here, and what you've learned already. You'll find the names of the regions in the table opposite.

1 What goes on where?

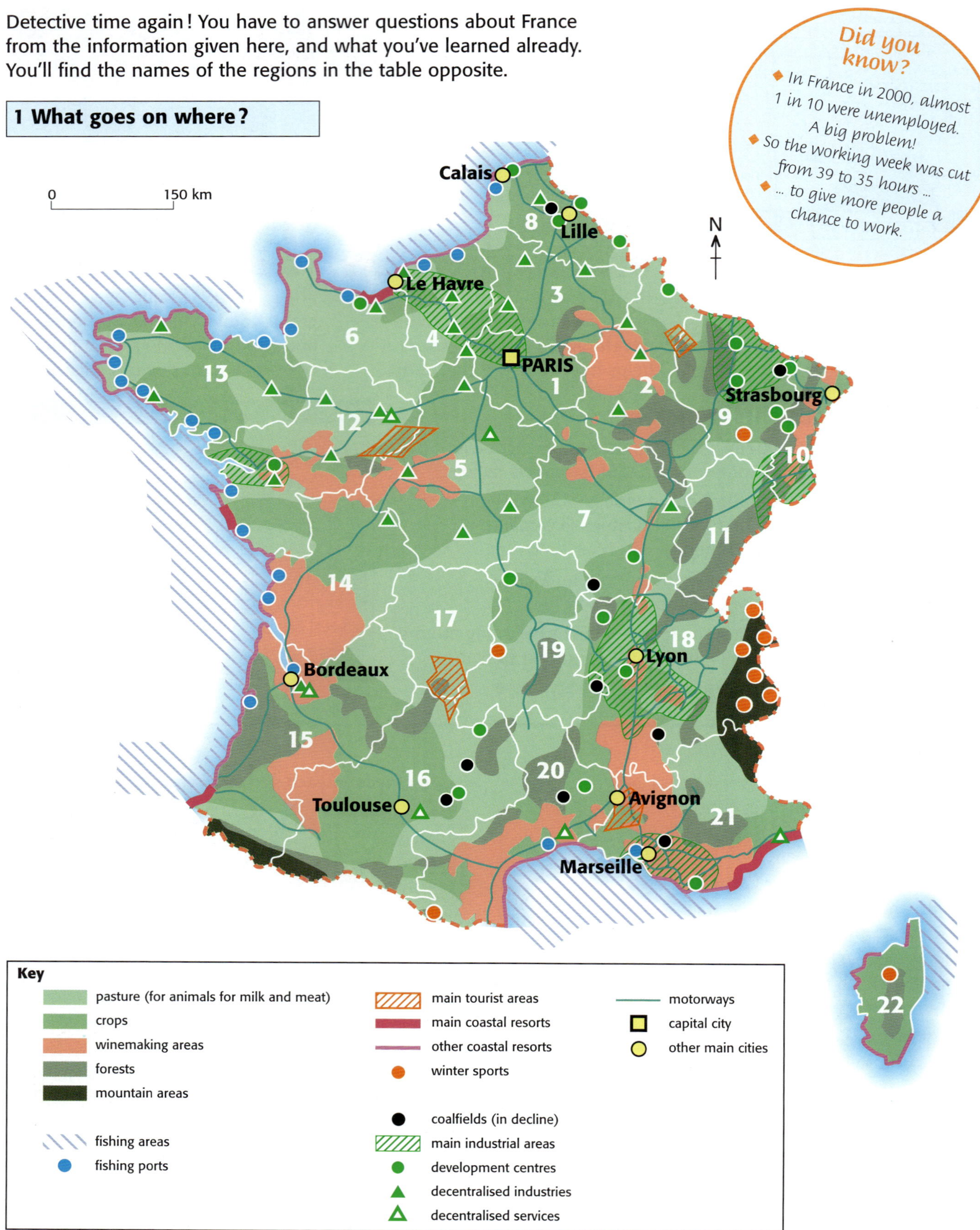

Key

pasture (for animals for milk and meat)	main tourist areas
crops	main coastal resorts
winemaking areas	other coastal resorts
forests	winter sports
mountain areas	
fishing areas	coalfields (in decline)
fishing ports	main industrial areas
	development centres
	decentralised industries
	decentralised services
motorways	
capital city	
other main cities	

2 Some data for the regions of France, 2000

	Region	% of France's total GDP it produces	% of working population in		
			agric.	industry	services
1	Île de France	28.4	0.5	18.7	80.8
2	Champagne-Ardenne	2.1	8.6	25.0	66.4
3	Picardie	2.7	4.9	29.1	65.9
4	Haute-Normandie	2.8	1.9	29.2	68.9
5	Centre	3.8	4.7	29.9	65.4
6	Basse-Normandie	2.1	9.4	24.9	65.7
7	Bourgogne	2.5	6.0	27.4	66.6
8	Nord-Pas-de-Calais	5.4	1.9	27.1	71.0
9	Lorraine	3.4	2.8	30.2	67.0
10	Alsace	3.1	2.4	33.4	64.2
11	Franche-Compté	1.7	4.7	35.5	59.8
12	Pays de la Loire	4.8	6.2	29.0	64.7
13	Bretagne	4.1	7.6	25.3	67.0
14	Poitou-Charentes	2.2	8.4	24.0	67.6
15	Aquitaine	4.4	7.5	21.3	71.2
16	Midi-Pyrénées	3.8	5.9	24.4	69.7
17	Limousin	1.0	9.2	24.4	66.3
18	Rhône-Alpes	9.7	4.1	28.0	67.7
19	Auvergne	1.8	8.1	28.4	63.5
20	Languedoc-Rousillon	3.0	6.9	18.1	75.0
21	Provence-Alpes-Côte d'Azur	6.8	3.0	17.9	79.0
22	Corse	0.34	5.7	15.6	78.7
	Average for France	**100%**	**3.2**	**24.5**	**72.3**

3 Migration within France, 1990 – 1999

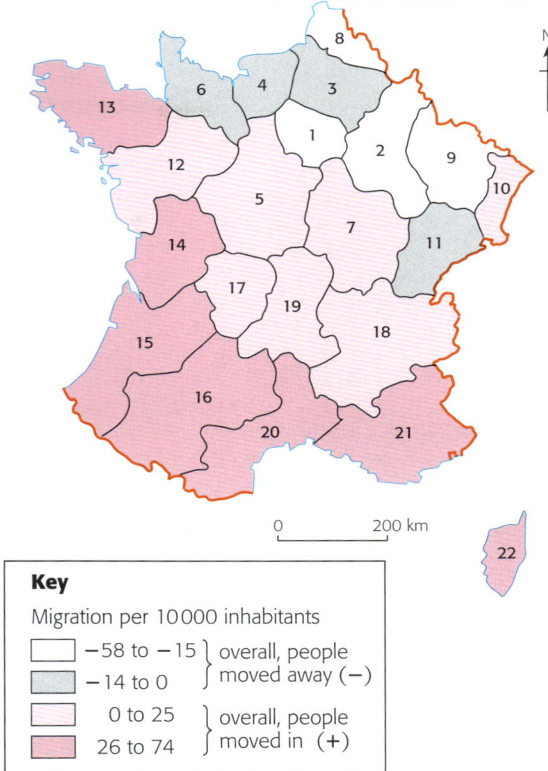

Key

Migration per 10 000 inhabitants

- −58 to −15 } overall, people
- −14 to 0 } moved away (−)
- 0 to 25 } overall, people
- 26 to 74 } moved in (+)

Your turn

1 *GDP* or *gross domestic product* is the total wealth produced in a country in a year.

  a Which *region* of France produces most wealth? Give reasons. (The map on page 50 will help.)

  b Which produces least wealth? Suggest reasons.

2 In which region is the % of the population working in agriculture: largest? smallest?

3 a In which region is the % of the population working in industry: largest? smallest?

  b The map shows some *decentralised* industries. What does that term mean?

4 In France, like everywhere, people move or **migrate** from one region to another.

  a Which appears to have been the main direction of migration, in the period 1990 – 1999?

    i from north to south   **ii** from west to east

  b Suggest some reasons for this pattern.

5 These pie charts show the employment structure in:

  a Île de France

  b Bretagne

  c Provence-Alpes-Côte d'Azur

But they're all mixed up!

Match each to its correct region.

6 This describes one of France's regions. Which one?

- ◆ hot dry sunny summers
- ◆ lots of people have moved here – partly for the sun!
- ◆ attracts a great many tourists
- ◆ lots of vineyards
- ◆ no very big cities (of over 500 000 people)
- ◆ a smaller % of its population work in industry than for most other regions

7 a Close your eyes, and pick a region from table **2**. (If you get the one in question **6**, try again!)

  b Using **6** as an example, write a set of 6 clues for it.

  c Now ask your partner to identify the region.

Employment structure for three French regions

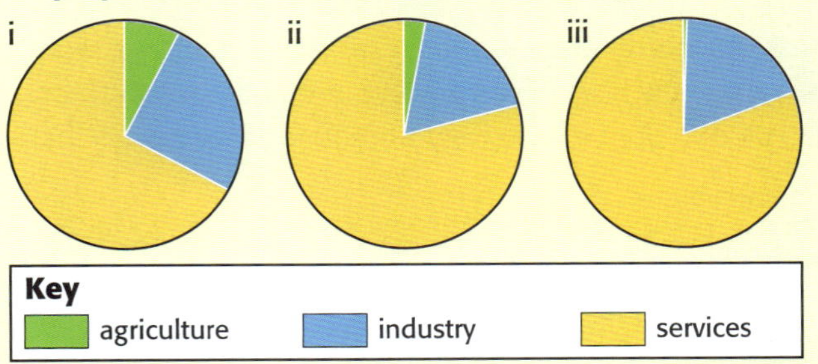

Key

- agriculture
- industry
- services

Letter from Langy

You saw on page 51 how people have migrated from one region of France to another – usually chasing work. Much of the migration is from rural areas, and it can lead to **rural depopulation**.

Le Bourg
03150 Langy
Auvergne

Mercredi

Ma chère Suzanne

So much has happened since I got your letter. We bought a new house at last !!! And this is my very first letter from Langy, right in the middle of France. Well, it's not exactly a new house. In fact over 100 years old and rather petite – here's a photo. But I really love it.

Langy is just a little village. With our arrival, the population went up to 201. An old man I met yesterday said it had been quite lively once, with a lot more people. It even had a shop – which closed after the war! The poor old primary school hung on for ages with only a handful of pupils, but finally gave up last year. It's the same with the church. Now it's used only for baptisms, weddings and funerals, and you have to get the key from one of our neighbours. As for transport – you could not manage without a car.

All this explains why the house was so cheap. I still can't believe how cheap, compared with Île de France. We saw some farmhouses further out that were almost falling down, and even cheaper. Some in the middle of huge fields of sunflowers. I felt so sad about all those families who'd worked hard on their little strips of land for years … and then had to sell to bigger farmers when they could no longer make a living.

We're not too far from Vichy. Marc hopes he'll be able to sell his pottery there – it gets quite a lot of tourists. And one day very soon, when we've settled in, I'll have to find a job myself – probably in Vichy. But what I'd really like to do is open a little village shop! (Shhhhhh.)

The house next door belonged to an old lady who lived alone. Her children had moved away years ago, to work in Paris. Now it's up for sale too, and we hear an English woman wants to buy it for a holiday cottage. There's a retired Swiss couple just down the road. We could get quite cosmopolitan !

We met the new mayor of Langy yesterday. Young and lots of energy. He's determined to attract people back to live here, and especially younger people. He has been sending out posters. We await the crowds.

Come down and see us soon. Fresh air, countryside, nightingales, cycling. And you know how Auvergne is famous for its extinct volcanoes. Vulcania – the volcano centre – is only an hour's drive away. You will really love it here.

Grosses bises

Jacqueline

▲ Jacqueline's new house (on the right).

▲ A view of Langy.

▲ The church in Langy. It was built in the 11th century.

1 Langy is suffering from *rural depopulation*. What does that term mean? (Look it up?)

2 Write down: **a** any causes **b** any consequences of rural depopulation, given in Jacqueline's letter. Give each as a full sentence.

3 This French road map shows the area around Langy. (Langy is in H5, about 46° 16′ north of the equator.)
  a Children from Langy now go up the N7 to primary school in Varennes. How far is that, by the shortest route? Measure to the centre of each settlement.
  b When Jacqueline runs out of coffee she drives down the N7 to a little shop in the middle of St Gérand-le-Puy. About how far?

4 A craft centre at Boutiron, just north of Vichy, is keen to sell Marc's pottery. It's at about 46° 9′ North. Draw a sketch map of the roads, with road numbers, telling Marc how to get there from Langy by car. Add distances where you think that will help.

5 This table shows data for the whole Auvergne region:

	1982	1990	2000
Population (millions)	1.33	1.32	1.31
Pop. density (people/sq km)	51.2	50.8	50.3
Natural increase in population (%)	− 0.01	− 0.06	− 0.12
Net migration	0.04	− 0.04	0.02
% of population			
aged 0 – 19	27.0	24.1	22.7
aged 60+	21.5	23.7	24.5
Life expectancy	74.6	76.7	78.2

  a Auvergne had fewer people in 2000 than in 1982. How many fewer? Give your answer as a full number. (No decimal points!)
  b The table shows *natural increase* and *net migration*. Explain what each term means, and say what a minus sign (−) shows. (Glossary?)
  c In both 1982 and 2000, more people moved *into* than *out of* Auvergne. But the population still kept falling. Why?
  d Overall, what is happening to:
    i the % of the population aged under 20?
    ii the % of the population aged 60 and over?
    iii life expectancy?
  e If these trends continue, predict what the population of Auvergne will be like in 2010.
  f What effects might these trends have on the region? Think of as many as you can.

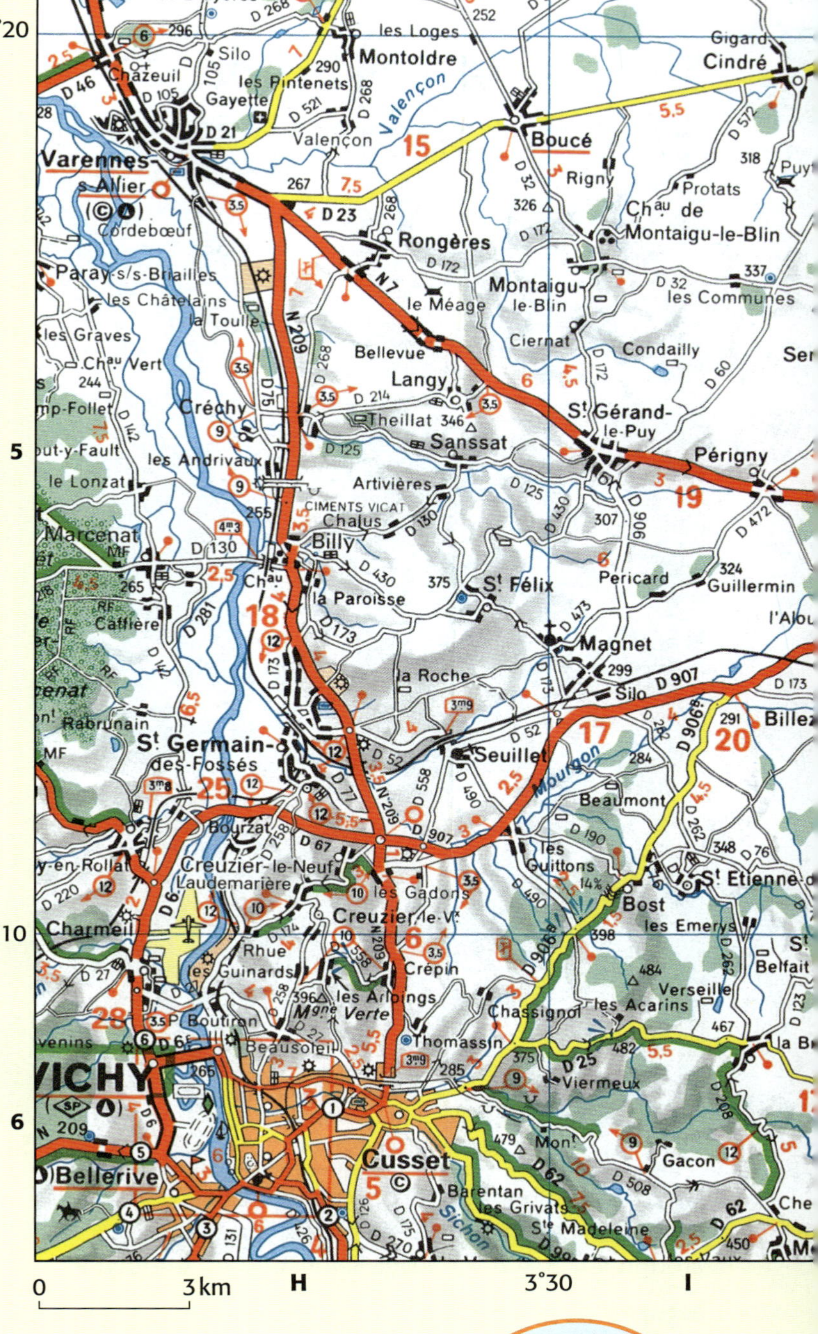

◄ *The mayor's poster.*

Did you know?
♦ France has 8000 km of motorways.
♦ On many of them you have to pay a toll.

Did you know?
♦ In France they drive on the right.

The Paris problem

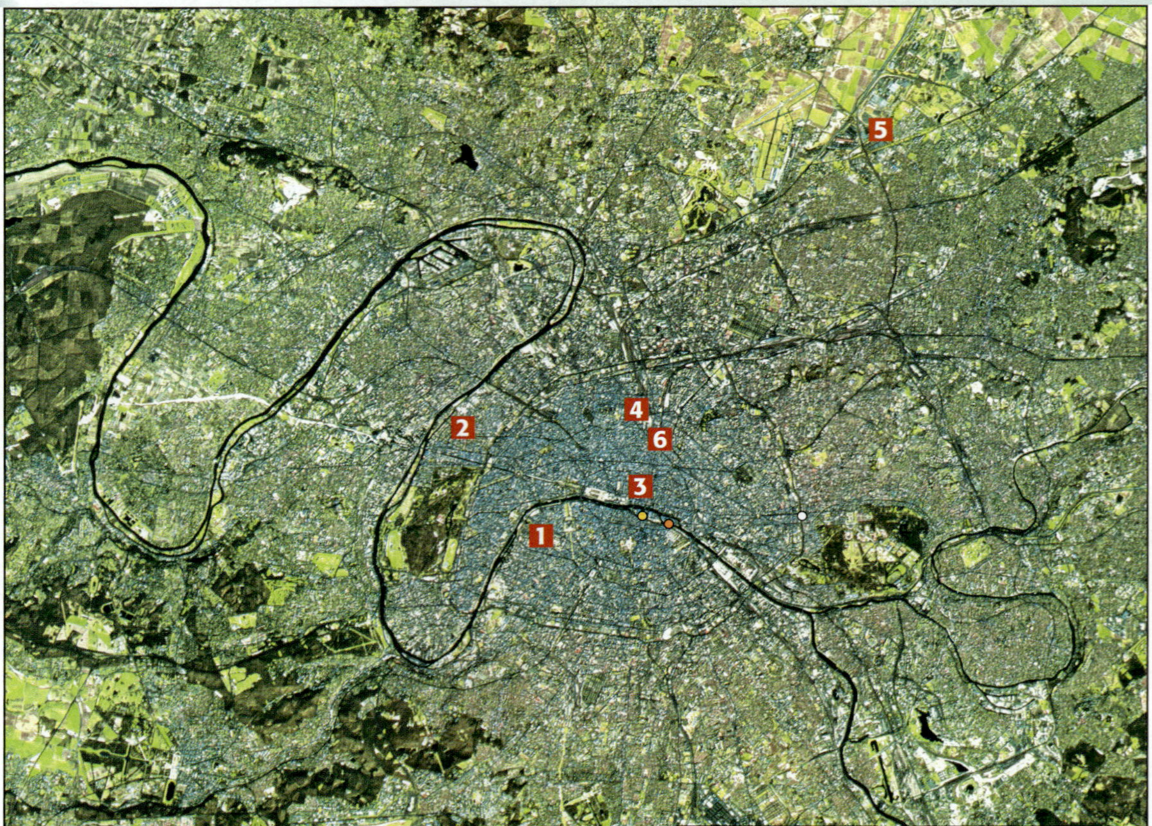

La Tour Eiffel

La Défense

Arc de Triomphe

Sacré Coeur

Gare du Nord

Charles de Gaulle airport

Key

- urban areas
- forests
- pasture (grazing)
- crops
- ○ ○ ● ○ see text below for these

Paris, one of Europe's most beautiful cities. Here is a satellite image of the city and the area around it. Look at the River Seine snaking through it.

How Paris grew …

◆ Paris began on two little islands in the Seine, now called the Île de la Cité (○) and the Île St Louis (●). People were already living on these islands, fishing, before the Romans got there over 2200 years ago.

◆ The settlement grew, spreading out in circles. By 1800, it had over half a million people.

◆ Today the ring road or **le Périphérique** (○) marks the boundary of the **City of Paris**.

◆ The City and built-up area around it form the **Paris conurbation**.

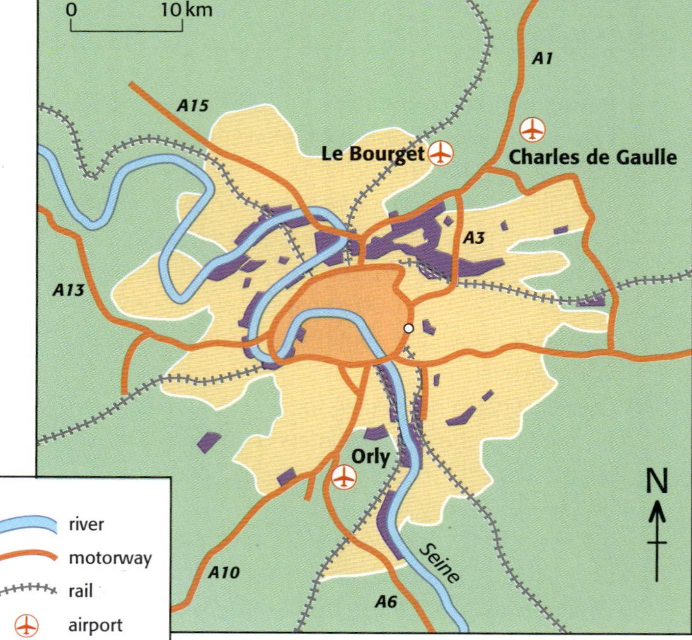

In the City of Paris most people rent apartments in blocks like these. (Even rich people.)

In the north and east of the City, many apartment blocks are run down and crowded.

The 1950s and '60s brought high-rise estates to Paris. Some are now very run down.

Today, on the edges of Paris, modern estates are being built for business people.

… and grew, and grew …

This graph shows how Paris grew in the hundred years from 1900 to 2000.

By 1970 it had big problems. Terrible traffic jams, pollution, lots of run-down housing, lots of poverty, and not enough homes.

The problems were worst in the north and east, in the 'working class' districts that had grown around the industrial areas. Look at the map on page 54.

(The west of Paris has always been wealthiest.)

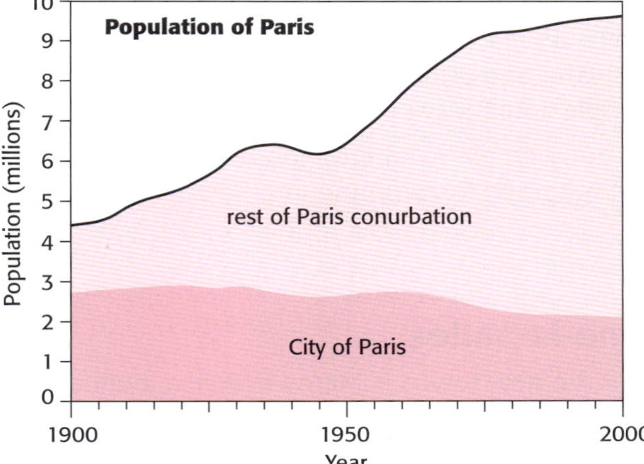

How they tackled the problem

The government decided to:

- redevelop the suburbs at key points or **nodes**, to give more housing, more offices, better shops, and more services such as health and sports centres. It chose La Défense (**2**) as one node.
- build five brand new towns outside Paris, all within easy reach. You can find out more about these in the next unit.
- get businesses to **decentralise** from Paris to other parts of France. (See page 49.) The aim was to help Paris *and* poorer regions.

▲ A traffic jam in Paris: faster by foot?

Your turn

1 What is a *conurbation*? (Glossary?)

2 Draw a *large* sketch map of Paris and its surroundings, based on the satellite image and map on page 54.

  a Mark in and label:
- **i** the River Seine
- **ii** the two islands at the heart of Paris
- **iii** le Périphérique
- **iv** the motorways out of the city
- **v** the location of the Eiffel Tower, La Défense, Arc de Triomphe, the three airports, and Gare du Nord where the Eurostar trains come in.

  b Shade in the built-up area – one shade for the City of Paris and another for the rest of the conurbation.

  c Add further shading (lines or hatching?) to show:
- **i** industrial areas **ii** farmland **iii** forests

  d Finally add a north arrow, a key and a label.

3 a Look at the graph above. Between which years did the *total* population of Paris grow fastest?

  b What kinds of problems would this growth have caused for Paris? (Think of things like water supply and schools, as well as traffic and housing.)

  c What is happening to the population of the City of Paris now? Suggest a reason for this.

  d Compare the population growth for Paris with that for France for the same period (page 47). What do you notice?

The new towns around Paris

Big problems need big solutions …

Five new towns

By 1970 Paris was crowded, polluted, and packed with traffic. Something had to be done to take the pressure off. The answer? Five new towns.

This map shows the five towns, built along parallel lines each side of Paris, and close to it. The aim was to create:

- clean, green, pleasant environments to live in …
- … with good public transport into Paris, so that people could leave their cars at home …
- … but with plenty of local jobs, so that people did not *need* to commute into Paris.

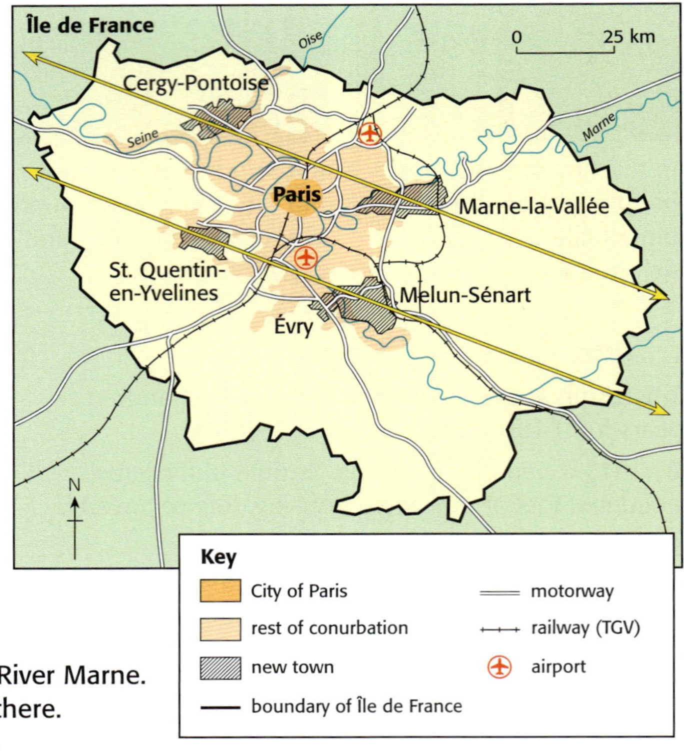

Marne-la-Vallée

One of the new towns is Marne-la-Vallée, built along the River Marne. It was developed around the villages and castles already there. Look at the map below and the photos on the next page.

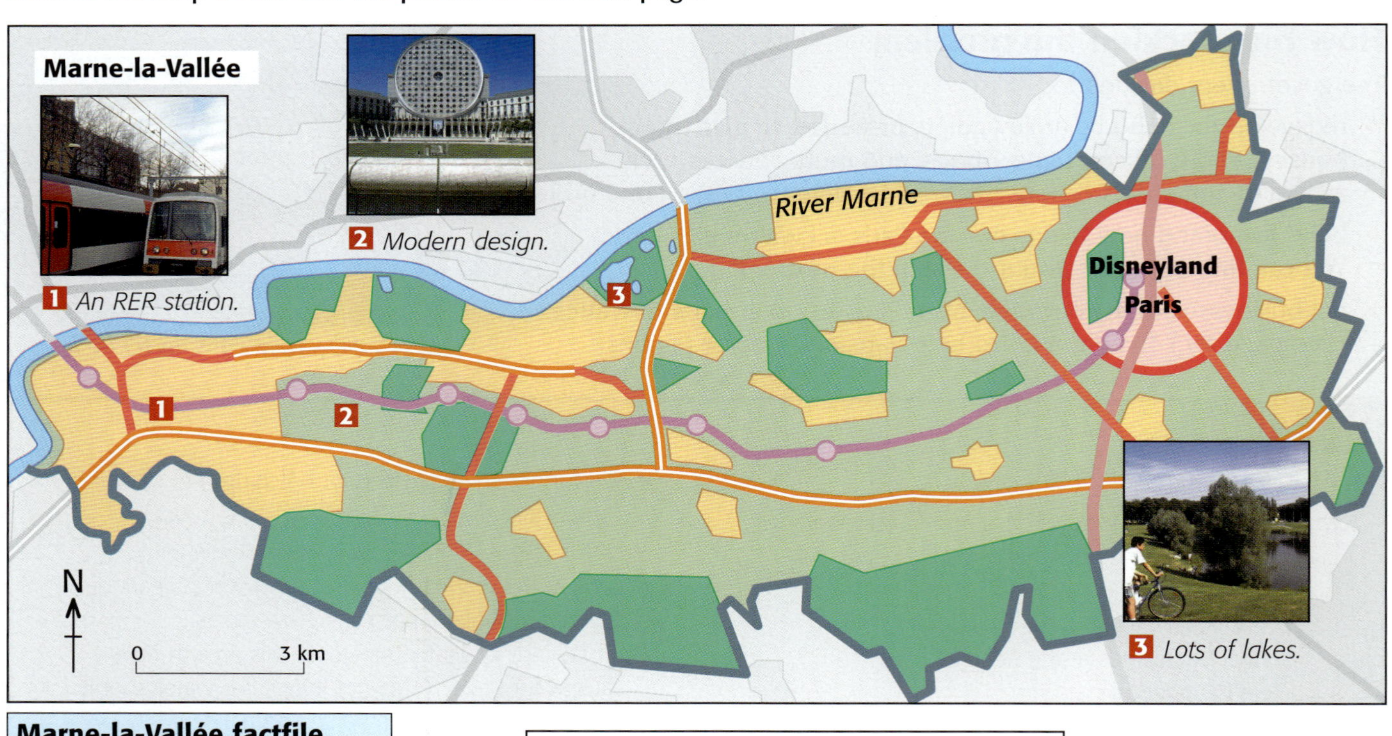

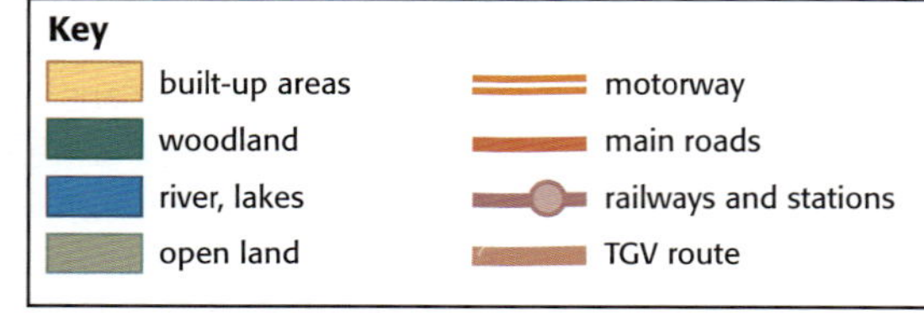
3   Lots of lakes.

Marne-la-Vallée factfile

- 13 km from Paris
- 15 000 hectares
- nearly 260 000 people by 2001
- over 2000 businesses by 2001
- over 107 000 jobs by 2001

▲ *Modern buildings in Marne-la-Vallée.*

▲ *It's a pleasant place to live …*

▲ *… and it has Disneyland Paris.*

Europe's Disneyland

Millions of people have visited Marne-la-Vallée already. Including you?
Because it's the home of Disneyland Paris, which opened in 1992.
It gets around 12 million visitors a year.

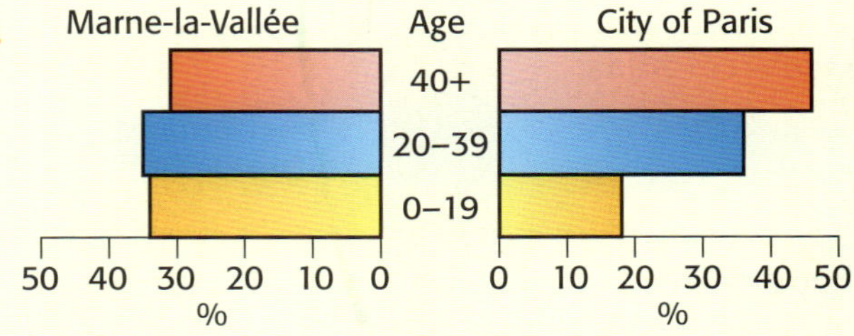

Your turn

1 The government hoped the new towns would help
Paris. In what ways could they do this?

2 The siting of the new towns allows *corridor growth*.
See if you can work out what that means.

3

Year	Population of Marne-la-Vallée
1975	103 000
1982	152 000
1990	211 000
1999	246 000
2001	256 000
2006	273 000
?	307 000 (maximum)

a Look at this table. The population numbers have
been *rounded off*. What does that mean?

b Some numbers are in blue. Why?

c Draw a line graph for the data. Mark the *Year* axis
up to 2020 and the *Population* axis up to 310 000.

d The town was planned with a maximum population
of 307 000 in mind. Around which year will it
reach that? How did you decide?

4 Compare the population structures.

a What differences do you notice?

b Come up with reasons to explain them.

c Name some services that might be in greater
demand in Marne-la-Vallée than in the City of Paris.

5 They could have built Disneyland anywhere in France
or the rest of Europe. Suggest reasons why:

a Marne-la-Vallée is a good choice

b the Marne-la-Vallée planners welcomed Disney.

6 You used to live in Paris, in the apartment block
marked ⬤ on page 55. But last month you moved to
Marne-la-Vallée, to the house marked ⬤ above.
Write a chatty letter to your friend Alice (who lived
next door in Paris) telling her your impressions of
Marne-la-Vallée so far.

France in the world

France has had a lot of influence on the world, for three reasons. It colonised many other countries, it helped to set up the European Union … and then there's all that culture!

France's political links

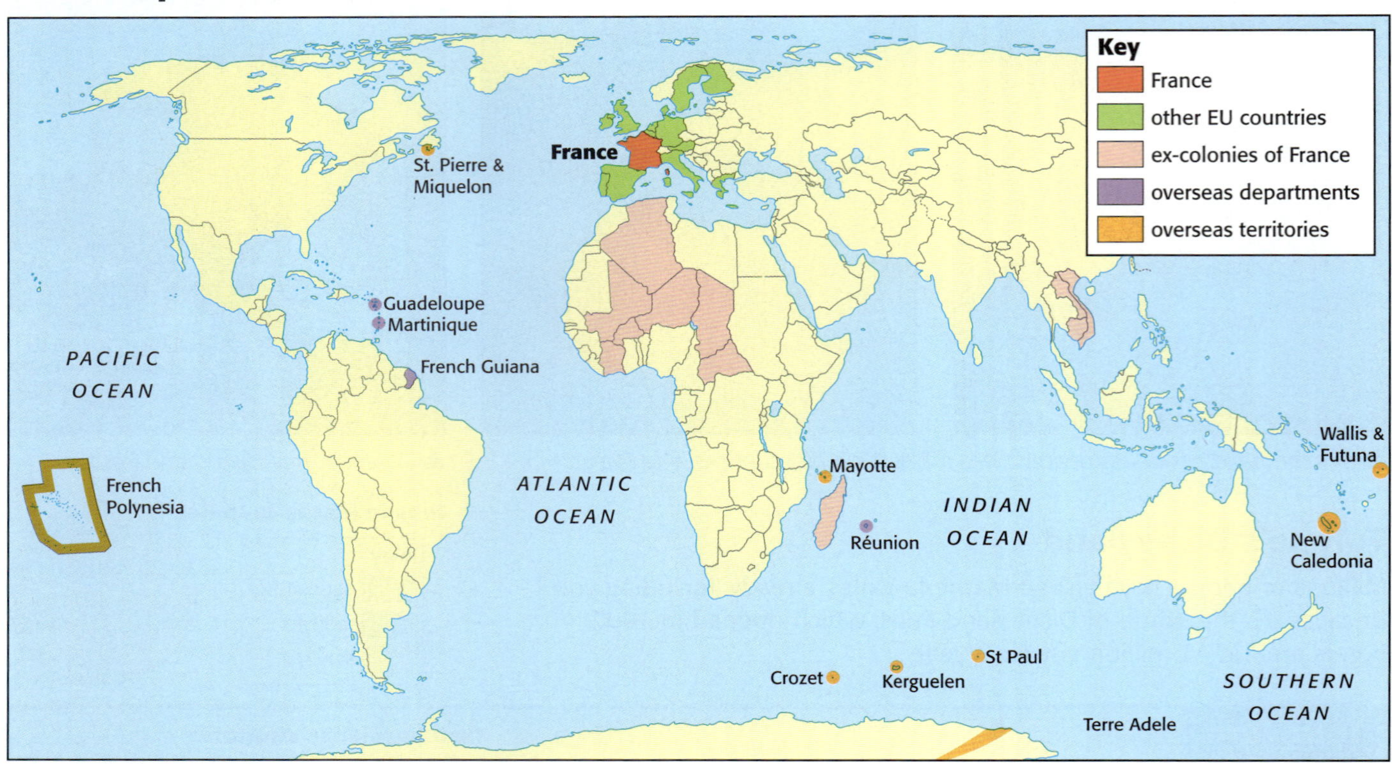

France's colonies

France was the world's second largest colonial power after Britain.

◆ Some of the places it claimed remain as overseas **departments** and **territories**, and send politicians to the French Parliament.

◆ They give France a base in every ocean – which could be useful one day!

◆ They, and most of the ex-colonies, also do most of their trading with France.

◆ French is widely spoken in many of these places.

▲ *Many people from its ex-colonies have settled in France.*

France in the European Union (EU)

France and Germany were the key founders of the EU.

◆ The countries in the EU trade freely with each other, without barriers. They also co-operate in many other ways. (You can find out more about the EU in the next unit.)

◆ Today, the European Parliament is based in France, at Strasbourg in Alsace.

▲ *The home of the European Parliament in Strasbourg.*

Et aussi …

These are other links between France and the rest of the world.

1 Culture

The world loves French culture.

◆ French cuisine and wines find their way almost everywhere.

◆ Paris is one of the world's main fashion centres.

◆ French writers, philosophers, painters and film makers have influenced the world.

3 Tourism

France is the most visited country in the world!

◆ Over 70 million foreign tourists arrive in France each year …

◆ … and over 14 million French people go abroad as tourists.

4 Treaties

France has signed many treaties with other countries. For example:

◆ to reduce global warming
◆ to protect the Antarctic
◆ to protect the ozone layer
◆ against dumping of waste at sea
◆ against whaling.

2 Trade

Like every country, France depends on other countries for trade. This shows its top 20 trading partners for 1997:

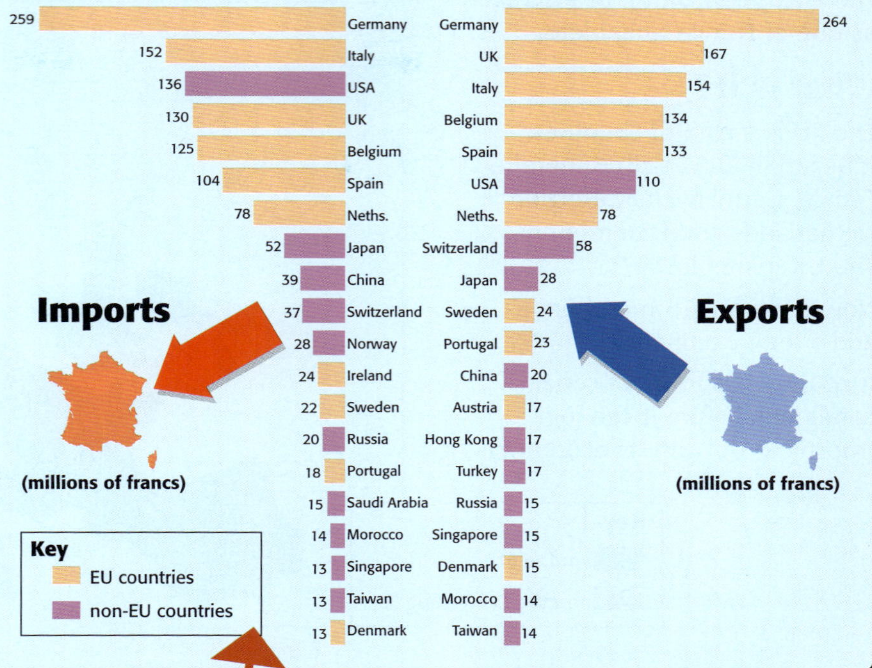

5 Aid

◆ Like most MEDCs, France gives some aid to poorer countries.

◆ In 1997 it gave $6.3 billion in aid.

◆ Most of this went to its ex-colonies.

GDP: how France compares *

Rank	Country	GDP ($ billion)
1	USA	9600
2	Japan	4600
3	Germany	1870
4	UK	1420
5	France	1280
6	China	1230
7	Italy	1040
8	Egypt	920
9	Canada	700
10	Brazil	590

* This is the total GDP (or wealth) for each country. It does not tell you how wealthy the people are. China has to share its wealth among far more people than France does!

Your turn

1 On which continent were most of France's colonies?

2 See if you can name the ex-colony from which France exported tonnes of elephant tusks. (Pages 124 – 125?)

3 Name four other ex-colonies of France.

4 Today France still has a base in every ocean. Try to think of some ways this could benefit France.

5 Look at France's trade for 1997.
   a To which country did it sell most?
   b From which did it buy most?
   c In its trade with China, which country earned more?
   d In its trade with the UK, which earned more?

6 Now write a short essay on *France's interdependence in the world.* (Glossary?) Not more than 250 words!

More about the European Union

The **European Union** or **EU** began as one of France's big ideas.

What is it?

The EU is a club of countries. It began in 1957 with 6 members: France, Germany, Italy, Belgium, Netherlands and Luxembourg. The UK joined in 1973.

Now there are 15 members – and a long waiting list!

A country has to meet certain conditions before it can join (mostly to do with its economy).

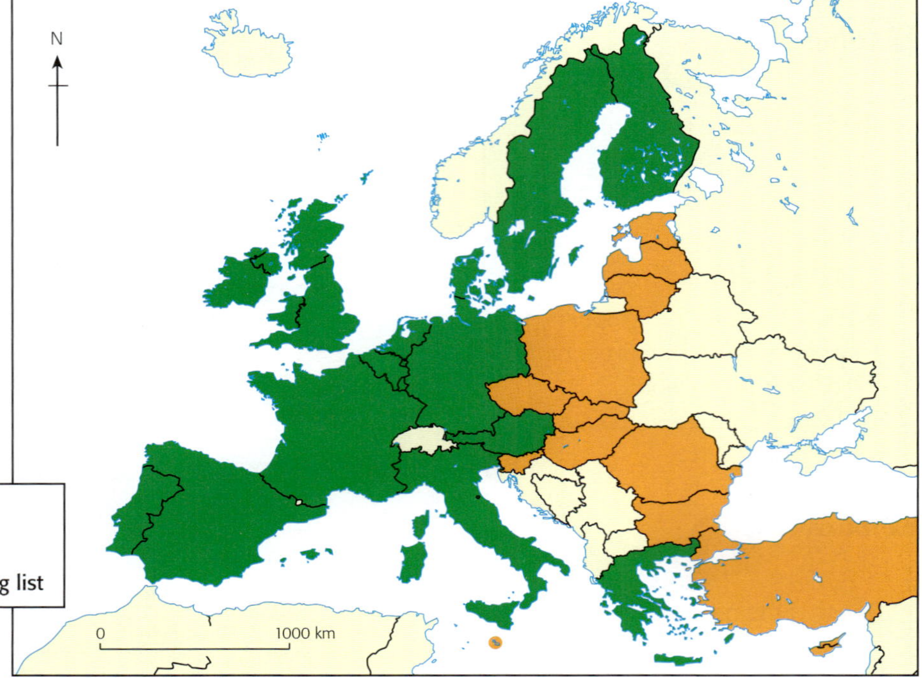

What are the benefits of being in the EU?

1 Helps trade

Companies in the EU can buy and sell goods freely across the EU, without long waits at borders, or extra taxes. That's good for business, and gives shoppers more choice.

2 Freedom to move around

An EU citizen has the right to live, work and travel freely anywhere in the EU. Great if you would like to work in Paris or Madrid, for example.

3 Help for poorer regions

The EU gives grants to poorer regions in the EU (for example with high unemployment), to help them develop.

4 Support for farmers

It gives grants to farmers to help them produce foods the EU needs, and to protect the countryside and wildlife.

Who pays?

All EU countries pay money into the EU Central Bank.
After lots of haggling, they agree on a budget.

The reason for helping the poorer areas is to make the whole EU stronger, and help it produce more.

This bar chart shows how much the member countries paid in, and got back in aid, in 2000.

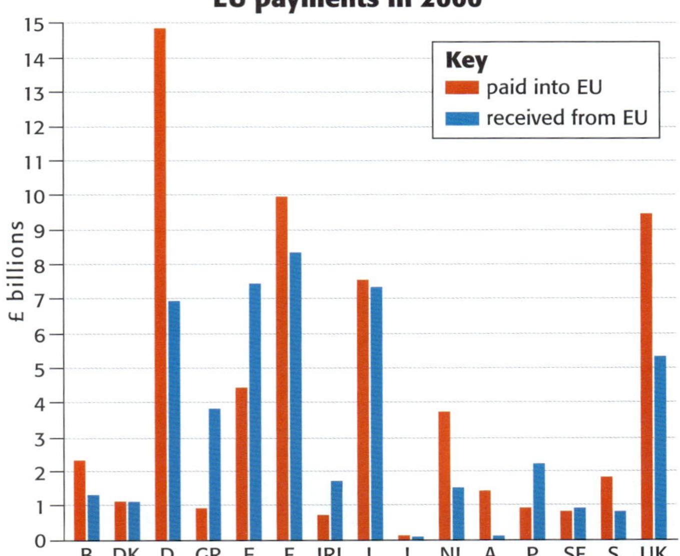

So is everybody happy?

Non! The EU has brought many benefits, but there are complaints.

It has lots of rules and regulations about goods that are traded. These have upset some people.

It has also rules and regulations about people's rights at work. Not everyone likes these either.

And some people are afraid that the EU will become a 'United States of Europe'.

Your turn

1 Using the map on page 122 to help, list the 15 countries in the EU. (You will need your list again for **3** and **5**.)

2 Name 5 countries waiting to join the EU.

3 Now look at the bar chart at the top of this page. It uses initials for the 15 EU countries. But which is which? Write the correct initial(s) after each name in your list from **1**. (Hint: It's España in Spanish!)

4 Look again at the bar chart.
 a Which country *paid in* most in 2000?
 b Which paid in least? Suggest a reason for this.
 c About how much did the UK pay in?

5 a What do these terms mean? (Glossary?)
  i net donor **ii** net recipient
 b On your list from **1**, underline the net donors in one colour and net recipients in another. Add a key.

6 Overall, which country do you think did best for EU aid, in 2000? Explain clearly how you decided.

7
From: a.collier@ashfield.org.uk
To: The Prime Minister@BigBen.org.UK
Sir, we give more money to the EU than we get from it. That doesn't make sense to me. Why don't we leave the EU and you send the money up here? We need it!

You are the Prime Minister. Write a serious reply.

Walter's global jeans

Walter, trying on his latest birthday present …

Getting Walter's jeans together

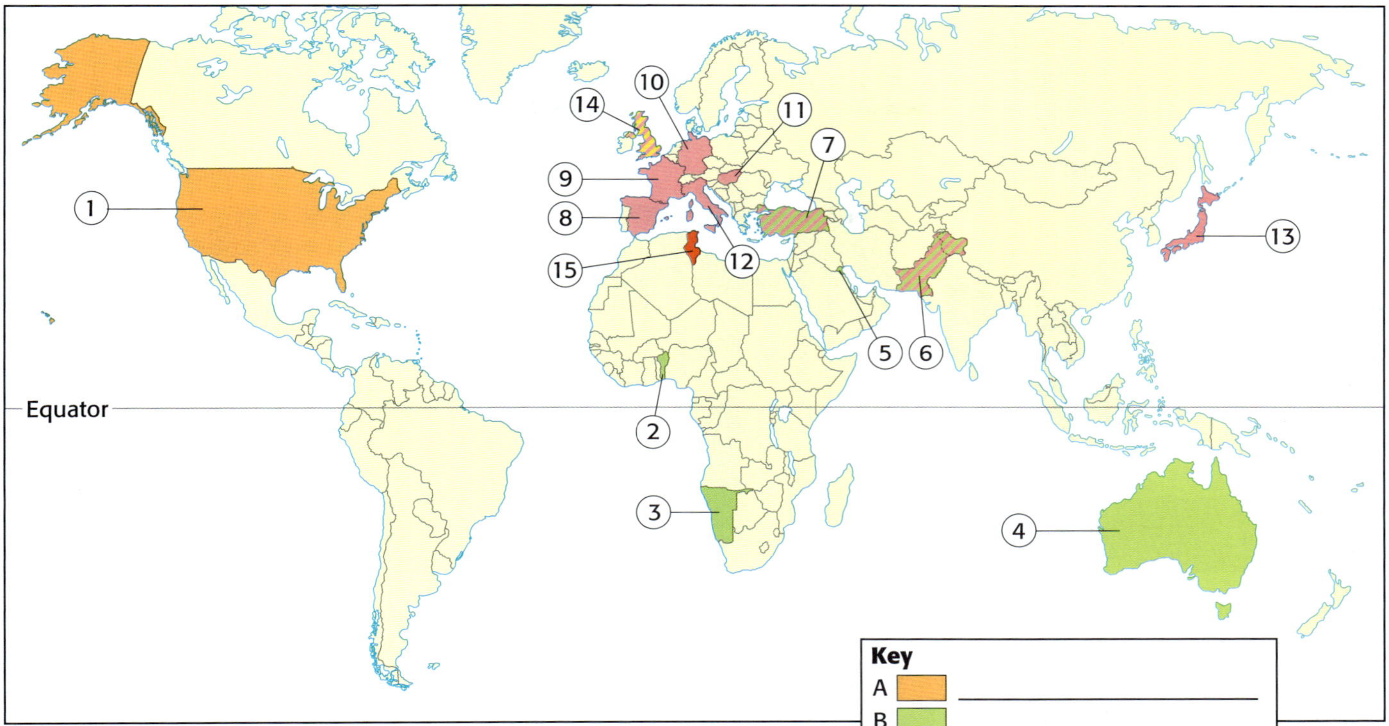

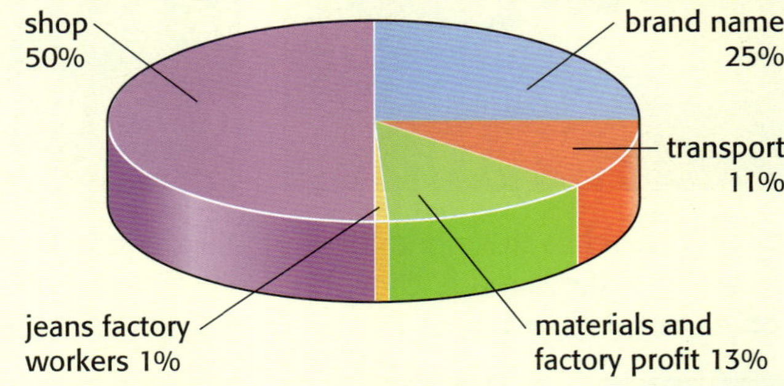

This map shows the 15 countries that were involved in producing Walter's jeans. Some of your clothes involve just as many countries. (In fact you're all kitted out in geography!)

Key

A		_____________________
B		_____________________
C		_____________________
D		_____________________
E		_____________________

Your turn

1 Which *continents* contributed to Walter's jeans?

2 Name the countries marked 1 – 15 on the map above. Pages 124 – 125 will help. Answer like this: ① = ____ Then, after each country, write what it contributed to the jeans. (For example, *zip*.)

3 The map key is not complete. Complete it by matching the letters to the terms in italics below. Give your answer like this: A = ________________
manufacture and processing of materials
source of a raw material
making and finishing the jeans
design and brand name
country where jeans sold
The glossary may help, if you're stuck.

4 Some countries on the map (for example the UK) have stripes of a second colour. Explain why.

5 The table on the right shows wages in clothing factories. Use it and the map above to explain why:
a the American company didn't make the jeans in the USA
b the denim was sent 1000 km from Italy to Tunisia, to be sewn into jeans.

Where the money goes when you buy a pair of jeans

shop 50%
brand name 25%
transport 11%
materials and factory profit 13%
jeans factory workers 1%

6 Look at the pie chart. Walter's granny paid £40 for the jeans for Walter. Of this, how much went to:
a the shop where she bought them?
b the American company whose label they carry?
c the worker(s) who sewed them?

Average hourly wage for workers in clothing factories

Country	Hourly wage (£)
USA	6.24
UK	6.05
Italy	6.01
Tunisia	0.92

Behind the swoosh

Let's look more closely at how clothes get put together.
We'll take a well-known label as our example: Nike.
Perhaps you have some Nike things?

the state
of Oregon

USA

The Nike operation

Nike is based in Oregon in the USA. This is the headquarters from which the business is controlled.

The people who run Nike are anxious to make as much money as possible. So Nike keeps on …

… bringing out new designs for its clothing and trainers. But it does not *make* these things itself.

Instead it searches the world for places to get things made cheaply, in other people's factories.

Nike goods are made in about 30 different countries, mostly by young women like these.

While they are working really hard, so is Nike – getting people like you to buy things with the swoosh on.

Nike spends around a billion dollars in total on advertising, in around 140 different countries.

It pays top athletes millions to wear Nike products, as another way to advertise.

It supplies its goods to 47 000 shops round the world. (It owns just a fraction of these shops itself.)

The spread of Nike

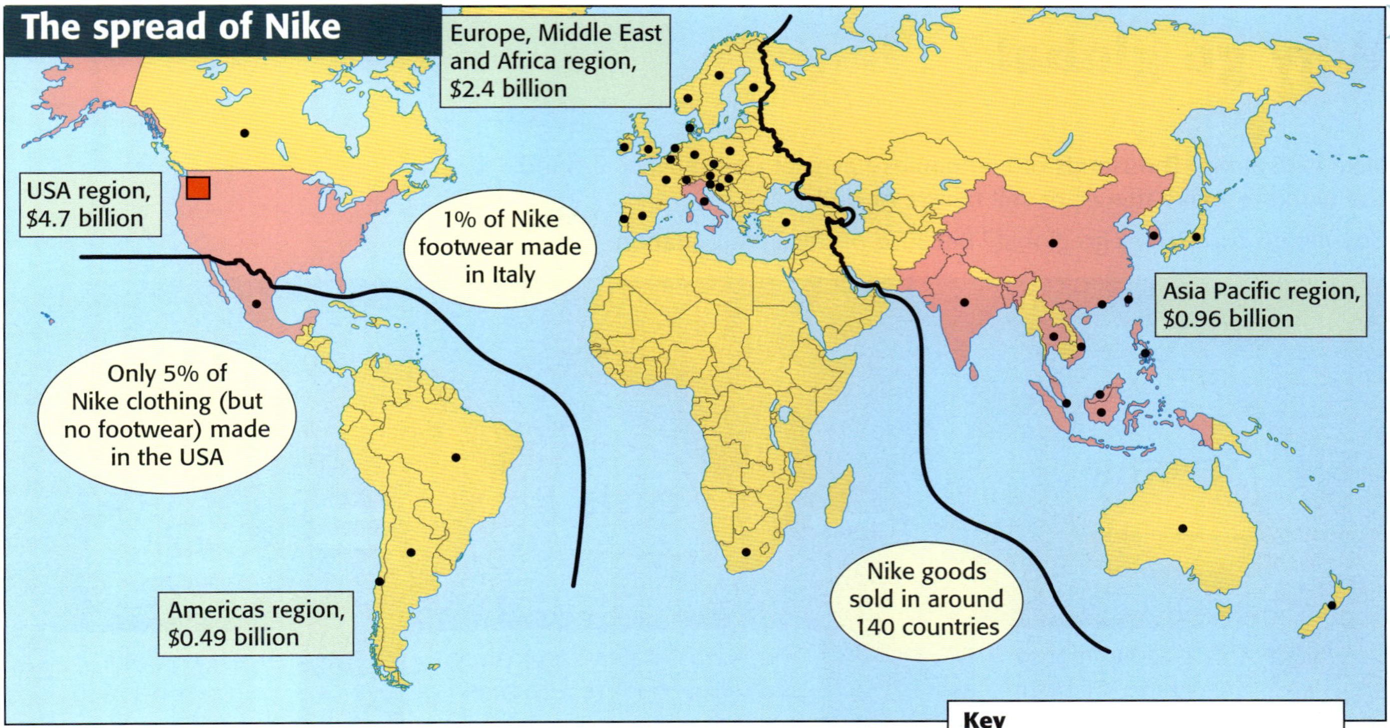

As this map shows, Nike is a **transnational corporation** or **TNC**. That means it is a company with branches in many countries.

The spread of Nike is an example of **globalisation**. Globalisation means the way companies, and ideas, and lifestyles, are spreading more and more easily around the world.

Globalisation affects *you*. It influences what foods you eat and clothes you wear. It links you to people all over the world. When *you* make a decision, like what to buy, you can affect people thousands of miles away.

Your turn

1 What kinds of goods does Nike sell? Write a list.

2 Using the map on pages 124–125 to help you, name:
   a six countries where Nike has a branch *and* gets goods made
   b two countries where Nike goods are made but Nike does not (yet) have a branch
   c eight other countries where Nike has a branch.

3 Nike is a *transnational corporation* or TNC. Its growth is an example of *globalisation*. Explain each of the two terms in italics.

4 Now compare the Nike map with the one on page 16.
   a Look at real GDP per capita for the countries where most Nike goods are made. What do you notice?
   b Suggest a reason why Nike chooses these countries.
   c On which *continent* does Nike *sell* most goods? Is it rich or poor?
   d Suggest a reason why Nike does not (yet) get goods made in countries like Ghana.

5 There are 191 countries in the world. In about what % of these are Nike goods sold?

6 The spread of Nike is an example of globalisation. See if you can give at least *four* other examples. (Companies? TV programmes? Examples from sport or politics?)

7 Now give six examples of how globalisation affects *you*. (Think about what you wear and eat, and what you do in your free time.) Give your answer as a drawing.

8 Each of these helps the process of globalisation. For each, write a short paragraph to explain why.

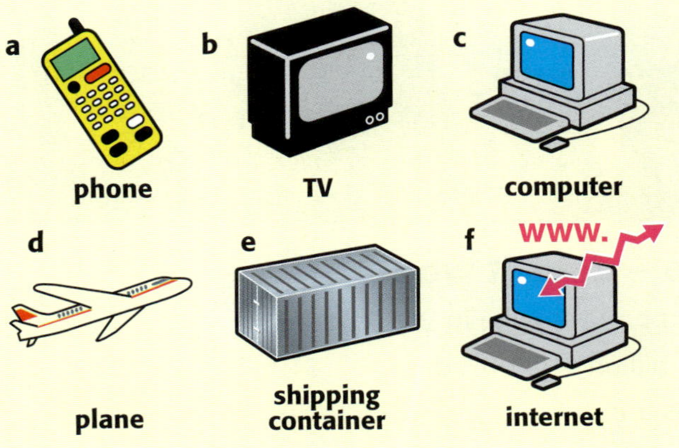

Nike isn't alone. Thousands of companies have set up branches around the world to make things, or sell things, or both.

So why do companies go global? Because of this little equation:

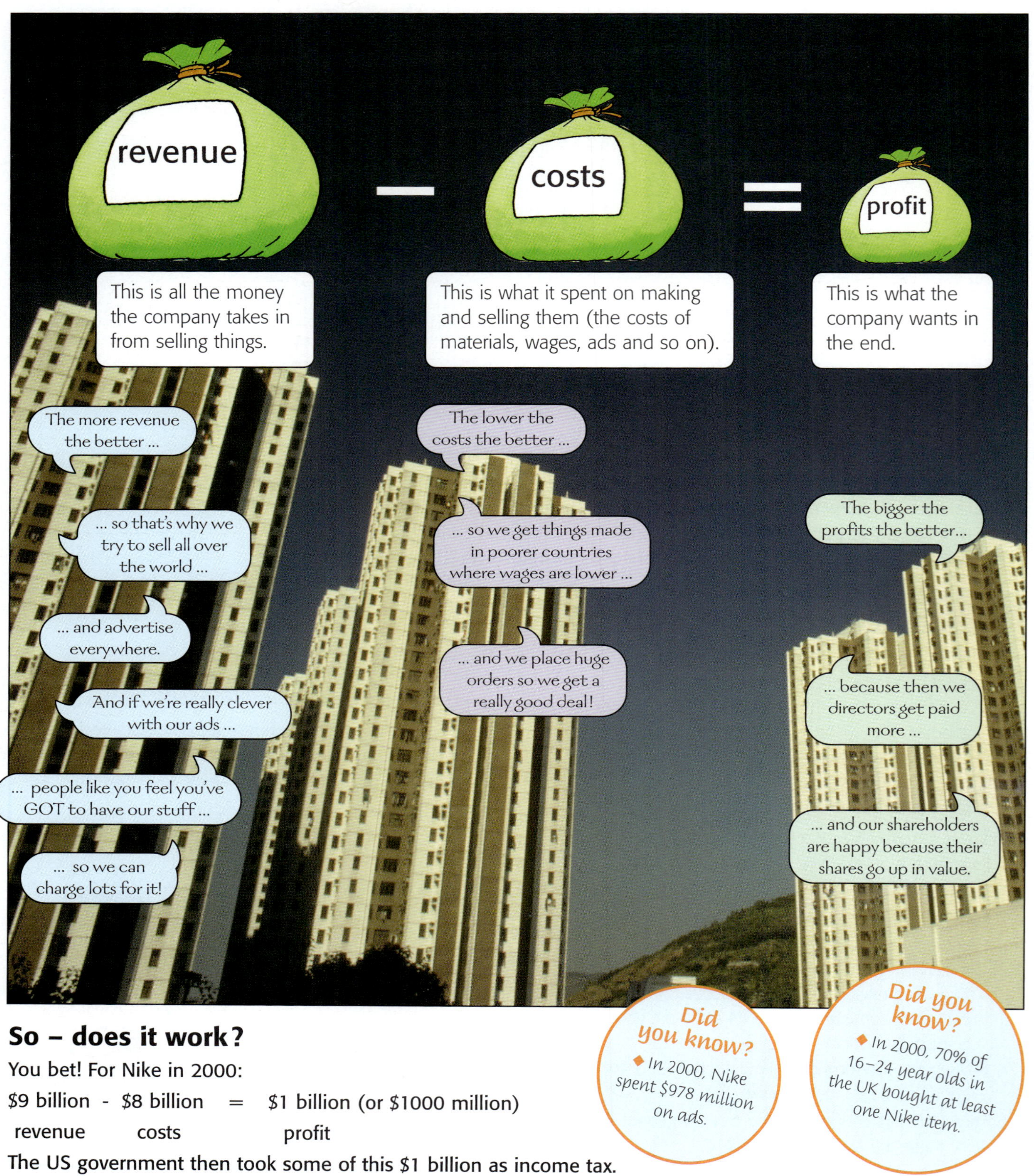

So – does it work?

You bet! For Nike in 2000:

$9 billion - $8 billion = $1 billion (or $1000 million)
  revenue   costs   profit

The US government then took some of this $1 billion as income tax.

Some other TNCs

Nike is very small compared with some TNCs, as this first table shows.
Exxon Mobil, the biggest company in the world, is over 20 times larger.

Revenues for 10 TNCs (in 2000)			
TNC	**Produces**	**Based in**	**Revenue ($ billions)**
Exxon Mobil	oil/petrol	USA	210
Ford	cars	USA	181
BP	oil/petrol	UK	148
Toyota	cars	Japan	121
Nestlé	foods	Switzerland	48
Microsoft	software	USA	23
Coca-Cola	you know what	USA	20
GAP	clothing	USA	14
McDonalds	you know what	USA	14
Nike	sports goods	USA	9

GDP for 10 countries (in 2000)	
Country	**GDP (or total wealth produced) ($ billions)**
USA	9595
India	1800
UK	1245
Belgium	237
Switzerland	191
Bangladesh	184
Nigeria	106
Tunisia	52
Ghana	34
Jamaica	8

Now look at the second table. It shows the GDP for some countries for 2000. Many of the TNCs produced more wealth than many of those countries!

In fact Exxon Mobil earned more that year than over 180 of the world's countries did!

The USA and Japan win for big companies. Of the 200 largest companies in the world, 59 are American and 58 are Japanese. (And all are TNCs.)

▶ *Guess who gets over 45 million customers a day, in 120 countries?*

Your turn

1 Copy and complete, using terms from the brackets.
The more _____ a company sells and the _____ its _______ the higher its _______ will be.
(*money   profits   losses   costs   goods   lower*)

2 Like every company, Nike aims to increase its profits.
  a Make a *large* copy of the Venn diagram on the right. (Use a full page.)
  b On your diagram, write in **A–H** below, *in full*, in the correct loops. (Small neat writing!) If you think one belongs in both loops, write it where they overlap.
    A It gets 40% of its trainers made in China.
    B It runs a website.
    C It sponsors top school sports teams.
    D It closed its trainer factories in the USA.
    E It now owns no trainer or clothing factories.
    F It employs sports scientists.
    G It brings out new styles regularly.
    H It opened a branch office in Australia.

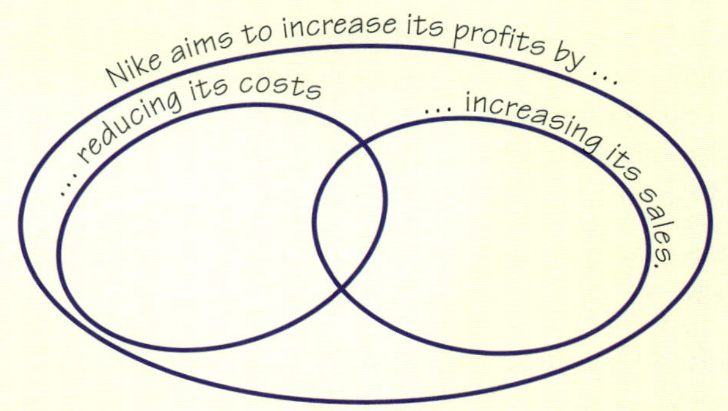

3 Now look at the tables at the top of the page.
  a What is *GDP*? Give your answer as a sentence.
  b Make *one* list showing the 20 companies and countries, in order of revenue / GDP. (USA first.)
  c On your list, underline the countries in one colour and the companies in another. Add a key and a title.

4 Which do you think has more power in the world, Exxon Mobil or Ghana? Explain your answer.

A fashion victim?

Nike is not the only company to get clothing made cheaply in poorer countries. Look at the list on the right.

So who are the people who make the clothes? Rosa in Manila is one.

Rosa's day

Rosa can hardly keep her eyes open. But she must must must concentrate. Otherwise she'll pierce her fingers. Or sew crookedly. If she does that, the supervisor will yell at her again.

She's tired because she worked overtime last night. Until 2 am. She didn't want to, but if you refuse they sack you on the spot. Everyone is forced to do overtime now for the big Christmas orders.

She dragged herself in again this morning, at 7 am. To sew non-stop, all day long, the side seams for sports joggers. Snatch a pair from the trolley beside you, slap them on the machine, race down each leg as fast as you can, throw them back on the trolley, grab another pair. On and on and on. By 8 her shoulders were aching. By 9 the heat was already stifling. And still an hour to go till the toilet break, when she can escape from the clatter of 500 machines for 10 minutes.

She thinks sadly about her family and village, like she does every morning. She left home just after her 16th birthday, 5 months ago. She was so excited about the job. They'd promised she'd earn enough to send some home. But the 280 pesos she gets (£4) for a 12-hour day is hardly enough to live on, when they take out rent and lunch.

Overtime again tonight. At 2 am she will leave the sewing section and drag herself past the guards, down the path by the barbed wire fence, to the room she shares with five others. Three bunk beds. No chairs. No wardrobe. She'll hang her clothes on the nails in the wall and climb into her bunk, too tired to talk to anyone.

Another working day tomorrow. It's usually six days a week, but in this busy period it's often seven. She's heard the clothes sell for high prices in Europe – more than she will earn for a hundred hours of sewing. She often wonders about the people who buy them. If they could see her, and her factory, what would they think?

She wishes she could give up and go home. But she can't. She must earn, and there's no work in the village.

Adapted from newspaper articles, 2000

Large % of clothing made in LEDCs *	
Calvin Klein	Timberland
Ralph Lauren	Tommy Hilfiger
The Gap	Next
Principles	Topshop
Warehouse	Oasis
Miss Selfridge	M & S

** This is not a complete list!*

▲ *No rest for Rosa till she gets back to the hut that's now her home …*

Just one of many …

Over half the clothing in UK shops is sewn in LEDCs by girls like Rosa. Many are from rural areas, with little education, and few other ways to earn a living.

Not all the clothes factories are bad. Some are more modern than UK factories. But there are many **sweatshops**, like Rosa's, where young women work in poor conditions, for very low pay. If the factory has no orders they get no pay. They can be sacked without warning.

How does it happen?

How does it happen that people like Rosa have to work in these conditions?
Again we take Nike as example – but it could be anyone:

Nike designs a new range of clothing. Next, it has to be made!

An executive goes to find a factory in an LEDC, where wages are low.

The factory owner takes on the work – and aims to make a profit.

The clothing gets finished on time. People like it. It sells really well.

The workers are not happy, but they need the jobs.

So he forces his workers to work very quickly, for very little pay.

Now shoppers are finding out about sweatshops, and protesting.
Nike and other companies have promised to inspect the factories they
use, and make them treat their workers better. But many thousands
like Rosa are still being exploited - all in the name of fashion.

Your turn

1 What's it like in Rosa's factory? Write a summary of the conditions there. (As a spider map, if you like.)

2 Rosa usually works a 6-day week, 12 hours a day.
   a How many hours a week is this?
   b How much does she earn for it?

3 Now look at the chain above. What would happen if:
   a the factory owner refused to work for Nike's terms?
   b the factory owner accepted Nike's terms, but decided to increase his workers' pay?
   c the workers went on strike?
   d the customers didn't like the new clothing?
   e the government of the LEDC passed a law that factories must pay higher wages?
   f customers refused to buy from Nike because of the sweatshops?
   g Nike forced the clothing factories to treat their workers better and pay them more?

4 Look again at the chain.
   Of all the people in it, who do you think:
   a has got *most* power to change things?
   b has got *least* power to change things?

5 

   Write down what you will say to each person in reply.

6 a Draw a development compass rose (page 5) and give it the title *How globalisation has affected Rosa*.
   b Write in questions you could ask, to explore how globalisation has changed Rosa's life.
   c Under your questions, write in any answers you can. (Use a different colour.)

Global actions, local effects

You saw how globalisation affects people like Rosa. Now let's look at the other side of the coin.

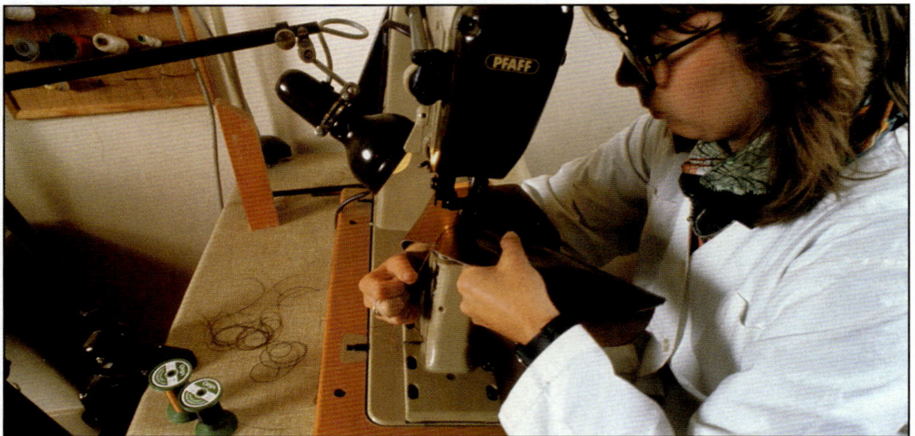

Annie's job takes flight

This is Annie at her machine. Or rather, it was Annie at her machine. But now the machine has gone. Annie's job has taken flight. Annie is unemployed.

The factory where Annie worked belonged to Dewhirst, the UK clothing manufacturer. It has just closed two of its factories – Annie's in Cheshire and another in Durham – with a loss of 1000 jobs. These factories made blouses, jackets, trousers and shirts, mainly for Marks & Spencer.

In fact 90% of what Dewhirst makes is for M&S. And that's the problem. Over the last two years, M&S has lost customers, and suffered a big fall in profits. So Dewhirst's profits have slumped too.

Now Dewhirst says it must cut costs to survive. It will still produce for M&S – but overseas. It is moving production to countries like Morocco, Indonesia and Malaysia, where costs are lower.

Not Annie's fault

A spokesman for Dewhirst said: 'These closures are no reflection on our UK employees. Their work has always been first class.' High praise, but it probably won't make Annie feel any better.

Other jobs under threat too

M&S sent out shock waves last year when it said *it* planned to buy more from overseas. For years it has tried to 'buy British', with 70% or more of its clothing made in the UK. Now that figure will fall to 30% in an attempt to cut costs. M&S then plans to lower its prices to lure customers back to its stores.

The UK clothing industry depended heavily on M&S. Annie's job is not the first to go, and won't be the last.
(Adapted from news reports, January 2000)

Did you know?

- In 2000, people in the UK spent £28 billion on clothing ...
- ... or about £470 for every man, woman and child.

Did you know?

- In the Middle Ages, wool and woollen cloth were Britain's main exports.

Did you know?

- The UK is the largest wool producer in Europe.
- It produces over 50 million kg of wool a year.
- Nearly 70% of it is exported.

Did you know?

- China is the world's biggest exporter of clothing (over 15% of the world's share).

▲ *For over 100 years M&S had strongly supported the UK clothing industry.*

Your turn

1 These five people are part of Annie's story.

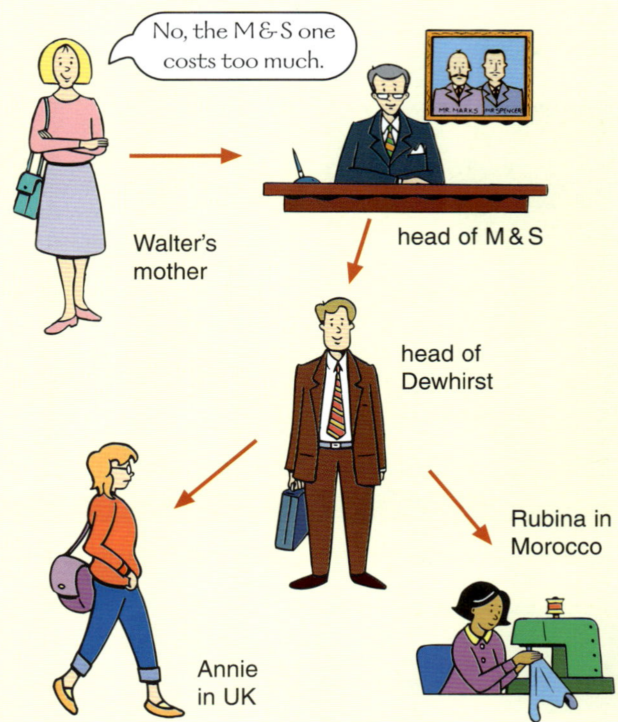

a What do you think the arrows mean?

b Make your own copy of the drawing, using stick people. Add thought bubbles for the other four people. (Big enough to write quite a lot in.)

c Fill in thoughts for the other four people.

2 Now do a reverse drawing, showing what the companies hope will happen as a result of the changes they have made.

3 Textiles and clothing have been important industries in the UK for centuries.
Study the 1950 map above. Then see if you can give reasons to explain:

a the main location for the wool industry (The map on page 121 may give you clues.)

b the two main locations for the cotton industry (Cotton is not grown in the UK!)

c the main location for hosiery (clue on page 38?)

d why the clothing industry was important around:
   i Liverpool **ii** London **iii** Newcastle

4 The table on the right shows exports and imports of clothing (in millions of dollars) for the UK.

a Show the export and import data on the same graph. (Choose any suitable type of graph.)

b Describe any trends you notice.

c Give reasons to explain these trends.

d If these trends continue, predict what the clothing industry will be like in the UK by the year 2020.

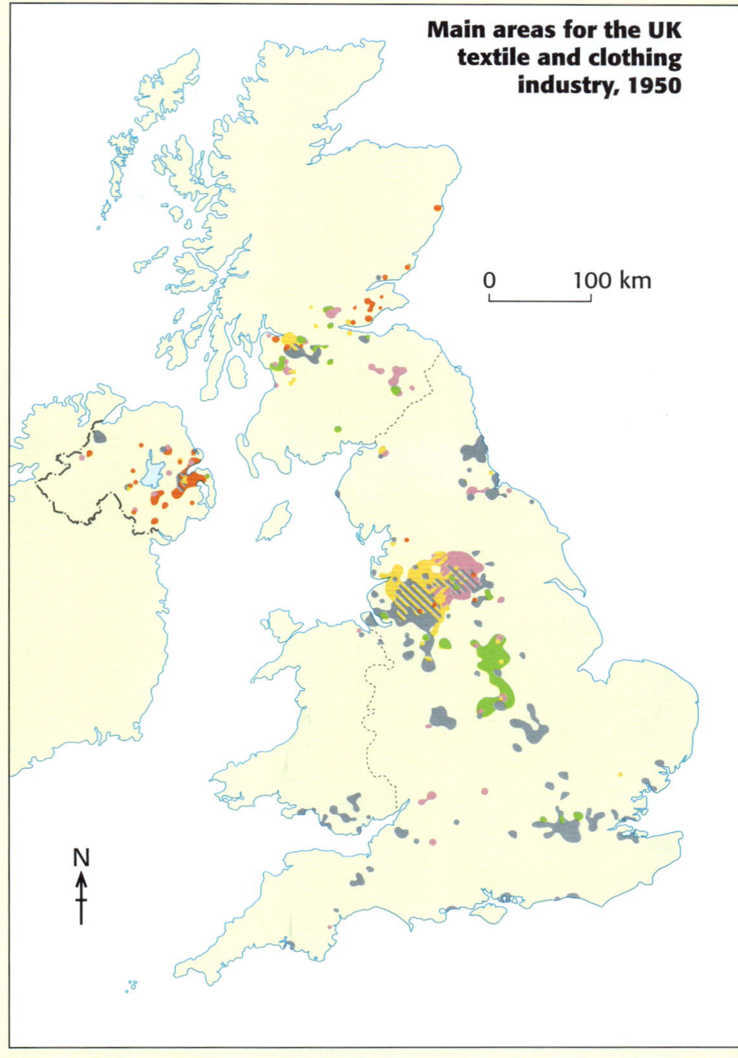

Key

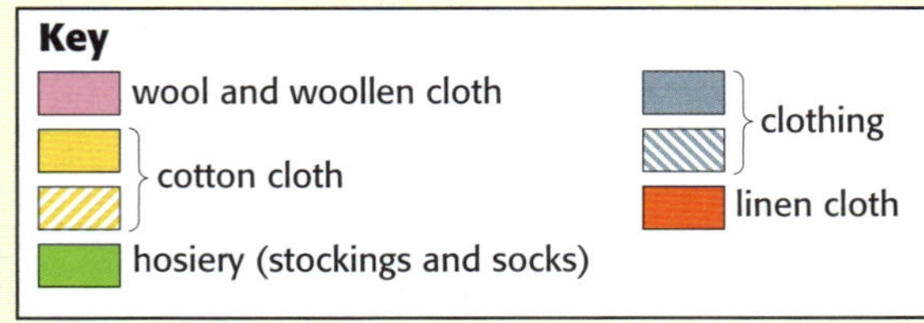

5 Now come up with some ideas to save the UK clothing industry. (You can't prevent imports.)
Think about things like the kinds of clothes that might sell well, designers, training schemes, grants.
Put your ideas in a memo to the Prime Minister.

UK exports and imports of clothing ($ millions)

Year	1990	1995	1998	1999	2000
Exports	3042	4648	4920	4487	4111
Imports	6961	8344	11977	12533	12992

Is globalisation a good thing?

Globalisation is going on in all kinds of businesses, not just clothing.
TNCs are spreading everywhere. Not just in LEDCs, but also in
MEDCs like the UK. Is this a good thing?

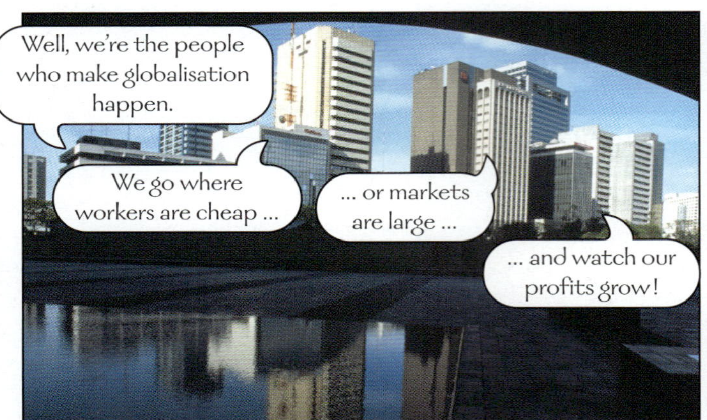

1 The TNCs think so. (They would!)

2 Many governments in LEDCs think so.

3 Many governments in MEDCs think so.

4 Many workers all over the world think so.

5 Many economists think so.

6 And the World Trade Organisation thinks so too.

So, many people are in favour of globalisation and think we all benefit.
But as you'll see in the next unit, many totally disagree!

More about the World Trade Organisation

The World Trade Organisation or **WTO** was formed to promote world trade. It is based in Geneva in Switzerland. Over 140 countries have joined it.

The WTO aims to remove barriers to trade between countries, so that companies can trade freely everywhere.

In the past, when countries fell out over trade they often went to war. The WTO aims to prevent this. For example if Europe tried to block imports of a crop from the USA, the WTO would try to settle the dispute peacefully.

Any country that joins the WTO has to sign an agreement to obey its trade rules.

▶ *Everyone here yet? Getting ready for a WTO meeting.*

Your turn

1 For each of these people, write down what you think is the *main* argument in favour of globalisation:

2 This is Asha. She works in Bangalore in India, doing accounts for UK companies.

They send her data via the internet in the evening (when it's morning in India). When they arrive into work next morning, the accounts are back, complete.

a Is this an example of globalisation? Explain.

b What argument do you think Asha would use in favour of globalisation?

c Asha wants more business from the UK. Write an e-mail for her to send to UK companies, telling them about the service she offers and the reasons they should employ her.

3 The UK is a member of the WTO.

a What is the WTO? Give its full name in your answer.

b Write down two aims of the WTO.

c Write a short section for the WTO website saying why globalisation is a good thing. (120 words max.)

Against globalisation

Lots of people are in favour of globalisation and TNCs –
and lots are against them!

1 Many politicians round the world are against.

2 So are some workers in LEDCs.

3 So are some workers in MEDCs ...

4 ... and many environmentalists everywhere.

5 Some economists are not too happy either.

6 Many people feel their culture is being eroded.

Protest goes global too …

Many people are worried about the effect of globalisation on the world's poorer countries.

They are especially worried about the World Trade Organisation, and its plans for free trade.

They say free trade just means TNCs are free to take over the world. And that it will help only the rich countries, and make poor countries poorer.

So protest has gone global too. When world leaders meet to discuss world trade these days, protesters from all over the world gather in their thousands.

For example in 2001, the leaders of the G8 group of nations met to discuss world trade and other issues at Genoa in Italy. Over 150 000 protesters turned up too. There were clashes between police and protesters. One protester was killed and 500 people injured.

(The G8 are the world's 7 richest industrial nations – the USA, Japan, France, Germany, Britain, Italy and Canada – plus Russia.)

▲ *Get the message?*

Your turn

1 Page 74 shows things people say against globalisation. Using these to help you, write:
   a a *social* argument against globalisation
   b an *economic* argument against it
   c an *environmental* argument against it.
   Give each as a short paragraph.

2 Globalisation is a complex issue.
   a From pages 72 and 74, pick out two arguments that are *exactly* opposite.
   b Now see if you can find *at least two more* pairs of opposite arguments. Write them down.

3 The photo above was taken at a big protest meeting against the WTO.
   a Name three groups of people you might expect to find there. (Would directors of TNCs turn up?)
   b Study the message on the placard. Then rewrite it as a short speech. (Not more than 100 words.)

4 On the right is Naresh, a security guard in India. He's guarding a building 4000 km away, in California! The CCTV pictures are sent by satellite. If he sees a problem he can quickly raise the alarm.
   You live in India. Write a letter to an Indian paper, in favour of *or* against the way the Californian company is employing Indian people.

5 And finally, you have a really important job. You are one of the G8 leaders. (Decide for yourself which one.)
   a First, do you think it is possible to halt globalisation? Write a note to another G8 leader giving your views about this.
   b You *are* worried about the power of the big TNCs. Write a set of guidelines you want TNCs to follow when they set up in LEDCs. (You will discuss these with the other G8 leaders.)
   Your guidelines should have at least 5 points.
   Think of big issues. Pay? Profits? The environment?

Coffee break !

Like a coffee? Espresso? Cappuccino? Caffe latte? Caffe mocha?
Caffe Americano? Or just instant?

While you read this, millions of cups of coffee are being drunk all over the
world. And hidden inside each one is months and months of toil.

When they get to their destination,
the beans must be roasted before
use. Some are then crushed and
processed to give 'instant' coffee.

5 There the beans are checked for
size and quality. Some are rejected.
The rest are packed again, ready
for export by ship.

4 The clean dry coffee beans are
poured into 60 kilogram sacks.
The sacks will then be brought to
a coffee centre.

1 Coffee grows on trees. The coffee
berries are called cherries.
They go from green to yellow to
red as they ripen.

2 They are picked by hand. It's slow:
they all ripen at different times!
If it rains the ripe cherries get
knocked off and rot on the ground.

3 Inside each cherry are two coffee
beans. The beans are removed,
washed well, then left to dry in
the sun.

Your turn

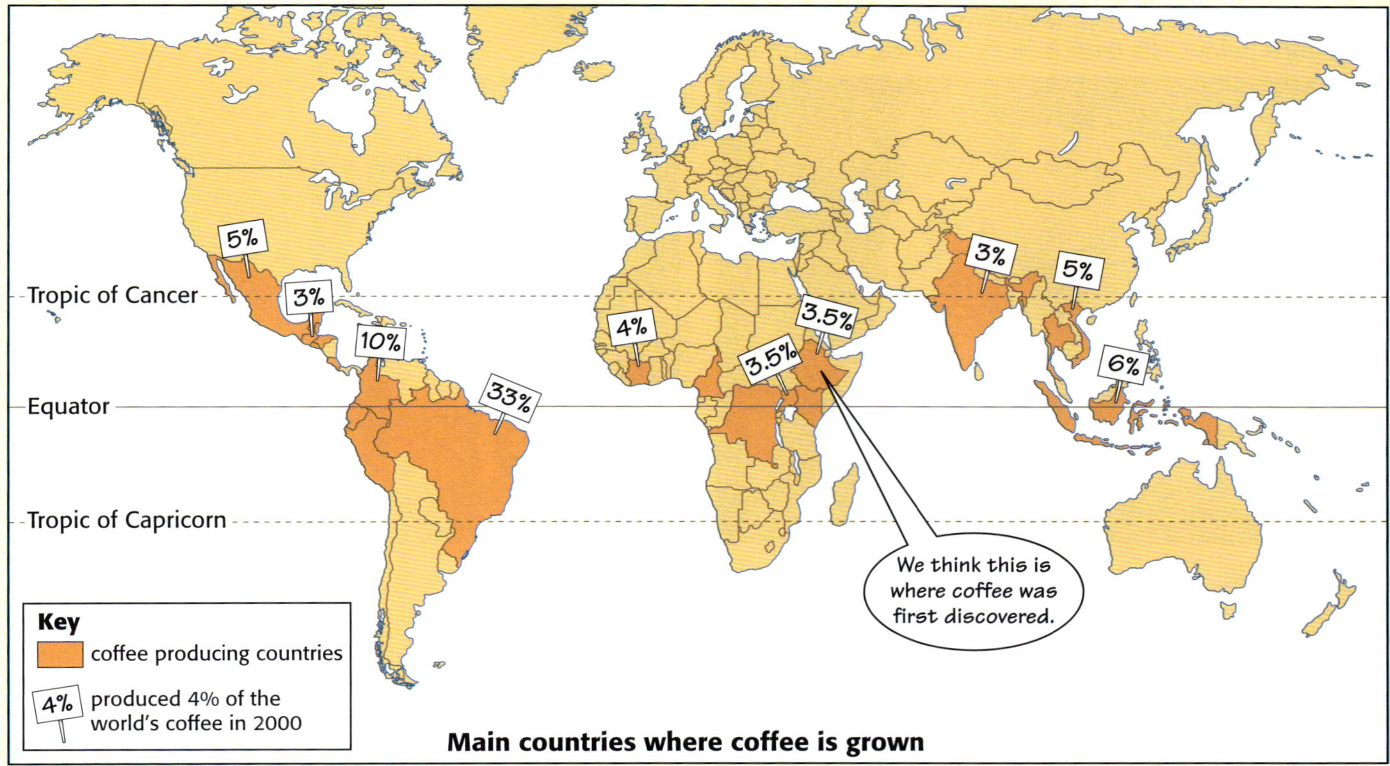

Main countries where coffee is grown

1 This map shows the countries that grow coffee.
It gives the % share for the top 10 that year.
  a List the top 10 coffee growing countries and their
  % in order, the main one first. (Pages 124 – 125?)
  b Now draw a pictogram to show this data.
  (Think of a good way to show 1% of coffee.)
  c Add a final row to your pictogram to show the total
  share for the remaining countries. Label it.
  d Which *continent* comes top for growing coffee?

2 Write down each statement. Then if you think it's false,
cross out the wrong part and correct it neatly.
(Use what you know already. Page 16 will help too.)
  A Coffee is grown in the tropics.
  B Coffee trees need a cool climate.
  C Coffee trees need quite a lot of rain.
  D A dry season is needed for the coffee harvest.
  E They grow coffee in the Philippines.
  F Ghana is the world's top coffee producer.
  G They think coffee was first discovered in Tunisia.
  H The coffee growing countries are all MEDCs.
  I The coffee you drink will have travelled by ocean.

3 Look at the table on the right.
  a What does it show? Answer in your own words.
  b Are there any coffee growing countries in this list?
  c Are there any LEDCs in this list? (Page 16?)
  d What can you conclude from your answers for **b**
  and **c**? Give your answer as a full sentence.

4

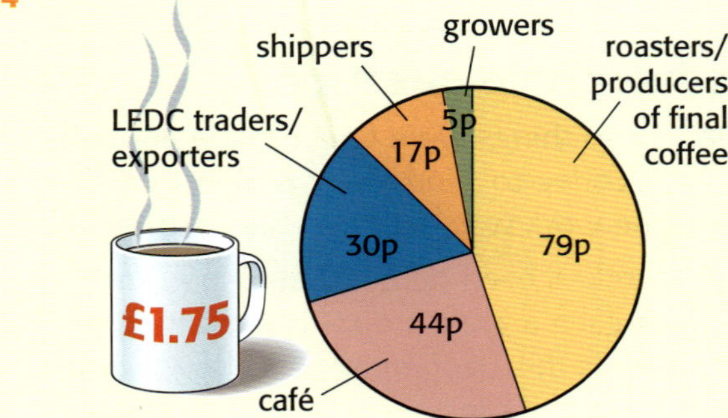

This pie chart gives you an idea where the money goes,
when you pay £1.75 for a coffee in a café.
  a What % does the grower get?
  b Who gets the largest share of the money?
  c Most of the money ends up in … ?
    i the LEDC that grew the coffee   **ii** an MEDC
  d Where do you think most of the hard work is done?
    i in the LEDC that grew the coffee   **ii** in an MEDC

Top 10 coffee consuming countries, 2000

	Country	kg/person		Country	kg/person
1	Finland	9.88	6	Netherlands	6.74
2	Norway	8.85	7	Germany	6.73
3	Denmark	8.58	8	Austria	5.46
4	Sweden	8.00	9	France	5.44
5	Switzerland	6.95	10	Italy	5.40

Bitter coffee

Most of the world's coffee is grown on small farms, by people like Pedro below. His farm is in Costa Rica, in Central America.

Growing coffee is hard work. Planting trees, watering in dry weather, spraying against disease, pruning, fertilizing, picking the cherries. But even when Pedro works really hard, it does not mean he'll earn more.

Because that is decided far away, in cities like New York and London, by people who'll never meet him. At Exchanges like this one, big buyers (mostly TNCs) buy coffee crops, often before they're harvested.

At the start of 2001, Pedro was feeling very worried. Look at the graph on the right to see why.

Pedro has some questions

A few years ago things were fine. I made enough money from coffee to send my two oldest children to school. The work was hard, but life seemed good.

Last year I worked even harder than usual, and my mature trees gave a great crop – but I earned hardly anything. Why is this happening? And how would you feel if you were me?

We'll have to keep the children at home this year – we can't afford to send them to school any longer. And at this rate our two little ones might never set foot in school. What kind of life will they have without education?

At least we grow our own vegetables to eat. But my neighbour up the hill has only coffee trees. Now he sends his children down to the main road, to beg from the cars. How would you feel if you had to send your children out begging?

It's a mystery

It's a big mystery. Pedro is earning less and less for his coffee – but coffee is not that much cheaper in the shops, and it costs more and more in coffee bars. So what's going on?

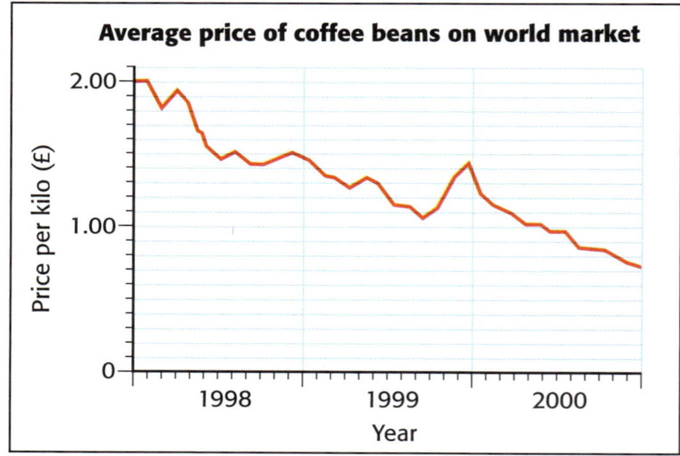

▲ *Many coffee farmers are barely surviving.*

Behind the coffee mystery

So why is Pedro getting poorer and poorer?

It's because there's too much coffee grown! There are tonnes of beans in store around the world.

This is partly because the World Bank and other bodies have encouraged LEDCs to grow coffee.

So countries have competed to grow more and more, instead of agreeing a plan between them.

With so much coffee on the market, the buyers can push the price right down. They pay less …

… so the coffee farmers earn less. Less money for food, and clothes, and education for their children.

Meanwhile more of us like to drink coffee in smart coffee bars. So they can charge us more for it.

Your turn

1 The coffee grown by Pedro and other small farmers is sold at trading centres called Exchanges.
   a Where might you find an Exchange?
   b Who buys up most of the coffee crops?

2 Look at the graph on page 78.
   a Why does this graph make Pedro feel anxious?
   b How much was a kilo of coffee beans worth:
      i at the start of 1998?   ii at the end of 2000?
   c Give a reason for the big fall in price.

3 The diagram on the right shows the % change in prices and profits for coffee, over a three-year period. (The figures for 1998 are taken as 100 %.)
   a How did the price of instant coffee change in that period? Do you think this was fair? Explain.
   b Now look at the company's profits. How did they change over the same period?
   c Suggest a reason for the change in b.

4 When too much coffee is grown:
   a who are the winners?   b who are the losers?

5 The price of coffee on the world market can rise as well as fall. Say how each of these might affect it.
   a All the coffee growing countries produce bumper crops.
   b A disease destroys all the stores of coffee beans.
   c A freak frost in Brazil kills all its coffee trees.
   d A medical report says coffee is really bad for us.

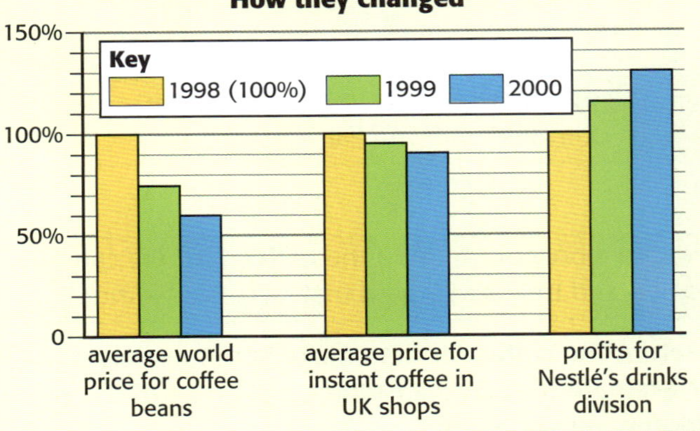

Fair trade for coffee growers

Coffee growers have been getting poorer and poorer, while the companies that sell coffee have been making big profits. Is this fair?

Making the coffee trade fairer

Here are suggestions from Oxfam and other groups, to help coffee growers:

Fairtrade coffee

Look at 4 above. An organisation called the Fairtrade Foundation is doing this already! It was set up by a group of UK charities (including Oxfam) to help people in poorer countries who grow or make things for export.

This is how it works for coffee:

The Foundation buys coffee beans directly from groups of coffee farmers.

It offers them a fair price for the coffee – enough to live on, plus profit.

It pays part of the money in advance, before the coffee is harvested, so that farmers don't run short.

It gets supermarkets to sell the coffee, stamped with the Fairtrade logo.

People who want to help the coffee farmers can buy it – and they don't mind that it costs a bit more.

In return the coffee farmers make some promises. For example to treat *their* workers fairly, and to look after the environment.

▲ *Fairtrade coffee on a shelf near you.*

Your turn

1

shopper supermarket manager Fairtrade worker coffee farmer

The people in this chain are linked by fair trade.
But who is thinking what?

a Make a larger copy of the chain. (Draw stick people.)
Give each person a thought bubble, big enough to
write a sentence in.

b Now write **A–D** below in the correct bubbles.

A By buying coffee beans directly we make sure
growers get a fair price.

B Now I can get on with growing coffee, without
worrying that my family will starve.

C I feel better about drinking coffee that gives
coffee farmers a fair deal.

D We make a fair profit on the coffee – so
we're happy to sell it.

2 Look at your drawing for **1**.

a Is there a loser in the chain? If so, who?

b Is there a winner in the chain? If so, who?

3 Now look at other suggestions on page 80.

a ① might seem a bit shocking. See if you can explain
how this action would help coffee growers.

b Which other suggestion aims to reduce the **supply**
of coffee? (Glossary?)

4 Together, the five suggestions on page 80 would help
the coffee growing countries.

a Which do you think would be the fastest to carry out?
(Perhaps weeks.)

b Which might take longest to carry out?
(Probably a few years.)

c Which might be the most difficult to carry out?
Explain why you think so.

5 Now look at suggestion ⑤.

a Explain why this would help the coffee growing
countries. (The pie chart on page 77 may help.)

b Now draw a consequence map like the one started
on the right, for suggestion ⑤.
Add as many boxes as you can.

6

Above is another suggestion for helping people
like Pedro.

a Which does it aim to increase?

i the **supply** of coffee **ii** the **demand** for coffee

b Do you think it's a good idea? Give reasons.

7 Some supermarkets sell Fairtrade chocolate (to help
cocoa farmers in Ghana and other countries) and
Fairtrade bananas (from the Caribbean).

You want to set up Fairtrade jeans, to help people
like Rosa on page 68.

a How will you do it? You can show your plan as
a flow chart or as bullet points.

b Write an ad for the jeans. Don't forget a logo.

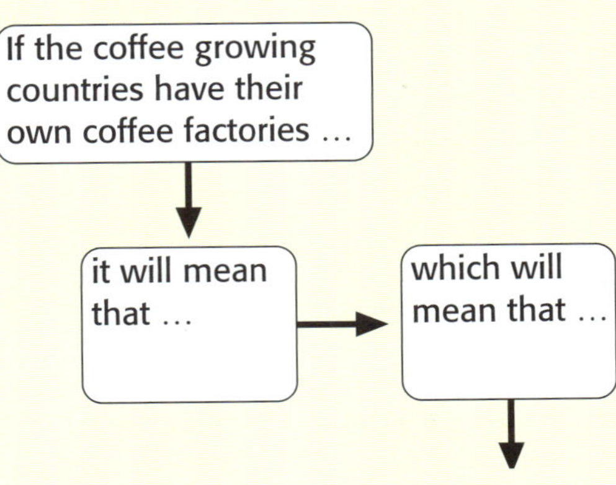

Planet Earth, your home …

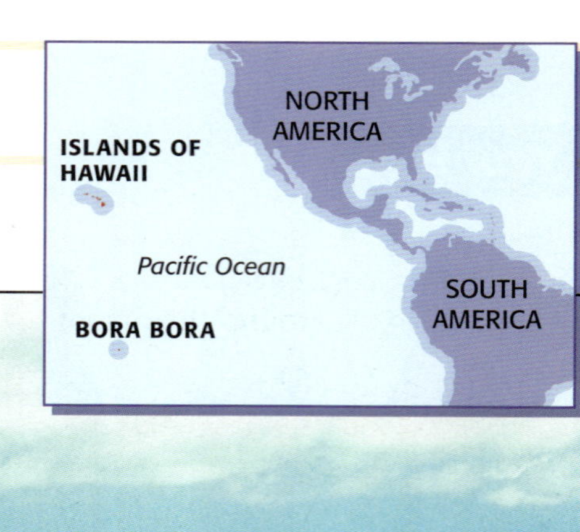

Planet Earth, your home … to protect and look after.

This is the beautiful island of Bora Bora in the Pacific Ocean.
It was formed by a volcano growing up from the ocean floor. (Those
plate movements again!) It is part of an overseas territory of France.

The humans arrive

We think the first humans evolved in East Africa about 200 000 years ago. (Or 64 million years after the dinosaurs had gone.) From there we spread slowly around the planet.

Our numbers are still growing. 200 years ago there were a billion of us. Today, over 6 billion. And about 150 more of us every minute.

Over the centuries, our clusters of dwellings have grown into towns and cities. Today over half of us live in cities.

By now we have explored almost all the land on our planet. We have ruined some of it, and made lots of mistakes – and learned some important lessons.

▲ *We reached the islands of Hawaii only 1700 years ago.*

Some lessons we have learned about looking after our planet

Local actions may have **global effects**. (Global warming is an example.)

We must live in a more **sustainable** way – or we will destroy the planet.

Each of us has a part to play in protecting the planet. Including **you**!

To protect places, we must **plan** and **manage** and **work together**.

This chapter has three case studies to show you these lessons in action:

◆ along the **River Rhine**

◆ in the **Peak District National Park** in the UK

◆ on the continent of **Antarctica**.

You will learn about the problems and conflicts in these places, and what is being done to protect them.

1 Look at the photo opposite. You are the very first human to arrive in that place. How do you feel? Nervous? Peaceful? Write an entry for your diary.

2 You want to find out more about the place opposite.
   a On a development compass rose (page 5) write down at least 6 questions you would ask.
   b Then see if you can answer any of them.

3 The human race is still growing. How many more people will there be on the planet:
   a by this time tomorrow?   b 7 days from now?

4 Now look at card **1** above.
   a What is *global warming*? (Try without the glossary!)
   b What do they think causes it?
   c Explain why global warming is an example of 'Local actions, global effects.'

5 Look at card **2**.
   a What does *sustainable* mean?
   b Give 3 things you could do to live more sustainably.

6 You are a protector of the planet. Design yourself a T-shirt that will remind you of this.

Case study 1: The Rhine

Our first case study is about the **Rhine**. It is Europe's busiest river. No wonder it needs protecting!

This map shows the Rhine's route from its **source** in the Alps to its **mouth** in the North Sea. Look how many countries it flows through, and how many more edge into its **drainage basin**.

Rhine factfile

- It is 1320 km long.
- Its drainage basin has an area of 185 000 km².
- Its drainage basin is home to about 55 million people. (About 58 million people live in Britain.)
- It provides water for 20 million people.
- It flows through the most densely industrial region in the world.

You will need to look at both maps in this unit to help you answer these questions.

Your turn

1 *glacier   source   delta   mouth   drainage basin*
These terms are used in this unit. See if you can explain what each one means, without looking it up.

2 Which country has the longest stretch of the Rhine?

3 Draw a large sketch map of the Rhine. Use a full page. On your sketch mark in:
  a the countries and main cities it flows through
  b the Alps
  c other mountainous areas
  d Lake Constance
  e the North Sea
  f industrial areas
  g agricultural areas
  h the names of the different sections of the river

4 As you have seen, each section of the Rhine has its own name. Which section:
  a has most industry around it?
  b do you think has most agriculture along it?
  c do you think has most people living around it?
  d has the narrowest, steepest, rockiest river valley? Explain your choice.
  e has most sediment deposited? Give reasons.
  f has least sediment deposited? Give reasons,
  g has most hydroelectricity stations? Why do you think that is?
  h has most water running through it?

5 Now choose two sections of the Rhine that you think may be liable to flooding, and give reasons.

6 The Rhine and its water are used for many different purposes – which means there is conflict.
  a Copy the conflict grid started below.
  b Add two more uses (where the dotted lines are) and then complete the rest of the labelling.
  c Now put ✓ where you think two uses are in harmony, ✗ where they conflict with each other, and *O* where they have no effect on each other.
  d Overall, would you say the level of conflict is high, or low?

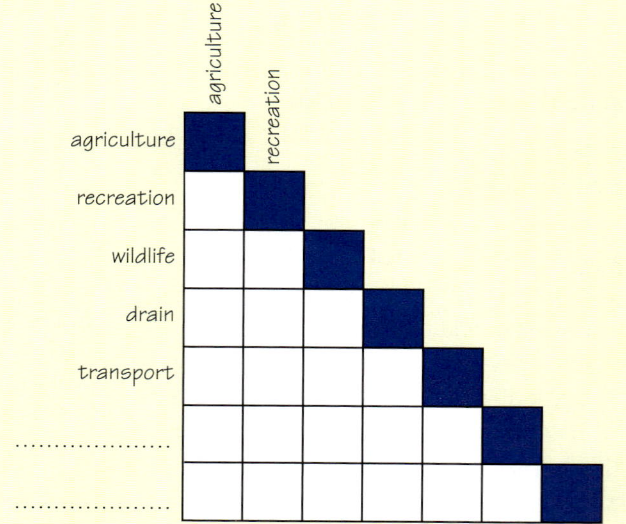

A hard-working river

Many demands are made on the Rhine …

9 It's a home to wildlife. 200 years ago it was world famous for its salmon.

10 It's a link between inland Europe and the rest of the world. Rotterdam at its mouth is the largest port in the world.

7 It acts as a motorway. Several hundred ships and barges sail up and down it every day carrying cargo. Ships can go up as far as Basel.

8 It's a recreation centre. Tourists take cruises on it. Local people sail on it and relax on its banks.

6 It acts as a drain – for sewage and other waste from homes and factories.

5 It provides water for hundreds of factories – mostly for keeping pipes and tanks cool. The water is drained back into the river.

4 It provides water for homes – for drinking, cooking and washing. (The water is cleaned up first.)

3 It provides water for farming. (10% of its water is used for irrigation, mainly in Holland.)

1 The Rhine rises in the Alps, fed by water from rain and glaciers. It runs into Lake Constance which acts as a huge reservoir.

The map:

2 From early in its journey, the Rhine is used to give hydroelectricity. Many of the reservoirs behind the dams are used for water sports.

Key

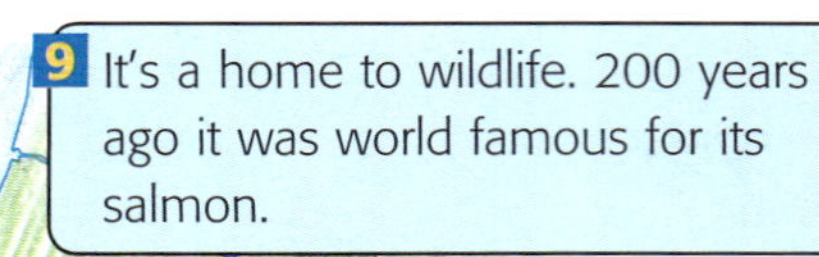

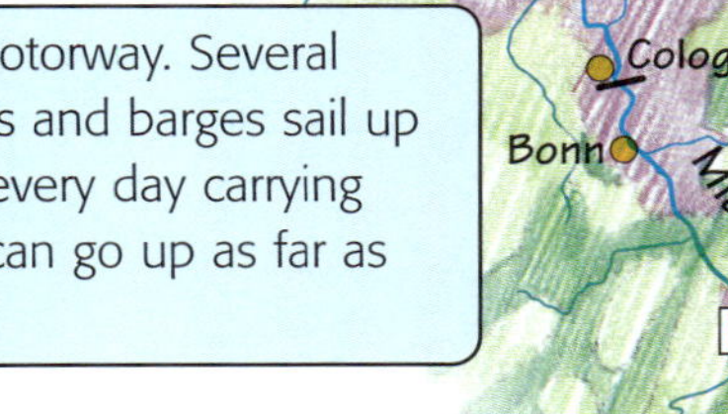

- —— rivers
- industrial areas
- agriculture (crops, pasture, vineyards)
- forest
- ● hydroelectricity stations
- ● cities and towns (not all shown)
- ● **A, B** needed for question 1 on page 89
- / end of named section of the river

Case study 1: The Rhine is dead …

Forty years ago, they said the Rhine was dead – killed by humans.

Poisoned by pollution

People living along the Rhine have always dumped their waste in it. But until 1800 there were not many people, and most of the waste was **biodegradable**. That means bacteria in the water could break it down.

Then the Industrial Revolution came to the Rhine basin. Mines were dug. Factories were opened. Towns and cities grew fast. More and more stuff ended up in the river – and much more of it was harmful.

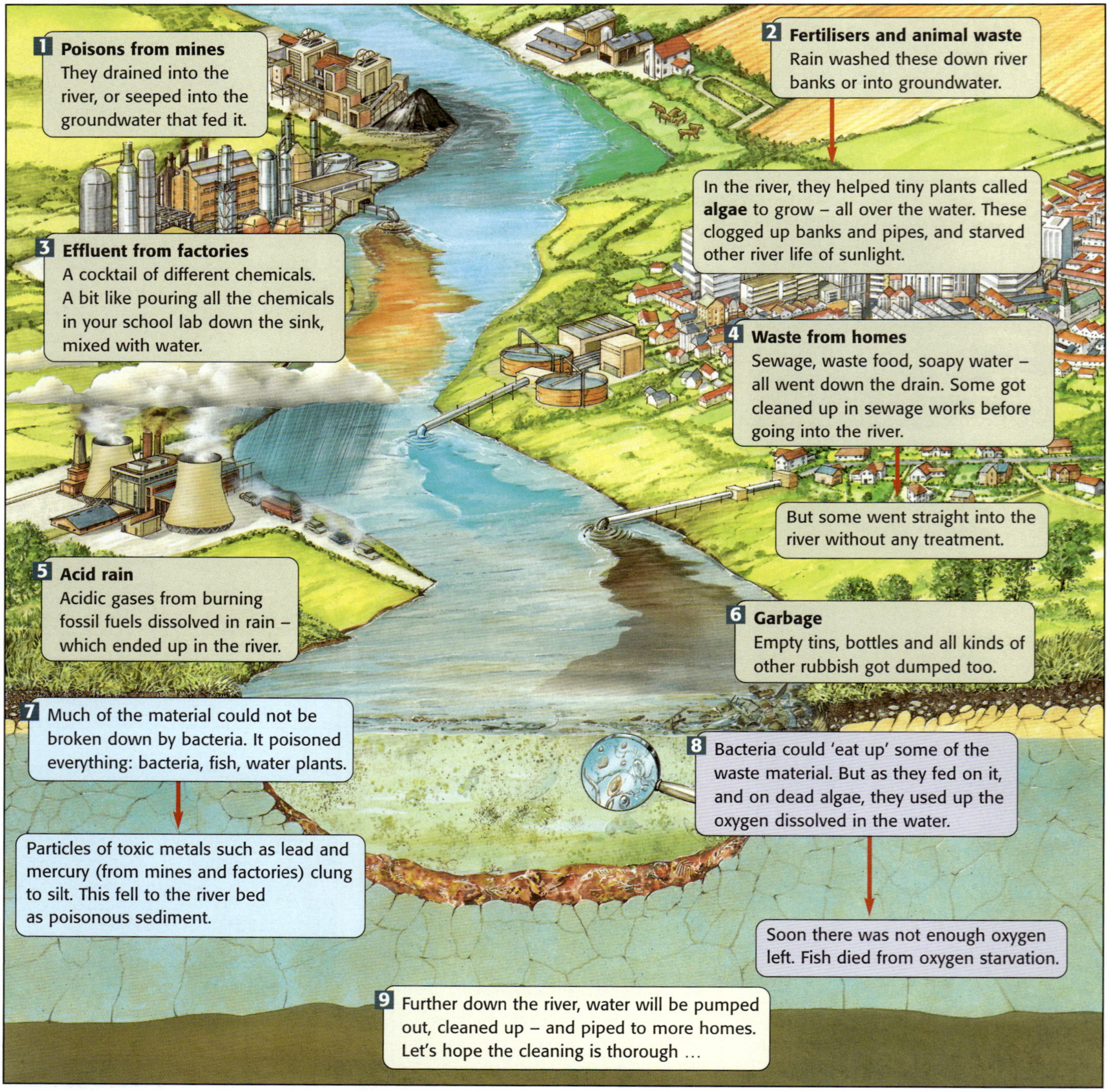

▲ *On its way to the Rhine. Nice …*

1 Poisons from mines
They drained into the river, or seeped into the groundwater that fed it.

2 Fertilisers and animal waste
Rain washed these down river banks or into groundwater.

In the river, they helped tiny plants called **algae** to grow – all over the water. These clogged up banks and pipes, and starved other river life of sunlight.

3 Effluent from factories
A cocktail of different chemicals. A bit like pouring all the chemicals in your school lab down the sink, mixed with water.

4 Waste from homes
Sewage, waste food, soapy water – all went down the drain. Some got cleaned up in sewage works before going into the river.

But some went straight into the river without any treatment.

5 Acid rain
Acidic gases from burning fossil fuels dissolved in rain – which ended up in the river.

6 Garbage
Empty tins, bottles and all kinds of other rubbish got dumped too.

7 Much of the material could not be broken down by bacteria. It poisoned everything: bacteria, fish, water plants.

8 Bacteria could 'eat up' some of the waste material. But as they fed on it, and on dead algae, they used up the oxygen dissolved in the water.

Particles of toxic metals such as lead and mercury (from mines and factories) clung to silt. This fell to the river bed as poisonous sediment.

Soon there was not enough oxygen left. Fish died from oxygen starvation.

9 Further down the river, water will be pumped out, cleaned up – and piped to more homes. Let's hope the cleaning is thorough …

Mangled by man

People polluted the river. And straightened, dammed and banked it, to make it do as they wished. Work was carried out at over 450 places along the river – mostly to help ships sail up it easily.

At the same time, the Rhine basin was being developed.

Each country carried out its own river projects without worrying about the other Rhine countries, or other parts of the Rhine. The result was … more problems.

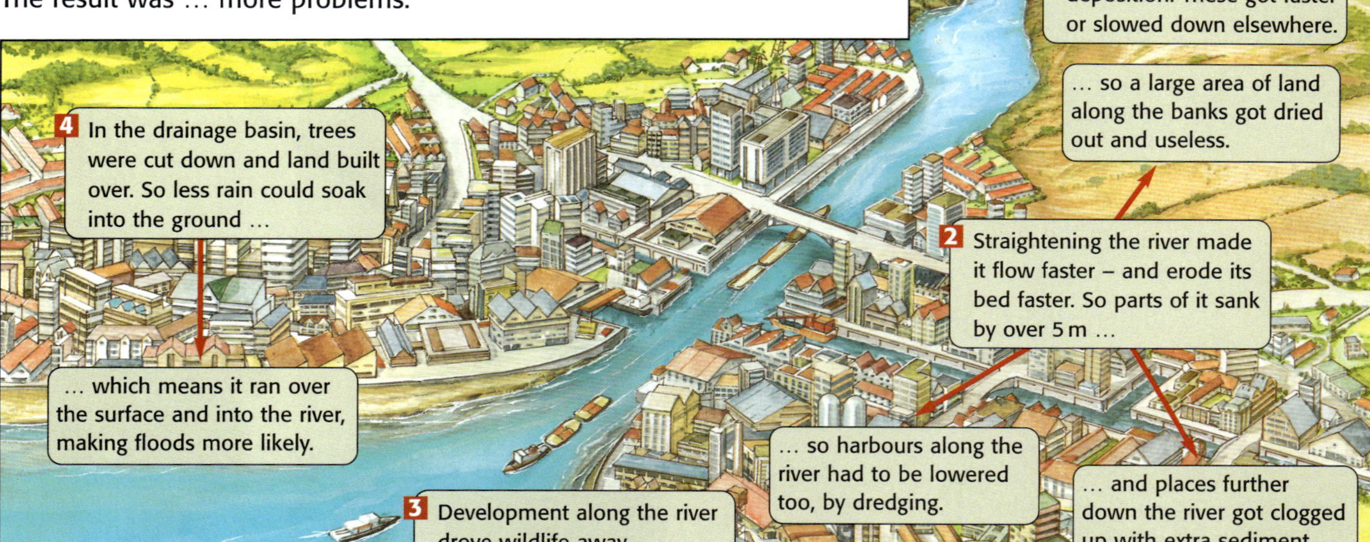

Your turn

1 What do these terms mean?
biodegradable *effluent* *bacteria* *Industrial Revolution* *groundwater*
Give each answer as a full sentence.

2 Pollution in the Rhine grew steadily worse from around 1850 onwards. Suggest reasons.

3 By 1960 the water of the Rhine tasted foul and smelled really horrible.
  a Make two lists side by side, as started here:

Pollution of the Rhine	
CAUSES	CONSEQUENCES
factory effluent	

  b Complete each list separately, in any order. (You don't need to match them yet.)
  c Now draw arrows linking each cause to *all* its consequences. (Your arrows will criss-cross.)

4 The Rhine used to be famous for salmon. By 1960 they had gone. Look at the information about salmon on the right. Then explain what part:
  a pollution
  b engineering works
  may have played in their disappearance.

5 Overall, which Rhine country probably:
  a suffered *least* from water pollution?
  b suffered *most* from poisonous sediment?
  Give reasons for your answers.

6 Could pollution in the Rhine affect:
  a the North Sea? b you?
  Give reasons for your answers.

7 You are the Prime Minister of the Netherlands. You want to save the Rhine. Write to the Prime Ministers of the other Rhine countries, suggesting some ideas.

Salmon lay their eggs in clean gravel on the river bed. The eggs hatch …

… into fish. 18 months later these swim down to the Atlantic Ocean.

After 4 or 5 years in the ocean they swim back up the river again …

… to the spot where they were born, to breed. Soon after, they will die.

Case study 1: Long live the Rhine!

Now the salmon are back and the Rhine is recovering – protected by an international commission.

Driven by disaster

By 1953 the Rhine was in a mess. The Rhine countries had each polluted it. Now they saw that the only way to clean it up was to work together.

So they set up the **International Commission for the Protection of the Rhine**, or **ICPR**.

The ICPR acted very slowly at first – so pollution got much worse! But 1970 saw a string of new sewage works being built along the river. These had a big effect. Life began to return to the Rhine.

Then on 1st November 1986, disaster. A fire broke out in a warehouse at the Sandoz chemical factory in Basel. Drums exploded in the heat. 30 tonnes of chemicals were washed into the Rhine by the water from the firemen's hoses.

All river life was wiped out for 150 km downstream. Water supplies were shut down as far as Amsterdam. The Rhine was back where it started.

The accident shocked people. They demanded action. Suddenly cleaning up the Rhine had top priority.

▲ *Firemen fighting the Sandoz fire, 1986.*

> **Did you know?**
> ◆ The presence of salmon is a good sign that a river is healthy.

The Rhine Action Programme

After Sandoz, ICPR launched an action programme. Its aim was to get the river back to health within 15 years. By steps like these:

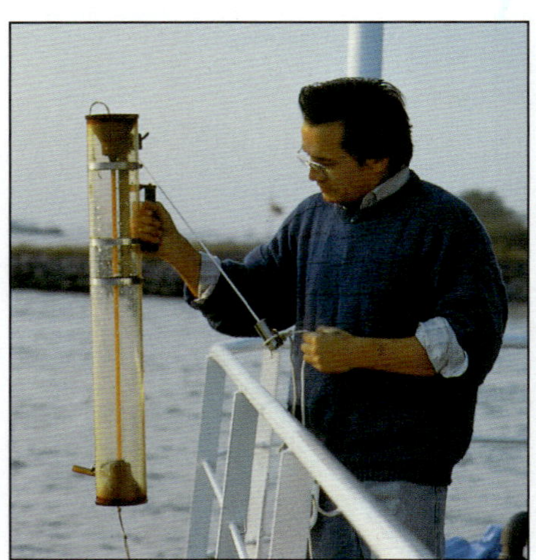

Strict limits for factory effluent all along the river. Frequent checks. Heavy fines for polluters.

Completing the scheme to build new sewage treatment works for cities and towns along the river.

Encouraging the construction of 'fish ladders' at dams so that fish can swim upstream.

It worked. By 2001 the oxygen in the Rhine was at a healthy level. And the salmon were back (but there will never be as many as before).

So is everything okay?

No. The Rhine is recovering. It's in better shape than before. But it still has problems and faces many threats. Like these …

◆ There is still plenty of pollution from some sources – for example farming.

◆ There's always a risk that factories will pollute it by accident.

◆ Global warming is causing more heavy storms – and that means more floods along the river.

◆ If global warming melts the glaciers that feed the Rhine, the river will depend on rain for its water. So the water level will vary a lot.

▲ *Heavy flooding on the Rhine, 1998.*

Your turn

1

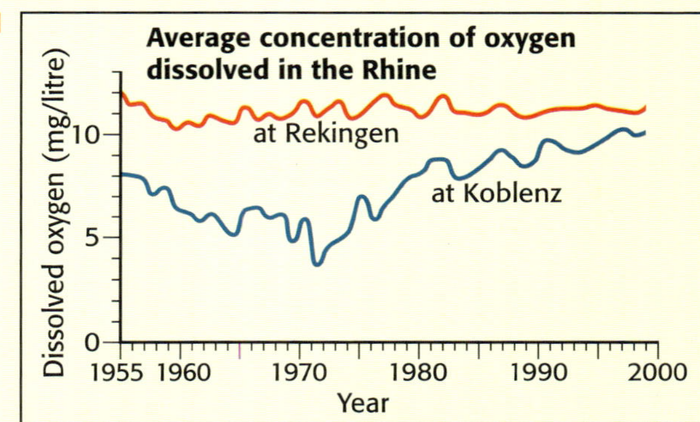

Look at this graph. Rekingen and Koblenz are two places along the Rhine.

a What causes the level of oxygen in a river to fall?

b Name one type of pollutant that can lead to a fall in oxygen.

c At which of the two places was the Rhine healthier? Explain why you think so.

d The two places are shown as **A** and **B** on the map on page 85. Which one is **A**? Explain your choice.

e In which year was the O_2 level at Koblenz lowest?

f Why did the level rise again after that?

g Do you think the O_2 level will ever be the same at both places? Give your reasons.

2 In the past the Rhine countries treated their river badly. Now they are working together to manage it in a more sustainable way.

a Draw a big table with headings like this. (Full page.)

Managing the Rhine	
Old way	Sustainable way

b Now look at statements **A – P** on the right. Which do *not* show a sustainable approach? Write these in the first column of your table.

c For each statement in your first column, choose the 'opposite' one from the list, and write it in your second column.

A If we want to dam the river we'll just do it.

B We will leave the river in its natural state as far as possible.

C If my country pollutes the river, it is no-one else's business.

D We will tame the river and make it behave as we wish.

E It's okay, rivers can cope with lots of rubbish.

F If we want to dam the river we will consult the other Rhine countries first.

G We think about the whole river.

H Before we do engineering work along the river we assess its impact on the environment – and may cancel it.

I We only worry about our stretch of the river.

J We don't worry about development in the drainage basin.

K Rivers are a fragile ecosystem and we must protect them from pollution.

L Let's do the engineering work, and sort out any environmental problems later.

M Let's make sure the salmon don't die off again.

N If my country pollutes the river it affects the other Rhine countries too.

O The river is fed by its drainage basin so we must think about that too.

P The salmon have gone. Too bad.

Case study 2: Britain's National Parks

Rivers need protection. So does the countryside.

We're lucky. Britain has a lot of beautiful countryside. But what if it got closed off so we could not visit it? Or eaten up by motorways and housing estates? To prevent that, some areas have been turned into **National Parks**.

What is a National Park?

A National Park is a large area of land that is protected by law, to benefit the whole nation. About 10% of England and Wales has been turned into National Parks. See the map on the next page.

▲ Take to the hills!

How the National Parks began

100 years ago, many people worked in dirty noisy crowded factories, 6 days a week. They looked forward to Sundays when they could escape to the countryside for fresh air.

But out in the countryside, landowners were busy enclosing the land, and trying to keep visitors away! This made people angry. They felt everyone had a right to enjoy the countryside. They held big meetings in the cities to protest.

At last, in 1949, the government passed a law setting up National Parks, to make sure people had access to the countryside. The first one to be set up was the Peak District National Park, in 1951.

Each National Park is managed by a **National Park Authority**.

Now use page 91 to help you answer these questions.

The National Park Authority
We aim to …
- conserve the beauty, wildlife and cultural heritage of the Park
- help vistors to enjoy it
- promote the economic and social wellbeing of the people who live in it.

Your turn

1 **a** What is a *National Park*?
  b How many National Parks does England have?
  c How many does Wales have?

2 Which National Park:
  a is largest? **b** is smallest?
  c has most people living in it?
  d has most built up areas (conurbations) close by?
  e is furthest from big cities?
  f is furthest from a motorway?
  g is best served by motorways?
  h is nearest the Scottish border?
  i is least crowded? (Some calculations needed!)

3 See if you can suggest reasons why some land in National Parks is owned by:
  a water companies (who provide our water supply)
  b the Ministry of Defence (which runs the army)

4 You live in central London. Using roads shown on the map, about how many km are you from the edge of:
  a Snowdonia? **b** the Peak District?

5 **a** What is a *National Park Authority*?
  b What are its aims? Write your answer in simple words that a six-year-old would understand.

6 What do you think of this point of view? Write a serious reply.

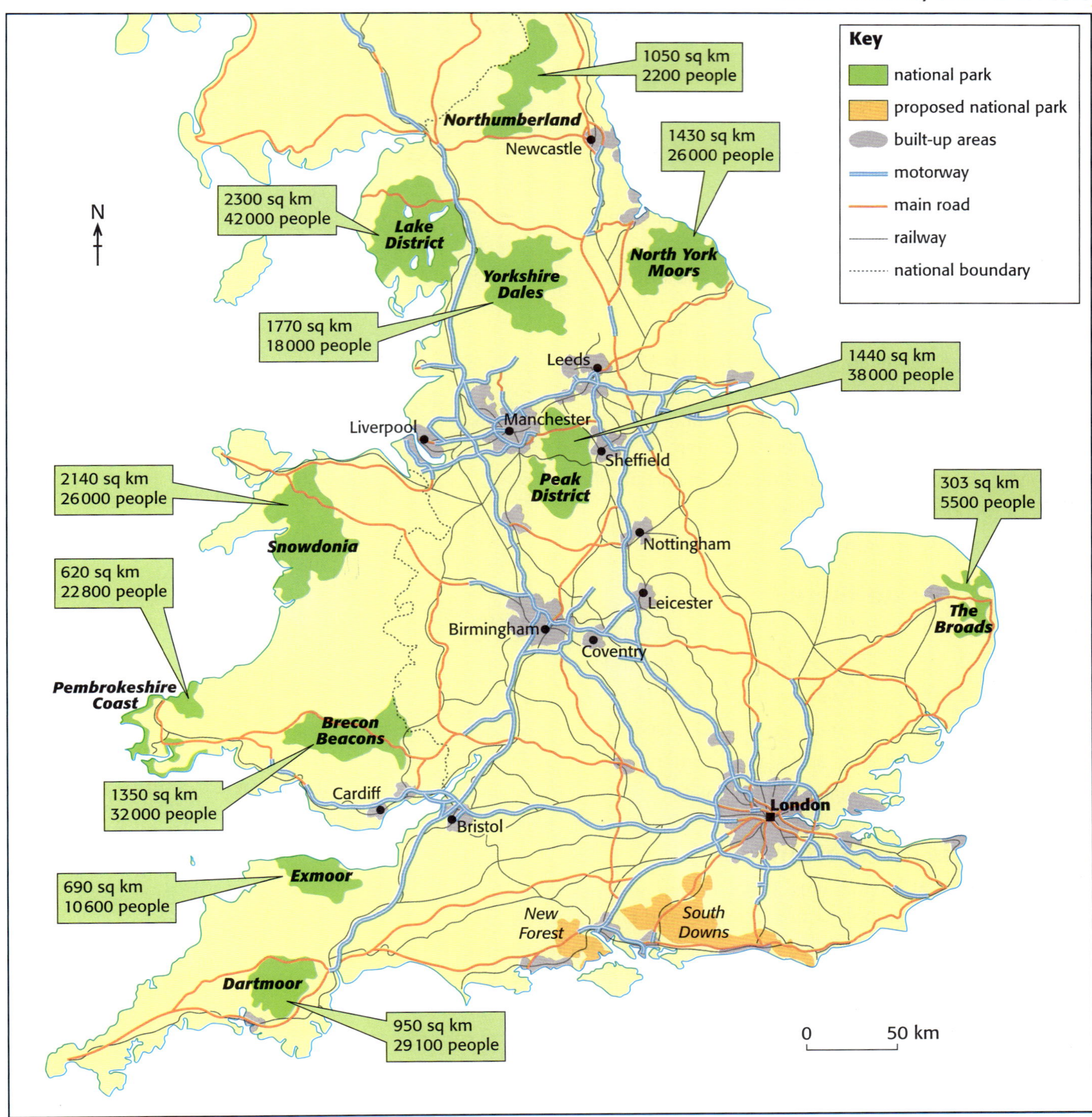

The National Parks are managed by National Park Authorities – but owned by a whole mix of people. Look at these examples.

Who owns it? (%)	Northumberland	Yorkshire Dales	Peak District
Private (farmers etc)	56.4	96.1	70.1
Forestry Commission	18.9	0	0.5
Ministry of Defence	22.6	0.3	0.2
Water companies	1.2	0.3	13.5
National Trust / English Nature	0.7	3.5	11.5
National Park Authority	0.2	0.1	4.2
Other	0	0.2	0

What are they like?

◆ Most of the National Parks are on high land. All have people living in them – see the map.

◆ All have great scenery – different in each.

◆ All have a mix of open land, farmland and woodland. The percentages vary.

◆ Almost all have reservoirs, storing water for towns and cities.

◆ One has lots of canals and rivers. Which one?

Case study 2: The Peak District

Now we focus on one National Park: the Peak District.

What's it like?

- The White Peak is a **limestone** area in the centre and south of the park. Here you'll find rolling hills and deep valleys.
- The Dark Peak forms an arch around the outside. The rock here is **gritstone**. The scenery is wilder, with high moorland, bogs and steep cliffs.
- Between the two is an area of **shale** rock with wide fertile valleys.
- There are around 2500 farms in the Park. Most are small. Most rear cattle or sheep.
- It has 2 towns and around 100 villages and hamlets.
- About 38 000 people live in it.
- It gets up to 30 million visits a year!

What can you do there?

What a choice!

☑ walking ☑ cycling ☑ climbing ☑ pony trekking
☑ sailing ☑ fishing ☑ windsurfing ☑ water skiing
☑ caving ☑ gliding ☑ hang gliding ☑ abseiling
☑ visiting historic buildings and stately homes
☑ exploring the towns, villages and hamlets

What else is it important for?

- **Water.** The Peak District gets plenty of rain, and has over 50 reservoirs. These supply water to towns and cities outside the park.
- **Quarrying and mining.** They have gone on here for thousands of years. Limestone is the main material quarried these days.

What's quarried / mined there?

Material	Used for
limestone	road building, making cement and chemicals, and in blast furnaces
shale	making cement
gritstone	building
fluorspar	making solvents, and fluoride toothpaste!

▲ *You'll find rolling hills in the Peak District …*

▲ *… and high wild crags too.*

A closer look at its geology

Look at the rock map at the bottom of the page. If you could slice through the Peak District along the red line AB, you'd see something like this:

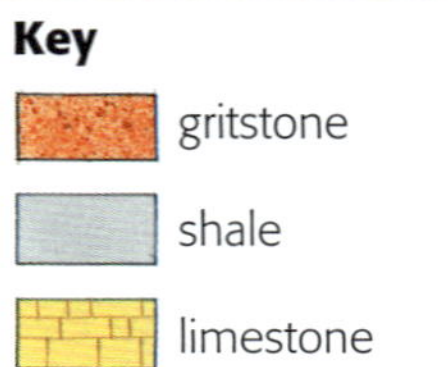

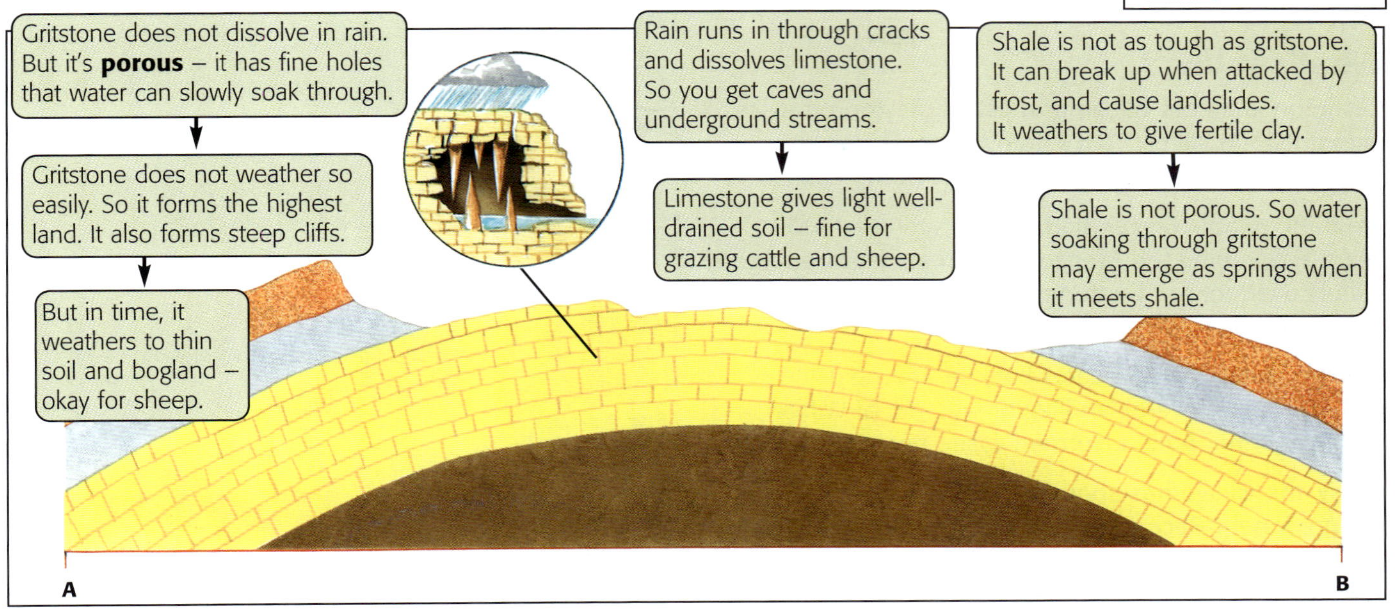

Check Unit 7.5 too?

Your turn

1 An American visitor asks you *where* the Peak District is. Write down your reply.
It must be clear and helpful – and include at least four geographical facts.

2 See if you can explain why the Peak District:
   a gets more visitors than the other National Parks (up to 30 million visits a year)
   b gets mostly day trippers
   c was the first National Park to be set up
   d has two very different types of landscape

3 These are some words to describe a landscape.

Facts		
small	large	vast
enclosed	open	exposed
smooth	quite rough	very rough
flat	rolling	steep
dead	calm	busy

Feelings		
ugly	pretty	beautiful
safe	disturbing	scary
boring	interesting	inspiring

Describe the landscapes in photos **1** and **2** on page 92, using at least two words from each set.

4 Now you have to match the two photos to **X** and **Y** on the rock map on the right.
Write a paragraph giving reasons for your choice.

5 Geology influences scenery – and activities! In the Peak District, in which rock type would you expect to:
   a go caving?   b do some serious climbing?
   c go pony trekking?   d go sailing on a reservoir?
   e go hang gliding?   f go potholing?

6 Now, time to recap. Draw a spider map to show what you have learned about the Peak District so far. (Check Unit 7.5 too?)

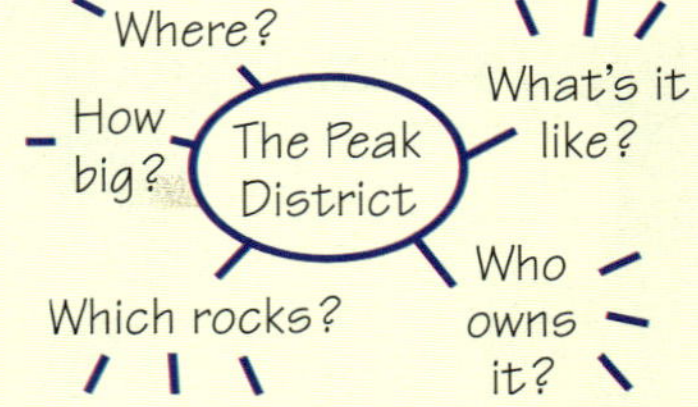

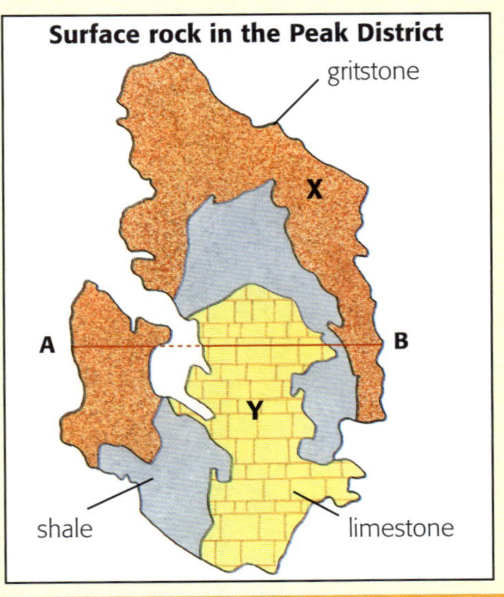

Castleton in the Peak District is a **honeypot**.
Visitors swarm to it!

What's it like?

Castleton is a neat village of mostly limestone houses, with gritstone slates. That's fitting, since it is at the edge of the White Peak, and near the Dark Peak.

We think people first settled on this site over 3000 years ago, during the Bronze Age. An ancient Iron Age hillfort overlooks it. Centuries later, the Romans built a fort not far away.

But the present village dates back to around 1080, when William Peverel, an illegitimate son of William the Conqueror, built a Norman castle here.

Today, the village has about 700 inhabitants. But they are not lonely. Because every year they receive over 2 million visits. Most visitors arrive in their cars on summer Sundays.

Services in Castleton		
For local residents		
Service	**Comment**	
Grocer	✔	2 general stores sell a range of foods
Butcher	✘	Nearest is 2 miles away
Baker	✘	Nearest is 6 miles away
Greengrocer	✘	Nearest is 2 miles away
Chemist shop	✘	Nearest is 6 miles away
Post Office	✔	
Church	✔	Two
Village hall	✔	
Library	✘	Mobile library visits once a week
Petrol	✔	

For visitors			
B&B / guest houses	7	Hotels	4
Camping / caravan sites	4	Youth hostels	1
Tourist shops	10	Cafés	6
Information centre	1		

For both			
Pubs	6	Fish & chip shop	1

One sunny Sunday

It is not surprising that visitors swarm to Castleton. There is lots to see there, including four exciting limestone caves. But it is not all sunshine …

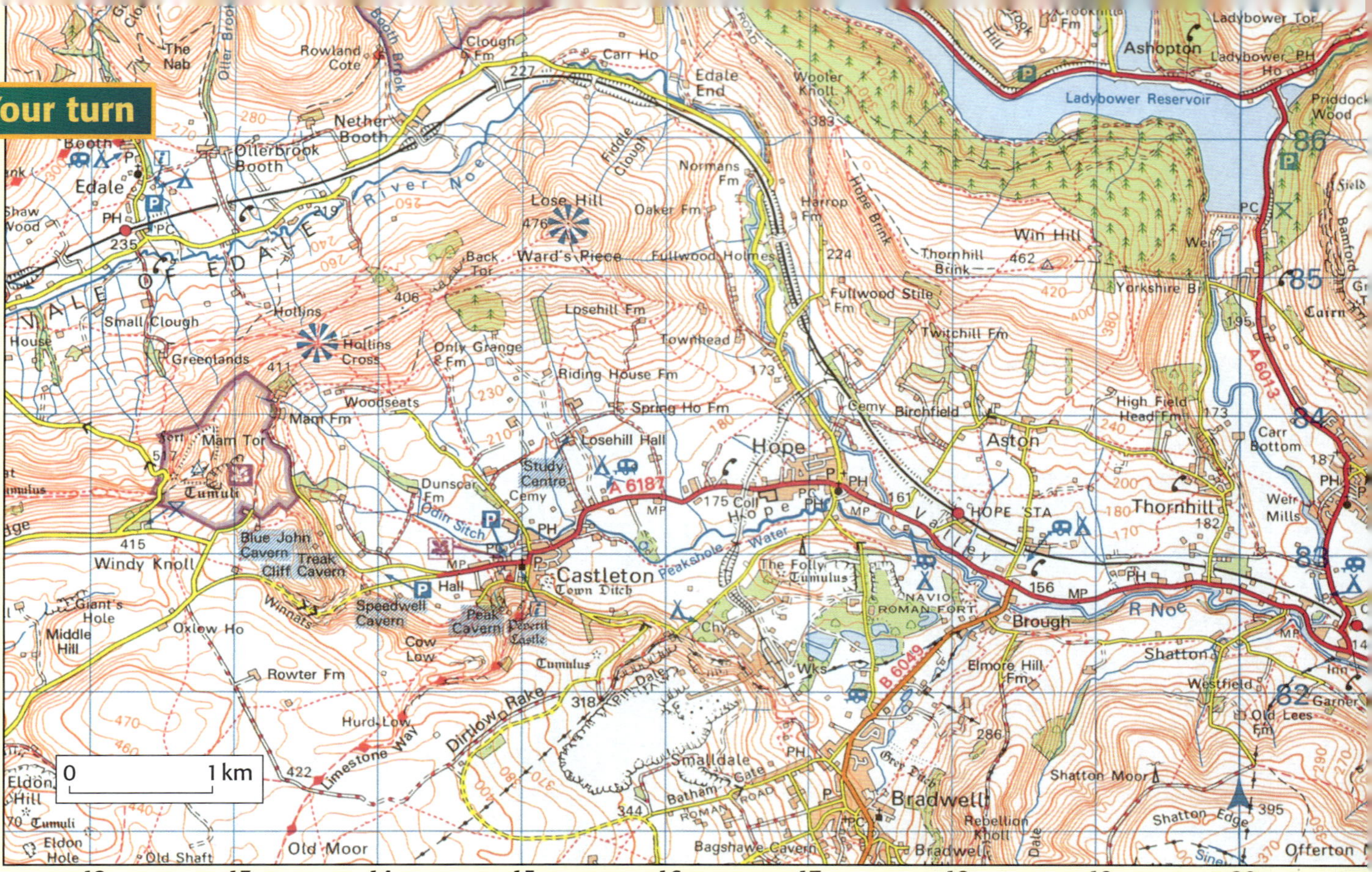

1 Look at Castleton on this OS map.
Is the village on high land, or in a valley?

2 Find Mam Tor to the west of the village.
This is where the Celts built their Iron Age hillfort.
  a Give reasons why they chose this spot.
  b A road used to run round the south of Mam Tor,
    until it was buried by a huge landslip in 1977.
    Mam Tor is made of either limestone or shale.
    Which one? Explain your choice.
  c What does the purple line around the site, and
    the purple symbol, mean? (Page 120?)

3 Now give as many reasons as you can why Castleton
was a good site for a settlement.

4 Look at the land to the north of Castleton.
(For example in square 1484.)
What evidence is there that this is *not* limestone?

5 Look at the land immediately south of Castleton.
Which type of rock is here? What is your evidence?

6 What signs of Roman occupation can you see on
the map? Give grid references.

7 a Castleton is a *honeypot*. What does that mean?
  b What evidence can you find on the map
    that Castleton gets lots of visitors?

8 This photo shows a famous ancient landmark on the
southern edge of Castleton. What is it? See if you can
work out which direction the camera was pointing in.

9 This is one resident's view.
Do you agree with her?
Give reasons.

10 Congestion is a big
problem for Castleton.
  a What does *congestion* mean?
  b Here's an idea for solving
    the problem. Is it a good idea?
    Give reasons.

11 You are in charge of managing tourism for Castleton.
Come up with a proposal for solving the congestion
problem. (The map might help.) Write it as a proposal
for the local council. Add a sketch map if that helps.

Case study 2: Conflicts in the Peak District

It is hard to protect an area *and* encourage tourists *and* keep the local people happy. These are some of the conflicts that arise:

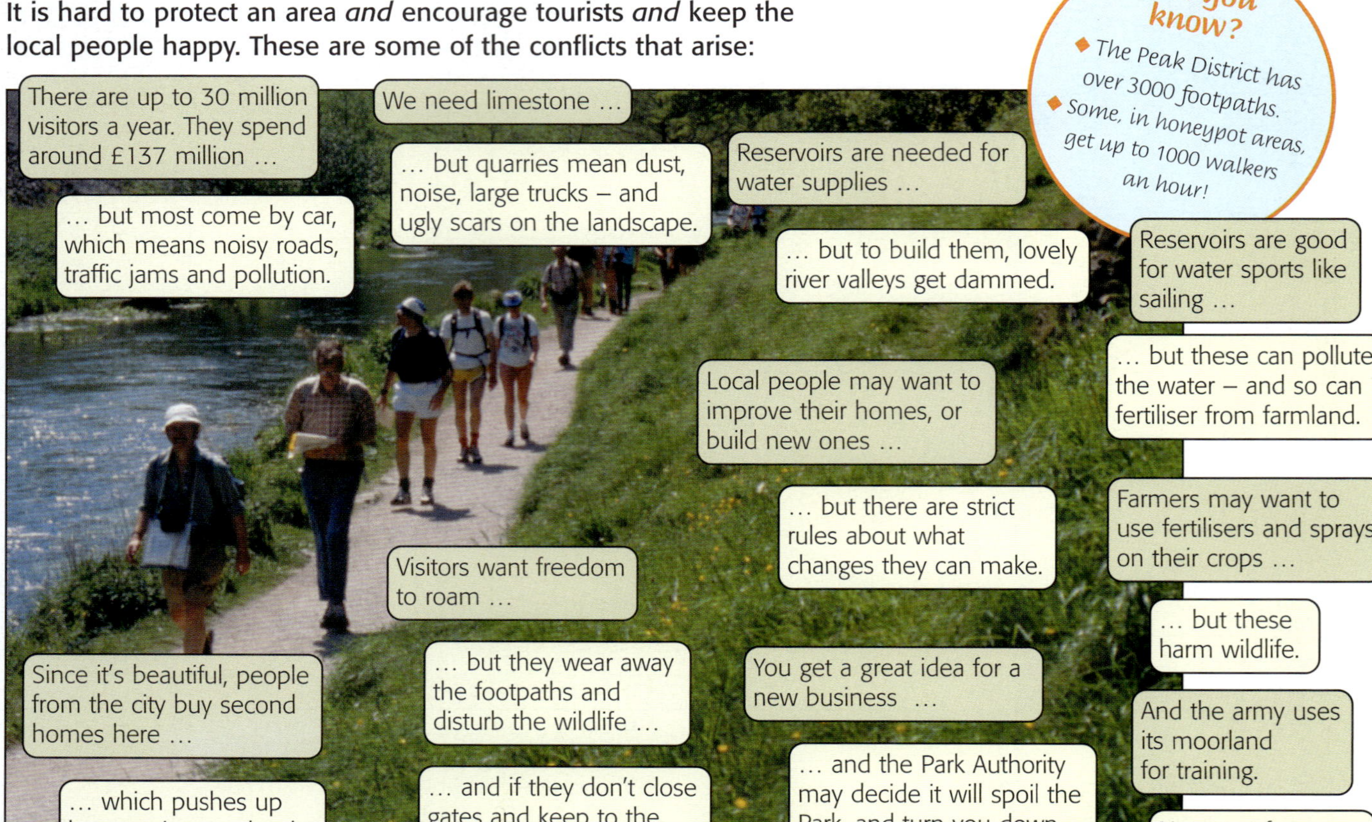

So – who decides?

As you saw on page 90, the National Parks were set up *to benefit the whole nation*. Each National Park has its own **National Park Authority** to manage it. Look at the diagram on the right.

The National Park Authority has to agree to any changes in how the land in the Park is used. It has to balance the needs of:

◆ the nation (for limestone, water and so on)

◆ local residents (for houses and jobs)

◆ visitors (for activities, freedom to enjoy the Park, and facilities like car parks and toilets).

And all the time it has to keep its aims in mind.

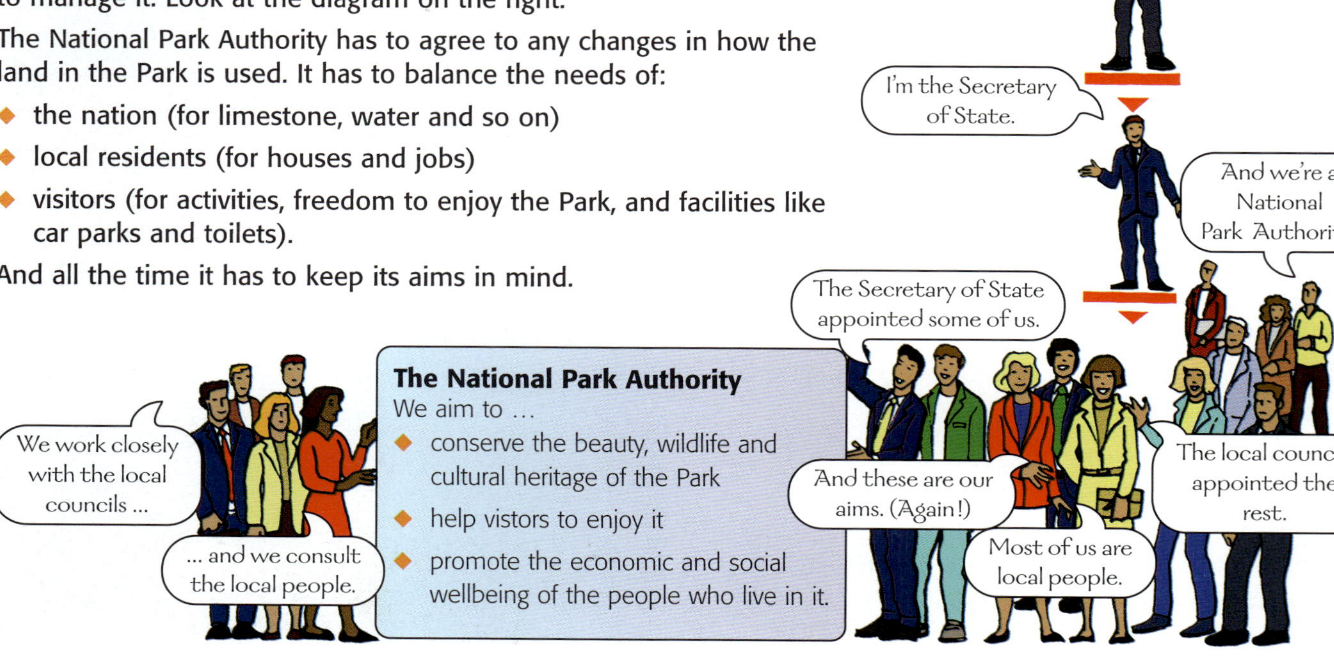

1 There are conflicting demands in the Peak District. Your first task is to show these on a conflict grid.

a First, check the conflict grid on page 84, to remind yourself how to draw one.

b Draw one for the Peak District. Write these on it:
farmers   other residents   visitors   tourist shops wildlife   army   quarries   water supply   fishing water sports

c On your grid, mark ✔ to show where groups or uses may be in harmony, ✗ where they may conflict, and **O** where they don't affect each other.

d Now write a short paragraph summarising the conflicts that arise from all those visitors.

2 The National Park Authority manages the Peak District.

a This Venn diagram is about how the Authority meets its aims. Make a larger copy of it.

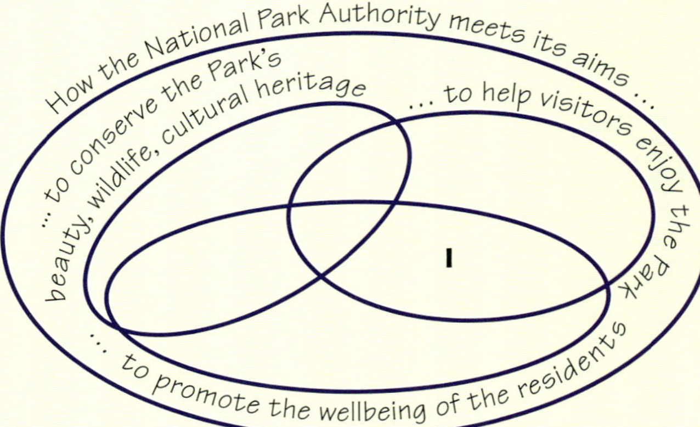

b Below are some statements about the Authority. You have to write each letter **A – K** in the correct loop of your Venn diagram. (One is in already.) If you think a letter belongs to two or even all three loops, write it in the overlap.

A It provides car parks and visitor centres.

B It encourages farmers to use traditional ways of farming.

C It gives grants to repair historic buildings.

D It has rules about materials and colours to be used for new houses.

E It aims to limit the number of new houses to keep the population at its present level.

F In deciding about new houses it gives priority to affordable homes for local people.

G It gets grants from the EU to help hill farmers.

H It forces quarry companies to plant a screen of trees around their quarries.

I It plans to get better bus services in the Park.

J It has given planning permission to several hundred new businesses in the last 30 years.

K It looks after all the footpaths.

▲ *Just one of those conflicts: a limestone quarry.*

3 Look at these pie charts.

Employment structure

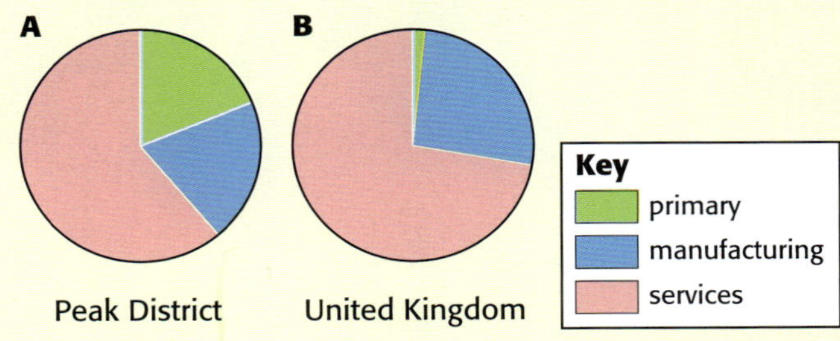

a How does the Peak District differ from the UK in general, for employment?

b See if you can explain these differences.

c **A** is for the Peak District overall. A pie chart just for Castleton would be different.
  i Explain why.
  ii What might Castleton's look like? Draw one roughly.

4 **Age structure of the population (%)**

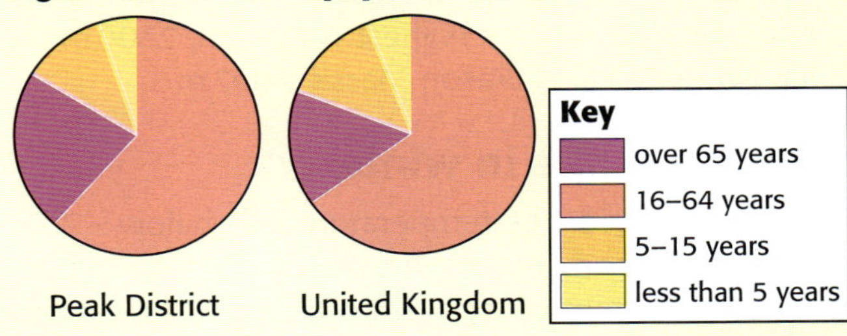

a This time, what differences do you notice for population?

b See if you can explain them.

5 Everything in life has bad and good points, or **costs** and **benefits**. Pretend to be *one* of these people:
- a retired person living in Castleton
- the owner of a tourist shop in Castleton
- the farmer living at 158847 on the map on page 95

a Write down a list of costs and benefits of living in a National Park, from your point of view.

b Now decide which wins out, the costs or the benefits. Give your answer as a 'Dear diary' entry.

Case study 3: Antarctica

Antarctica, the white continent. Almost as big as Europe. Its land frozen under a sheet of ice over 2 km thick on average. Try to imagine that!

Like the land below it, the ice sheet has mountains and valleys. It makes Antarctica the world's highest continent, 2300 m high on average. Its highest peak is Vinson Massif, 4897 m.

What's it like in winter?

Cold, cold, cold. The temperature falls below – 70°C in places. Take off your gloves and your fingers freeze in seconds. Touch anything and they stick to it instantly. Get bad frostbite and they'll need to be amputated!

In winter (around June) it's dark there, because it is tilted away from the sun. No planes fly in. For thousands of km around it, the ocean freezes over. So no ships can reach it either. If you are there in winter, make sure you have enough food and other essentials. Or else – goodbye.

What's it like in summer?

Still cold, cold, cold. Even the warmest parts don't get far above freezing. So you still need your special clothing. But now it's bright. Some places are light all night long for a time. (The diagram on the right shows why.) Sunlight on snow can damage your eyes, so keep your goggles on.

But now planes fly in again. The ice on the ocean melts so ships can sail in. You can relax a bit. Help is at hand.

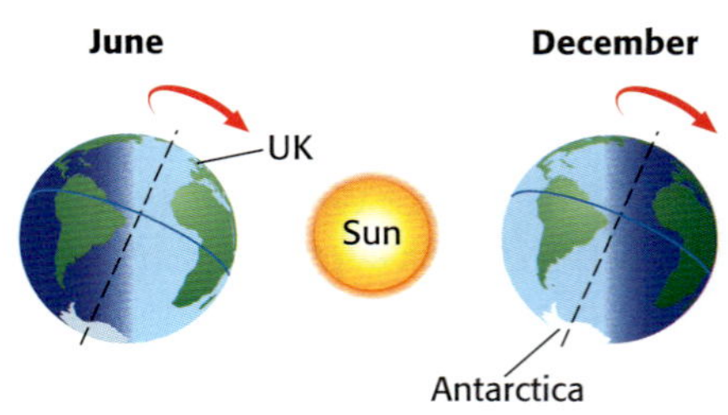

▲ *Because the Earth is tilted, summer in the UK is winter in Antarctica, and vice versa.*

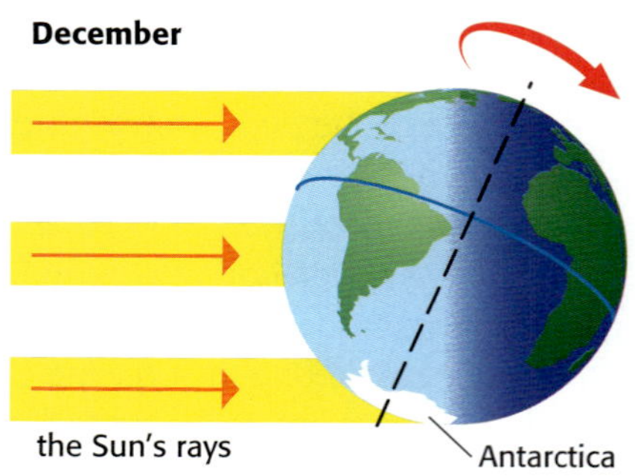

▲ *In the Antarctic midsummer, some places get sunlight 24 hours a day.*

A map of Antarctica

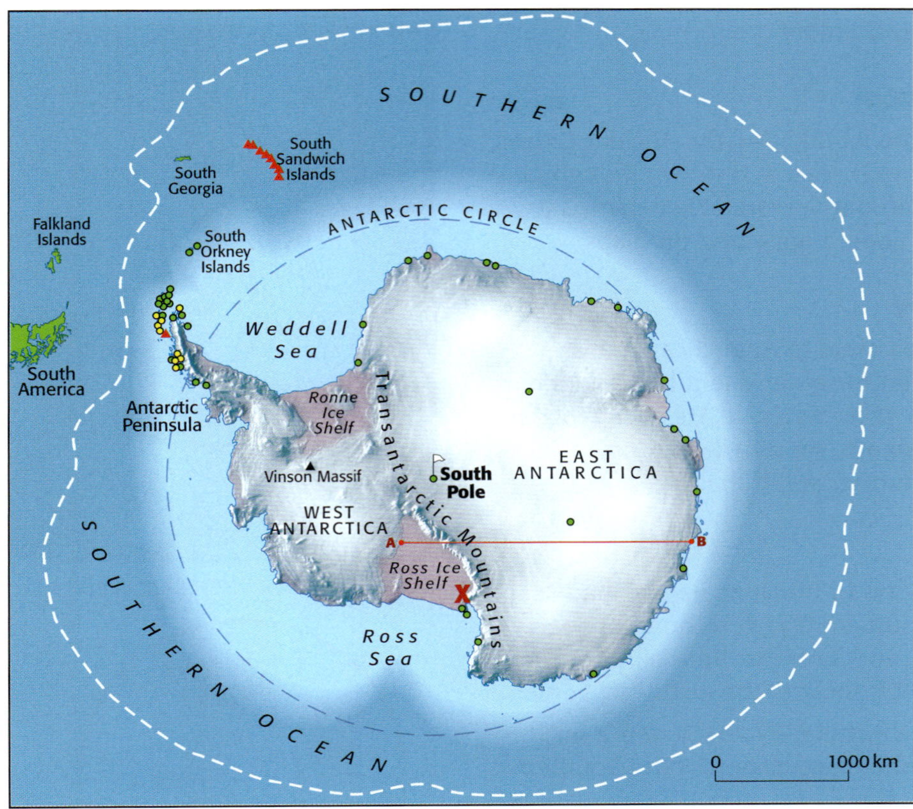

▲ *One of the Norwegian team who were first to reach the South Pole – on 14 December 1911, 34 days before the British team led by Captain Scott.*

Key
- ice shelf
- ocean iced over in winter
- rest of ocean
- Antarctic Polar Front
- ▲ active volcano
- South American continent
- ● main science research stations
- ○ main tourist destinations
- — see cross-section in 'Your turn'

Look at the Southern Ocean. It is always cold, and much of it freezes over in winter. Its boundary is called the **Antarctic Polar Front**. When you cross into another ocean, the water suddenly gets warmer.

Your turn

1 A small green visitor from another planet asks you where Antarctica is. Answer!

2 You're planning an expedition to the South Pole from **X** on the map. (That's where Captain Scott started.)
  a About how long is the journey, in a straight line?
  b Will you be able to go in a straight line? Explain.
  c In which part of the year will you travel? Why?
  d You reach the South Pole and rest overnight. What's it like there? Write an e-mail home.
  e You leave the South Pole again. In which direction are you travelling?

3 Now draw a sketch map of Antarctica. Show and label:
West Antarctica   East Antarctica   the South Pole
the Southern Ocean   the two seas   Ross Ice Shelf
Ronne Ice Shelf   the Transantarctic mountains
Vinson Massif   the Antarctic peninsula   a volcano
a bit of South America   the Falklands   South Georgia

4 What do you think an *ice shelf* is? (Glossary?)

5 Which oceans meet the Southern Ocean? (Page 124?)

6 At the South Pole there's daylight 24 hours a day in December and darkness 24 hours a day in June. Explain why, as if to a nine-year-old. (Use diagrams?)

7 This is a cross-section through part of Antarctica (along the red line on the map above).

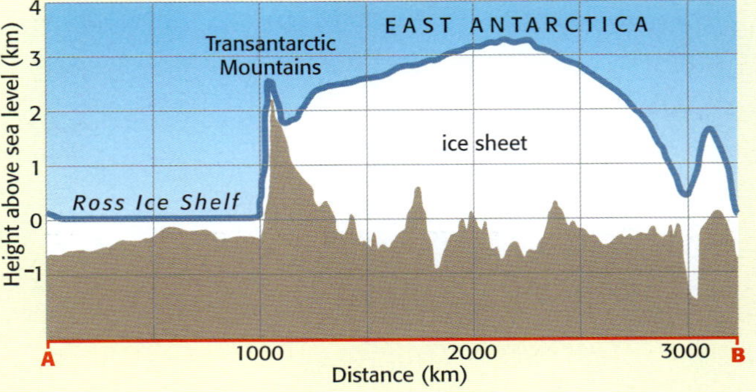

  a Is the land mostly *above* or *below* sea level?
  b About how thick is the ice at its thickest point?
  c If global warming makes the ice melt, will the UK be affected? Give reasons for your answer.

Case study 3: The history of Antarctica

For thousands of years, Antarctica was just theory …

Named by the Greeks

'There is a continent at the bottom of the world,' said the Ancient Greeks, several thousand years ago. They had never seen it. But they thought it *must* exist, to balance the land at the top of the world. They named it *Anti-Arkitos* (or the opposite of *Arctic*). Soon it appeared on maps.

Captain Cook goes sailing by

Captain Cook was the first person to sail close to Antarctica, on his Second Great Voyage (1772 – 75). The British government had asked him to see if it existed. He sailed across the Antarctic Circle. He saw penguins, seals, whales and icebergs. But no continent. He sailed away again, certain that no human would ever get further south than he.

Then come the hunters

Captain Cook and his men sent back news of the animals they had seen. Soon ships were on their way to the Southern Ocean to hunt for seals. Some species were killed for their skin, and some for their oil. Thousands and thousands were slaughtered. By 1900 most of the seals had gone.

Whales were next. Their oil was worth a fortune. By 1965, over a million Antarctic whales had been killed. The whale population of the Southern Ocean was almost wiped out.

To find their prey, the sealers and whalers also had to be explorers. They mapped their routes, so the world learned more and more about the geography around Antarctica.

▲ *Captain Cook: no sign of Antarctica.*

▲ *Whaling in the Southern Ocean. The whales were nearly wiped out.*

▲ *Curves to kill for? A strong flexible material from the whale's mouth was used in 'whalebone' corsets.*

Arguing over Antarctica

While the hunters were chasing seals and whales, there were many other expeditions to Antarctica. Many were sponsored by governments, keen to find out what resources it had – and get a share!

By 1950, seven countries had laid claim to slices of Antarctica. Two others, the USA and Russia, were threatening to take it over. Tension grew.

But in 1957, twelve countries agreed to work together in Antarctica for one year, on science projects. It was a great success. So in 1961 they signed the Antarctic Treaty. This sets aside all claims to Antarctica, and protects it as a place of peace and science.

43 countries have now signed the Antarctic Treaty.

▲ *Flags around the South Pole – a sign of peace.*

Your turn

1 Time to draw a time line for the history of Antarctica.
  a Draw a long line, with lots of space beside it to write in. (Turn your book sideways and use two pages?)
  b Mark the line from 1770 to 1970, with a division for every 10 years.
  c Now write in the information below, at the correct places on your time line. Use small neat writing.
  d Where information covers more than one year, find a way to show this using shading.
  e And finally, give your time line a title.

1819–21 Russian expedition is first to see and circle Antarctica.

1950–58 Disputes between countries over claims to Antarctica.

1943 Argentina claims part of Antarctica.

1923 New Zealand claims part of Antarctica.

1839–43 British expedition led by Captain James Clark Ross explores around the Ross Ice Shelf.

1982 Commercial whaling is banned all over the world.

1800–1900 Seals hunted until almost wiped out.

1772–75 Captain James Cook is first to sail inside the Antarctic Circle.

1908 Britain claims part of Antarctica.

1924 France claims part of Antarctica.

1911 Norwegian explorer Roald Amundsen and his team are first to reach the South Pole.

1838–42 American expedition confirms Antarctica exists.

1904–1965 Whales hunted until almost wiped out.

1931 Norway claims part of Antarctica.

1933 Australia claims part of Antarctica.

1940 Chile claims part of Antarctica.

1898–1900 British expedition is first to spend a winter on Antarctica.

1961 Antarctic Treaty to protect Antarctica as a place of peace and science.

1957 Twelve countries agree to co-operate for a year on Antarctica science projects.

1912 British explorer Captain Robert Scott and his team reach the South Pole, 34 days after Amundsen. They perish on the return journey.

1897–99 Belgian expedition is first to winter inside the Antarctic Circle (trapped in ice).

Case study 3: Antarctica today

A region of beauty, peace and science, protected by a treaty …

Why is Antarctica important?

It is important for many reasons. Like these …

- It is the world's last great wilderness. Humans have not spoiled it (yet).
- It is very beautiful. (So tourist ships now stop off for short visits.)
- Since it is unspoiled, scientists can learn a lot from it about the history of our planet, and how life evolved.
- It is a symbol of how nations can work in harmony.

Science in Antarctica

Today 19 countries have research stations in Antarctica, and about 1100 people live there right through the winter. They are mainly scientists. They do many different kinds of research. For example …

▲ *Releasing a weather balloon in Antarctica.*

Air gets trapped in ice. So they drill out plugs of ancient ice to learn about the atmosphere 500 000 years ago. It helps us understand climate change.

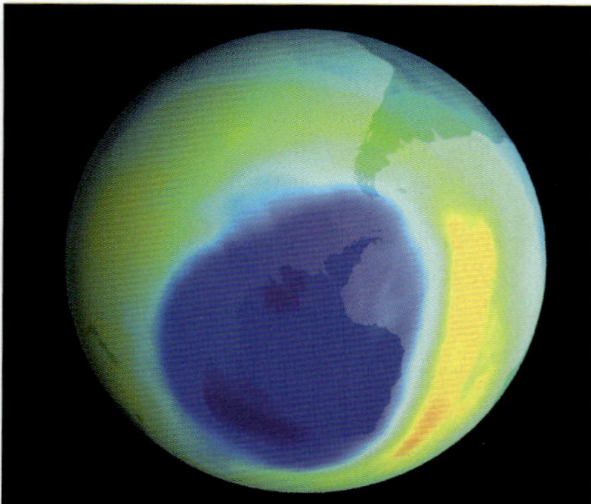

They've also learned a lot about today's atmosphere, including the ozone layer, with help from satellite images. And about how pollutants get carried around.

Using satellite images, they have discovered lakes hidden under the ice. These must contain ancient species that would help us understand how life evolved.

Antarctica and the ozone layer

Research in Antarctica has already helped us all.

Ozone is a form of oxygen, with the formula O_3. It collects high in the atmosphere, in the **ozone layer**. This acts as a sunscreen, protecting us from the sun's more harmful radiation.

Without ozone we'd get more skin cancers. Crops would suffer. The tiny sea plants that fish feed on would die off, so life in the ocean would collapse.

The amount of ozone changes naturally through the year. But in 1985 scientists noticed the layer had a big hole in it, above Antarctica. That meant danger! (The hole is the blue patch on the satellite image above.)

They found the cause: solvents called **CFCs**, used all over the world (for example in sprays such as hair sprays, and as coolants in fridges). When CFCs escape into the atmosphere they destroy ozone. They are now banned, but there are still some left in the atmosphere.

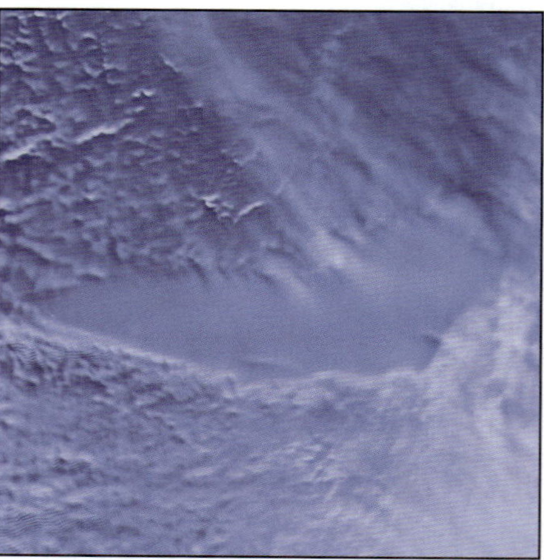

▲ *The smooth shape in this satellite image is Lake Vostok, an ancient lake under the ice. Scientists plan to study the life in it, without contaminating it.*

So is Antarctica safe?

Antarctica is still unspoiled. But will it stay that way?

The Antarctic Treaty aims to reduce these threats, and protect Antarctica. For example under the treaty:

◆ rubbish must be removed from Antarctica – except waste food and sewage. (Long journeys for those would pose a health risk.)

◆ many substances are not allowed there. For example polystyrene.

◆ all proposals for new projects must be checked, to make sure they won't harm the environment. (So some get turned down.)

◆ countries have set aside their claims to Antarctica.

◆ mining for minerals is banned for the foreseeable future.

◆ fishing in the Southern Ocean is controlled.

▲ *Barrels of waste ready for removal.*

Your turn

1 Look at all the reasons why Antarctica is important. Which reason do *you* think is the main one?

2 Local actions can have global effects.

a Explain how Molly's action may have affected people living in Australia.
b Now do the same for Joe.

3 Now list the threats facing Antarctica. As bullet points, in order, with the most serious one first.

4 Above are some of the Antarctic Treaty conditions to control human impact on Antarctica. Put them in what you think is their order of importance (main one first).

5 a Now list the **costs** and **benefits** of humans being in Antarctica. (Glossary?)

b Decide which win out.
c So should humans leave Antarctica alone? Write a newspaper article giving your opinion, with reasons.

Introducing tourism

All these people have something in common – they are all **tourists**.
You have probably been one too – even if you've never seen an airport.

So what is a tourist?

A tourist is a person who travels to and stays in a place that is not his or
her usual place, for a short period, for leisure, business or other purposes.
Look at the box on the right.

So not all tourists are people on holiday – but most are.

What is tourism?

Tourism means all the activities that tourists take part in, and the services
that support them. Tourists, hotels, airports, taxi drivers and ice cream
sellers are all part of the tourism industry.

Tourism is big business

For people on holiday, tourism means fun. For the people who look
after them, it is a very serious and important industry.

In 1999, countries earned a total of $555 billion from international
tourists. For over 80% of the world's countries, tourism is one of their top
five money earners. They want to keep those tourists rolling in.

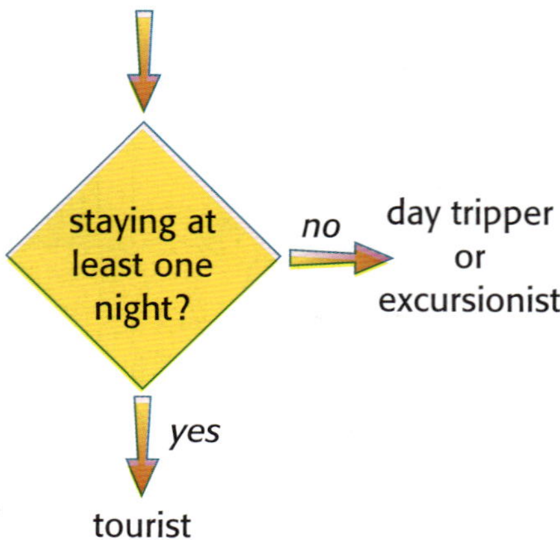

Where do they go?

Look at this table and map.

Rank	Country	Tourist arrivals (millions)
	Top 10 tourism destinations, 2000	
1	France	75.5
2	USA	50.9
3	Spain	48.2
4	Italy	41.2
5	China	31.2
6	UK	25.2
7	Russian Federation	21.2
8	Mexico	20.6
9	Canada	20.4
10	Germany	19.0

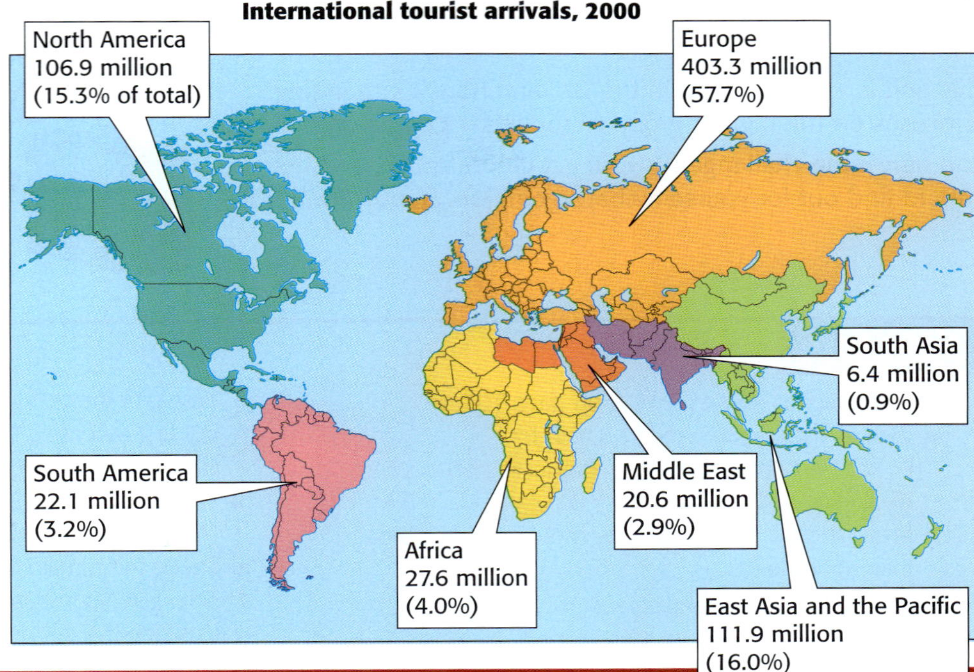

Your turn

1 Define these terms: **a** tourist **b** tourism

2 Now decide whether this person is a tourist or not.
   a Emile on a school trip from Paris to London
   b Chris from Oxford, in Greece for a fortnight's sun
   c Walter in Leeds for the day, at a football match
   d Annie on the way to Sweden for an eye operation
   e Alex in Antarctica for 3 months, to study penguins
   f Sachin on tour in the UK with the India cricket team
   g Jill from Scotland Yard, in the USA to track a thief
   h Andy from Bath at his mum's in Suffolk for Easter
   i Zia from Watford off to Mecca on pilgrimage

3 a What do these terms mean?
   (Try to answer without using the glossary.)
   i international tourist **ii** domestic tourist
   iii inbound tourist **iv** outbound tourist
   b For each term give one example from the list in **2**.

4 Look at the tourist arrivals on the map above.
   a On a pie chart 100% is shown by a full pie
   or 360°. What angle represents 1%?
   b Show the data on the map as a pie chart.
   Arrange the slices in order of size.
   c Which region was by far the most visited, in 2000?
   d *Europe had about ___ times more international
   tourists than South Asia did.*
   Complete this statement and give as many reasons
   as you can to explain it.

5 Now compare the map above with the one on
   page 16, showing real GDP per capita.
   What conclusions, if any, can you draw?

6 a Draw any suitable graph for the destinations in the
   table above, to help you compare their popularity.
   b Now write a paragraph comparing their popularity.
   Use terms like *least, most, 50% more than …*
   c For each destination, see if you can give reasons
   why it is popular. (Warm? exotic? full of history? …)

7

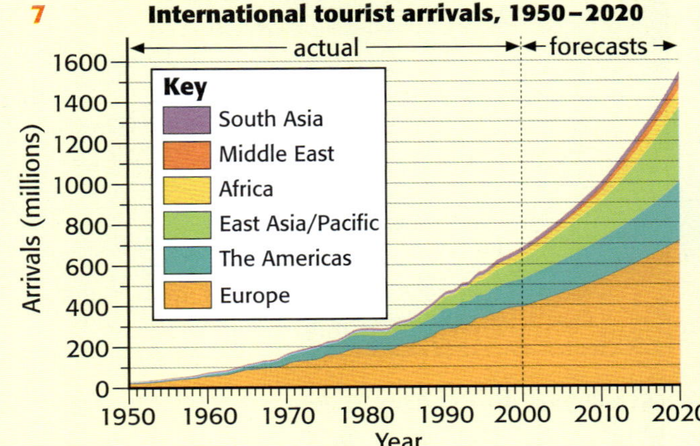

This graph shows how tourism is growing.
   a What does the term *The Americas* mean here?
   b About how many international tourists were there:
   i in 1950? **ii** in 1980? **iii** in 2000?
   c How many are predicted for 2020:
   i in total? **ii** for Europe? **iii** for East Asia / Pacific?
   d Write a short report (max 200 words) on the trends
   shown in the graph, and suggest reasons to explain
   them. (Think about the overall trend *and* the trend
   for each region.)

The UK on holiday

This unit is about tourism in the UK, and how it's changing. It focuses on the biggest group of tourists – people on holiday.

And here's the challenge for *you*: act the detective, and use the data to find out for yourself what's going on. Happy hunting!

Did you know?

- About 2.1 million people in the UK work in tourism.
- That's about 7% of UK jobs.

Your turn

1 This question is about graph **A** on page 107.
 a What is the *overall* trend in Britain for:
  i total holidays taken? **ii** domestic holidays?
  iii foreign holidays?
 b In which year did people take more holidays abroad than at home?

2 Now see if you can suggest reasons why:
 a the total number of holidays increased
 b the number of foreign holidays increased
 c the *total* line is not smooth, but zig zags.
 There are clues in the box below, but see if you can also come up with reasons of your own.

CLUES

The UK economy is in better shape some years than others.
Jumbo jets can carry more people faster, further, and at less cost per person. First introduced in 1971.
Fierce competition among tour operators
Households with use of car: 31% in 1971, 72% in 2000
UK population: 55.9 million in 1971, 59.8 million in 2000
If there's a chance you'll lose your job …
TV holiday programmes
School?
Wages have been rising steadily since 1971.
Most people like sunshine
Dishwashers, tumble driers, microwave ovens, freezers …

3 Look at table **B**. You have to draw a graph for this data. (A bit like the graph at the top of page 35.)
 a Make a *much* larger copy of the diagram below. Add the two missing numbers for the lower axis.
 b On your diagram, plot the points for % of people taking *no* holidays. Join them with a smooth curve. Shade the area under your line.

c Now plot the points for % taking *only one* holiday. But first you need to do some sums! (Hint: 41 + 44 = 85, and see page 35.)
 d Shade in the area between your lines for **b** and **c**. (Use a different colour than before.)
 e Shade the remaining blank area in a third colour.
 f Now give your graph a key and a title.
 g Describe the trends that show up in your graph and try to explain them. (Will the clue box help?)

4 Look at map **C** on page 107.
 a Which region of Britain was the top destination for domestic holidays? See if you can name any of its counties and attractions. (Page 91 might help.)
 b *'For domestic holidays in Britain, most people prefer to go to the big cities.'* Do you agree? Give evidence to support your answer.

5 Table **D** shows where we like to go for foreign holidays.
 a Which two countries are the most popular?
 b From the other named countries pick out:
  i three that seem to keep growing in popularity
  ii two that seem to be losing their appeal.

6 So far you have focused on holidays that are 4 or more nights long. But are they the *most* popular? Table **E** has the answer!
 a Show the data from *the first two columns* of the table using a suitable type of graph.
 b Try to give reasons for the pattern it shows.
 c Using table E to help you, copy and complete this statement using the correct term from the brackets: *The longer the holiday, the ______ it works out per day. (cheaper   more expensive)*
 d Try to give reasons for the statement in **c**.

7 Meanwhile, lots of tourists from other countries come to the UK. Look at table **F**.
 a Which is more important to the UK economy, domestic or foreign tourists? Give your evidence.
 b On average, which of the two groups takes longer holidays here? Suggest reasons for this.

8 Draw a suitable bar chart for table **G**. (Think hard!) Explain any patterns you notice. (Language? distance?)

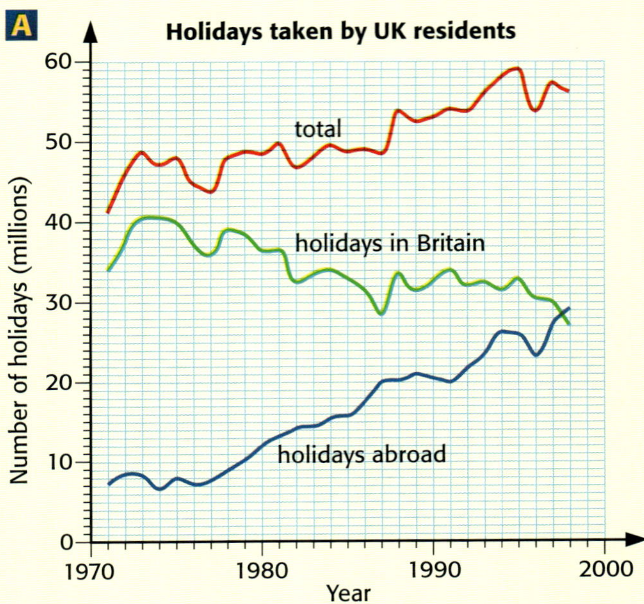

A

Holidays taken by UK residents

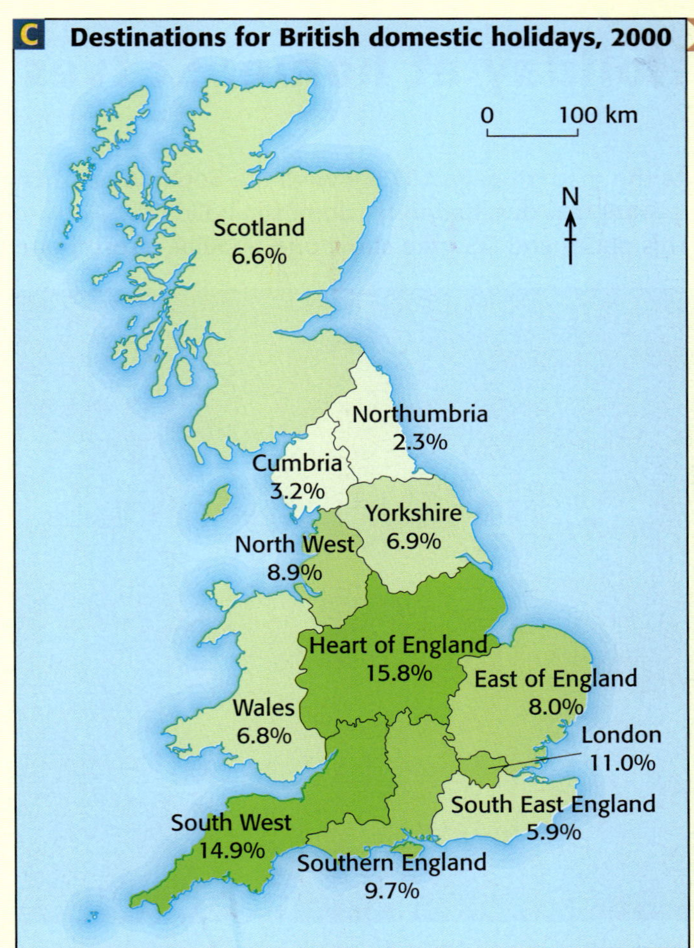

C

Destinations for British domestic holidays, 2000

B

% of UK residents taking holidays (4 nights or more)

Year	No holiday	1 only	2 or more
1971	41	44	15
1974	39	44	17
1977	41	42	17
1980	38	43	19
1983	42	38	20
1986	40	40	20
1989	41	37	22
1992	41	35	24
1995	39	35	26
1998	41	34	25

D

Where UK residents took their foreign holidays (4 or more nights) (%)

Country	Years		
	1981	1991	1998
Spain	21.7	21.3	27.5
France	27.2	25.8	20.2
USA	5.5	6.8	7.0
Greece	6.7	7.6	5.3
Italy	5.8	3.5	4.0
Portugal	2.8	4.8	3.6
Irish Republic	3.6	3.0	3.5
Turkey	0.1	0.7	3.0
Netherlands	2.4	3.5	2.7
Cyprus	0.7	2.4	2.6
Belgium	2.1	2.1	2.3
Germany	2.6	2.7	1.8
Malta	2.6	1.7	1.3
Austria	2.5	2.4	1.3
Other countries	13.7	11.8	13.9

E

Holidays taken by UK residents in 2000

Length of holiday	Number (millions)	Spending (£ billions)
1–3 nights	67.2	7.86
4–7 nights	29.8	6.29
8+ nights	8.9	2.35
Total	**106.0**	**16.50**

F

Holidays taken in the UK in 2000

	Trips (millions)	Nights (millions)	Amount spent (£ billions)
By UK residents	106.0	392.7	16.5
By overseas tourists	9.3	67.0	4.3

G

Top 10 countries of origin, for visitors to the UK in 2000 (all numbers in millions)

Country	Population	Visitors to UK
Australia	19.2	0.8
Belgium	10.2	1.0
Canada	31.3	0.8
France	60.0	3.1
Germany	59.3	2.8
Irish Republic	3.8	2.1
Italy	57.6	0.9
Netherlands	15.9	1.4
Spain	40.0	0.8
USA	281.4	4.1

Holiday at home: St Ives

As the map on page 107 showed, the South West of England is a popular destination for domestic holidays.
This photo and OS map show one popular resort there: St Ives.

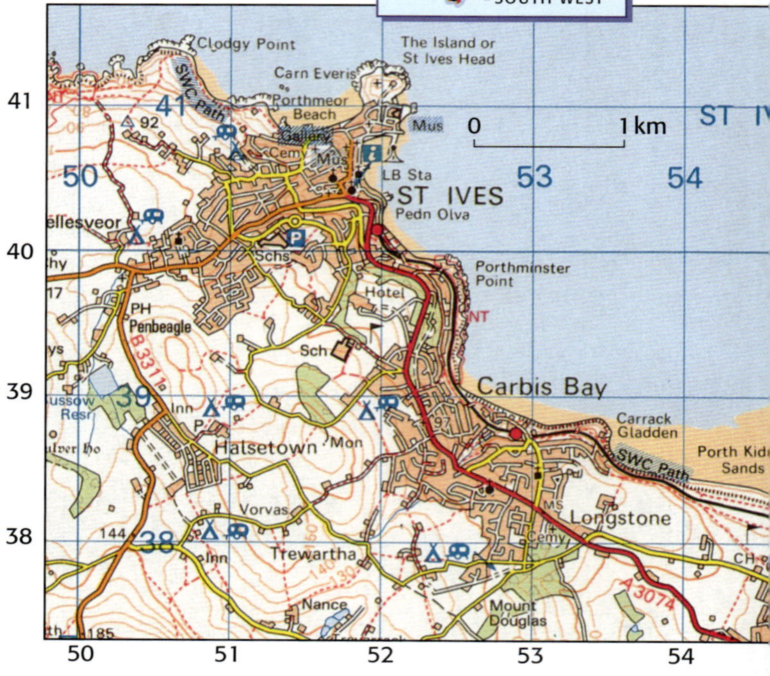

How is it doing?

More of us are going abroad for our holidays. And when foreign tourists come here, most don't head for the seaside! This means that some British seaside resorts are suffering.

St Ives is lucky. It attracts tourists because of its charm, and the unspoilt coast and countryside around it. The number of tourists is holding up. But Cornwall County Council knows it must fight to keep it that way. So it aims to:

♦ improve existing accommodation for tourists (rather than build more)

♦ ensure that any new tourist development is sustainable. That means it must attract tourists, but not spoil St Ives, or harm the environment, or lower the quality of life for local people.

Tourists in St Ives:
age profile for a typical year

Age	% of tourists
0 – 14	25.7
15 – 24	9.6
25 – 34	12.3
35 – 44	19.8
45 – 54	15.6
55 – 64	8.4
65+	8.6

What the brochure says ...

Welcome to St Ives. Its sandy beaches, turquoise sea, scenic harbour, cobbled streets and secret corners will delight you.

At its heart is the fishing harbour and four magnificent beaches. One, Porthmeor, is famous for its surfing. Behind the harbour lies a maze of narrow streets and alleyways. This is the hold part of town, where you can explore for hours.

Fishing, farming and mining have all helped to shape St Ives. The mines have closed now, but you can still watch the fishing boats unload their catches. Later, treat yourself to fresh fish from the menu in one of our wonderful restaurants.

With its clear bright light, it is no surprise that the town has long attracted artists. It is famous for its art galleries, studios and craftshops.

At the Tate Gallery, by Porthmeor Beach, you can see work of well-known artists who spent time here.

Explore the coastline too. Ride the scenic railway from Lelant to St Ives to see it at its most breathtaking. Take some wonderful walks. And don't forget swimming, biking, golf, horseriding. Make it a holiday to remember.

Your turn

1 Where exactly is St Ives? Answer as fully as you can.

2 Look at the building marked with a red dot on the photo. Where do you think it is on the OS map? Give a six-figure grid reference.

3 Draw a sketch map of St Ives, showing the main physical features, the built-up area, the main road through it, the railway, and attractions for tourists.

4

Visitor attractions in St Ives	
Outdoor	Indoor

Make a large table with headings like this and fill it in, using any clues you can find on these two pages.

5 Let's think about the people. Look at table **A**.
  a What can you say about the number of tourists at peak season each year, compared with the number of residents?
  b What problems might result from this? You could give your answer as a spider map.

6 Tourists visit other parts of Cornwall too. Table **B** shows data for a typical year for the whole county.
  a What do you think *number of tourist nights* means?
  b Now make a *large* copy of the diagram started below. The two vertical axes should be exactly the same height but different colours. (You choose.) Fill in the rest of the numbers and months.

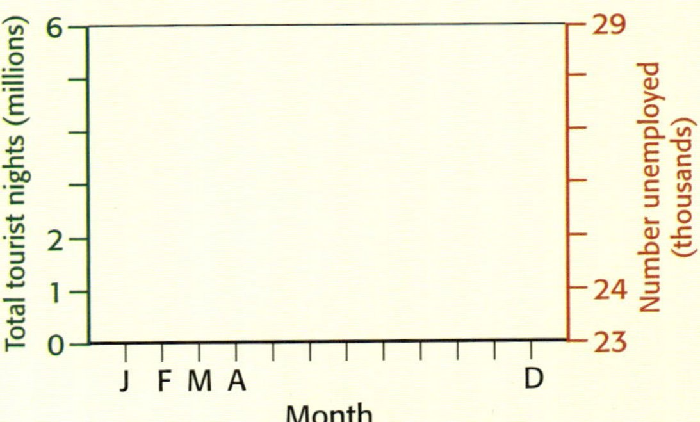

  c On your diagram plot points for the number of tourist nights, using the left axis. Join them to give a smooth line the same colour as this axis. Add a label to the line to make it clear what it shows.
  d Repeat for the number of unemployed residents, but this time using the right axis.

7 Look at your diagram for **6**.
  a Explain why the line graph for tourist nights is the shape it is. Try to think of more than one reason.
  b Can you see any connection between the shapes of your two graphs? Explain.
  c Much employment around St Ives is *seasonal*. What does that mean?
  d Give at least four examples of jobs in St Ives where you expect employment to be seasonal.

A

St Ives / Carbis Bay

Year	Number of residents	Number of tourists at peak season
1961	7900	8650
1971	8600	11 900
1981	9430	12 500
1991	9970	13 200
1994	9770	12 800
1996	9780	13 630

B

Cornwall through one typical year

Month	Total number of tourist nights (millions)	Number of unemployed residents (thousands)
Jan	0.3	29.0
Feb	0.4	28.1
March	0.7	27.4
April	1.7	26.4
May	2.3	25.0
June	3.0	24.0
July	4.4	23.9
Aug	5.6	23.9
Sept	3.0	23.6
Oct	1.4	24.1
Nov	0.4	25.1
Dec	0.8	25.8

8 Now look at the table on page 108, showing the typical age profile of tourists who visit St Ives.
  a Display this data in the form you think most suitable. (Line graph? bar chart? pie chart? pictogram?)
  b From the data, which group do you think St Ives attracts most?
    A retired people
    B families with young children
    C families with older (late teenage) children
    D young single working people

9 It's your job to bring more tourists to St Ives, especially in the quiet months. Here are three suggestions:
    A open a large hotel and conference centre. (Remember, tourists include people on business.)
    B open a 'Harry Potter boarding school' where tourists can stay – and get lots of surprises!
    C open a 'Smugglers' Cove' telling all about the history of smuggling in Cornwall, and its famous smugglers and pirates.
  a Which do you think would be best for St Ives? Explain why you chose it and *not* the other two.
  b Prepare a short proposal for the project, to send to Cornwall County Council. Briefly describe your idea. Say which age group(s) of tourists it is likely to attract. You can even suggest a site for it.

Beautiful Benidorm?

Tourism can change a place completely and forever …

Benidorm in 1960: a fishing town with 6200 residents, two great beaches and just a few hotels.

Benidorm in 1995: 55 000 residents, and 350 000 tourists at its busiest time. (Most of them British!)

The package holiday arrives

In 1950, only 3% of people in the UK went abroad on holiday. But wages were rising. War planes from World War II were being converted to carry passengers. A few astute businessmen toured the Mediterranean looking for good holiday places … and the **package holiday** was born.

In 1957 the first package tour, from the UK, arrived in Benidorm. The tourists loved its sunshine, peace and quiet. News spread. Soon hotels and apartments were springing up all around it to meet demand. Many had grants from the Spanish government. But there was little planning or control, and much of the building was poor quality.

How the package holiday works

- A tour operator selects a hotel.
- It books a block of rooms for next season (or several seasons).
- It also books some planes (or may even buy its own).
- Then it sells a complete holiday (flight + hotel and at least some meals) to tourists.

Benidorm heads downhill

By the late 1980s, millions of tourists later, Benidorm had a poor image.

So tourists began to stay away.

Benidorm today: doing better!

Benidorm is *really* important to Spain: it contributes 1% of its GDP!
So the Spanish government got worried about its reputation.

Now the government has taken more control of development around
Benidorm. Bad hotels have been improved. New posh ones have been
built. A new theme park has been set up close by, to attract visitors all
year round.

Now Benidorm is getting more tourists than ever. It has loads of
activities, and a lively night life – but still not much peace and quiet!

Is the growth in tourism sustainable?

There is one big problem facing the Benidorm area: water shortage!
Benidorm uses huge amounts of water for tourist swimming pools
and showers. This diagram shows what's happening:

Your turn

1 a Make a *large* copy of the 'vicious circle' on the right.
  b Write the sentences below in your boxes, in the right
    order, to show how tourism can ruin a place.
    (Hint: start by writing sentence **C** in box 1.)
    A In the end, no tourists want to go there at all.
    B So developers rush to build new tourist facilities.
    C Tour operators offer cheap packages to a resort.
    D But development isn't managed or controlled ...
    E Now many tourists are put off.
    F Tourists rush to book because it's so cheap.
    G ... so the resort's natural attractions get ruined.
    H So the tour operators have to slash prices further.

2 Look at your vicious circle in **1**.
  a A government *could* object at step 1.
    Give a reason why it might not wish to.
  b At what point did the Spanish government intervene
    in Benidorm's development?
  c At what step do you think it *should* have done so?

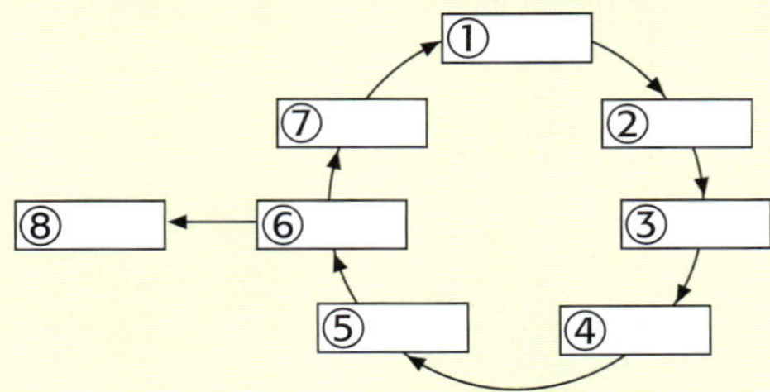

3 If tourism ruins a place, whose fault is it?
  Using your vicious circle to help you, list all the groups
  you think may be to blame. And give your reasons.

4 You grow almonds near Benidorm. You are worried:
  the soil is growing salty and your trees are dying.
  a Draw a diagram to show why this is happening.
  b Now write a letter to the Spanish government
    explaining why you should get compensation.

5 Benidorm is beside the sea, and gets lots of sun.
  Come up with a sustainable way to give it as much
  clean water as it needs. (Hint: solar power, evaporate,
  condense.) Include a drawing of your scheme.

Gambling with Gambia?

Today many package holidays are in poorer countries … like Gambia.

Where is Gambia?

Gambia is a small country of only 1.2 million people, in West Africa. It was created by a treaty between Britain and France in 1900 – by drawing lines on a map! Gambia was a British colony until 1965.

Today Gambia is colonised in a different way. Its climate and beautiful sandy beaches attract thousands of tourists in search of winter sun.

Gambia is keen to earn money from tourism. The first package tour arrived (from Sweden) in 1965. Now Gambia gets over 90 000 tourists a year.

So is everyone happy?

No. Tourism has brought conflicts. Like these …

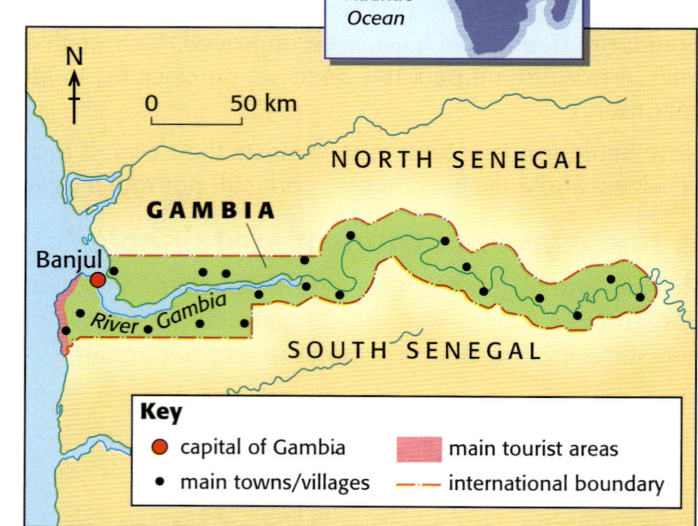

A very leaky business

For poorer countries like Gambia, there's a high level of **leakage** in tourism. In other words they get very little of the money that tourists pay. It leaks out all over the place, like this …

So does tourism really help Gambia – or just exploit it?

1 Using the map on page 112, write a paragraph on the geography of Gambia: where it is, its main features, roughly how long and wide it is, and so on.

2 One of Gambia's main attractions is its climate. Look at the climate graph at the top of this page.
   a Which two months are likely to bring most British tourists? Why?
   b In which three months are hotel staff most likely to be laid off? Why?

3 Look at this table.
   a What is *real GDP per capita*?
   b On average, compared with a Gambian, how many times better off is:
      i a Ghanaian?
      ii someone from the UK?
      iii someone from Spain?
   Give your answers to 1 decimal point.

Real GDP per capita ($US)	
Gambia	1010
Ghana	1760
UK	20910
Spain	16500
Sweden	20120

4 a In tourism, what does *leakage* mean?
   b You book a package holiday to Gambia: £350 for the return flight and two weeks in a British-owned hotel. Less than £100 of the money you paid makes it into Gambia's economy. Explain this.

5 For each of **A–D** below, write down what you think is:
   a the main advantage   b the main disadvantage
   of tourism:
      A the prime minister of Gambia
      B a Gambian farmer
      C a waiter in a tourist hotel in Gambia
      D a strict Muslim mum in Gambia, with four teenagers

6 The government of Gambia decides to invite twenty foreign companies in, to set up luxury hotels all along the coast. In return it will charge them very low taxes. Is this a good idea? Give as many reasons as you can to support your answer.

7 You are Gambia's Minister of Tourism. You want Gambia to gain more benefit from tourism. What steps will you take? Write your answer as a speech to the Gambian parliament.

Towards sustainable tourism

Holidays are fun. But behind the fun are real conflicts – over money, the environment, and respect for people and their cultures.

▲ The jump dance is a traditional war dance of the Masai of East Africa.

Sustainable tourism

Tourism can earn a lot of money – and do a lot of harm. It can take a place over and give little in return. Now people are starting to see that it must be made more **sustainable**.

Sustainable tourism means tourism where:

◆ tourists have an enjoyable holiday, while respecting the place, people and culture

◆ local people are involved in decisions about tourism, and get a fair share of the earnings from it

◆ there is as little damage as possible to the environment.

Sustainable tourism is important for all countries, rich and poor – for the UK as well as Gambia. But it is especially important for poor countries, where it could help thousands of people to climb out of poverty.

Below are some examples of sustainable tourism.

1 Community tourism

In **commmunity tourism**, small groups of tourists go to stay with local people in their villages. They eat local food. They see how the people live. They learn about their culture and customs. The money they pay for food, guides and accommodation goes straight to the local people.

So you could find yourself sleeping in a tent in the desert, or in a thatched hut on a Pacific island. You could stay with a tribe in the rainforest and learn how they survive. You could help harvest cocoa in Ghana, or trek in the Kenyan savanna with the Masai.

Community tourism is a form of fair trade – like the coffee on page 80.

▲ Community tourism: you could stay in a hill village in Thailand like this one.

2 Ecotourism

This is where you spend time in an **ecosystem** to learn about its animals and plants. You could end up tracking monkeys in the rainforest in Costa Rica, or bird watching in Belize.

There are usually strict rules. For example stay with your guide, keep to pathways, no smoking, leave no rubbish.

Ecotours aim to protect the ecosystem *and* make a profit. Sometimes local people gain a fair share of the profit. But *that does not always happen*. It depends on who's running the tours.

▲ *Ecotourists enjoying the wildlife in Coast Rica.*

But what about the rest?

Package tours to holiday resorts are still the most popular kind of holiday.

Now even package tour operators are starting to think about sustainability. Some show videos about local culture and customs, and advise tourists how to behave (like *'Ask permission before taking people's photos. Do not wear skimpy clothing in the streets.'*) Some support local schools and orphanages.

But these are only small steps. Many resorts around the world are still suffering unsustainable development. The rights of local people are ignored. Environments are wrecked. And one time bomb is ticking away in many resorts: the problem of water shortage.

▶ *Yes, I'm a Costa Rican toucan.*

1 a What is *sustainable tourism*? Give your answer in your own words.
  b Who wins in sustainable tourism? Who loses?

2 a What is *community tourism*?
  b Look back through the photos of places in LEDCs, in earlier chapters of this book. Find one where you think community tourism might be a success, and explain why you think so.
  c Suppose you went there on holiday.
    i How do you think *you* would benefit?
    ii How would the local people benefit?
  d Suppose lots of people hear about the place – and arrive every week in their hundreds. Do you think this would be a sustainable situation? Explain.

3 a What is the main difference between community tourism and ecotourism?
  b Can these two types of holiday solve all the problems of tourism? Give reasons.

4 

A travel agent shows you this photo from a brochure, to persuade you to buy a package holiday. Using a development compass rose (page 5) to help you, write down at least 8 questions to ask, to find out whether that package operation is sustainable.

5 Look at the slogan on this suitcase.
  a What message is it trying to put across?
  b Write the slogan as a heading in your exercise book. Below it write a set of guidelines for tourists on how to behave when they go on holiday.

You, citizen of the world

Citizen Walter …

Like Walter, you too are a citizen at many levels.
Being a citizen brings rights – and responsibilities.
For example as a citizen of the UK you have a right to free education and health care. You have a responsibility to obey the UK's laws.

Citizens of the world

The world is full of beauty. We all have a right to enjoy it.
But it also faces many problems – like the poverty endured by millions of people. As citizens of the world, we have a responsibility to help to solve its problems.

Local actions, global effects

As you have seen throughout this course, you are linked to people and places everywhere. That includes millions of people you will never meet, and places you will never visit. But you can still affect them, because **local actions can have global effects.**

Through local actions, we help to create many of the world's problems. Through local actions we can help to solve them.
For example through our actions as …

Did you know?
◆ Superman was born on the planet Krypton and sent to Earth when still a baby.
◆ His astonishing powers didn't develop until he was a teenager.

Did you know?
◆ The UK is a democracy.
◆ That means it is governed by the people for the people.
◆ You get your say by voting (once you reach 18).

… shoppers …

… energy users …

… tourists, and …

… voters (from age 18).

So what kind of future will you choose?

Each of us can help to solve the world's problems – or make them worse. It is easy to feel you have no power, and that what **you** do, or don't do, does not matter. But suppose 100 people like you take action … then 1000 … 10 000 … a million … 50 million … 500 million … a billion people. That could change everything.

So, your actions may seem small – but they count. By working together, you can change things. The future is in your hands.

Your turn

1 Choose one major problem facing the world. Draw a large consequence map like the one started here (use a full page) to show:
   a the problem. (Write it in the problem box.)
   b what the future will be like, if nothing is done to solve this problem. (Give as many consequences as you can.)
   c steps that could be taken to solve the problem. (No violence permitted.)
   d what the alternative future might be if these steps are carried out.

2 So what's your ideal future for the planet? Write an essay about the state you'd like to leave it in, for your grandchildren to enjoy. Add drawings?

3 You have to make a speech on School Open Day to convince parents that we all have responsibility for solving the world's problems. What will you say?

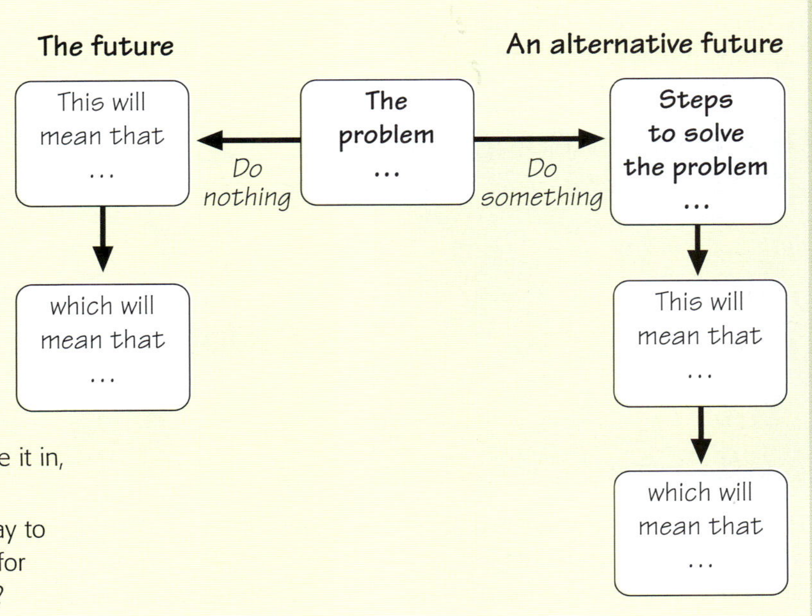

117

Going places with geography

It's getting near the end of your geography course – or is it just the end of the beginning?

So what have you learned?

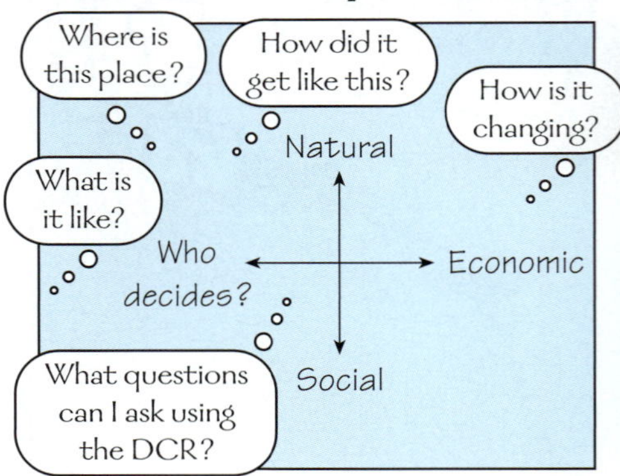

You've learned to be nosy, and ask questions about the world around you and how it's changing. A very important thing to have learned!

And how the Earth's surface is shaped by plate movements, and the actions of rivers, waves, wind, glaciers, weather.

About the resulting physical features such as beaches and volcanoes, and hazards such as earthquakes and floods.

Climate, ecosystems and other natural resources – and how we humans interact with and exploit these, to meet our needs.

How conflicting demands on environments arise, and the harm we do – and how we are learning we must live more sustainably.

About some of the places on our planet – regions, countries, cities, towns, rivers. Where they are, what they are like, and why.

How and why countries are at different stages of development. And how to compare them using development indicators.

Skills like map reading, carrying out enquiries, interpreting and presenting data, and drawing conclusions from it.

And finally, about the problems facing our planet and how we can help solve them – through local actions with global effects.

Going forward with geography

Geography is a brilliant subject. It helps you understand what's going on in the world. It helps you make sense of the news. It makes travel more exciting. It even makes a walk round your local area more interesting.

But that's not all. Studying geography leads directly to dozens of careers, and is a big help for many others. Careers like these …

▲ *Vulcanologist (volcano scientist).*

▲ *Meteorologist (weather scientist).*

▲ *Town planner (shaping settlements).*

▲ *Sailor. (Which way is land?)*

▲ *Travel agent (sends you packing).*

▲ *Reporter (questions, answers …).*

So geography helps you go places! We hope you have enjoyed what you've learned in this course, and that it will help you on your travels.

Your turn

1 In what ways will the geography you have studied help *you* in your life? You can give your answer as a set of drawings, a spider map or a short essay.

2 See if you can list 10 careers (*excluding* those above) where a knowledge of geography and geographical skills is a help, or essential.

3 a Write this T-shirt slogan in your exercise book. Then explain why it is true, in about 50 words.
   b Now make up another slogan to encourage young people to study geography. Add a logo if you like.

Ordnance Survey symbols

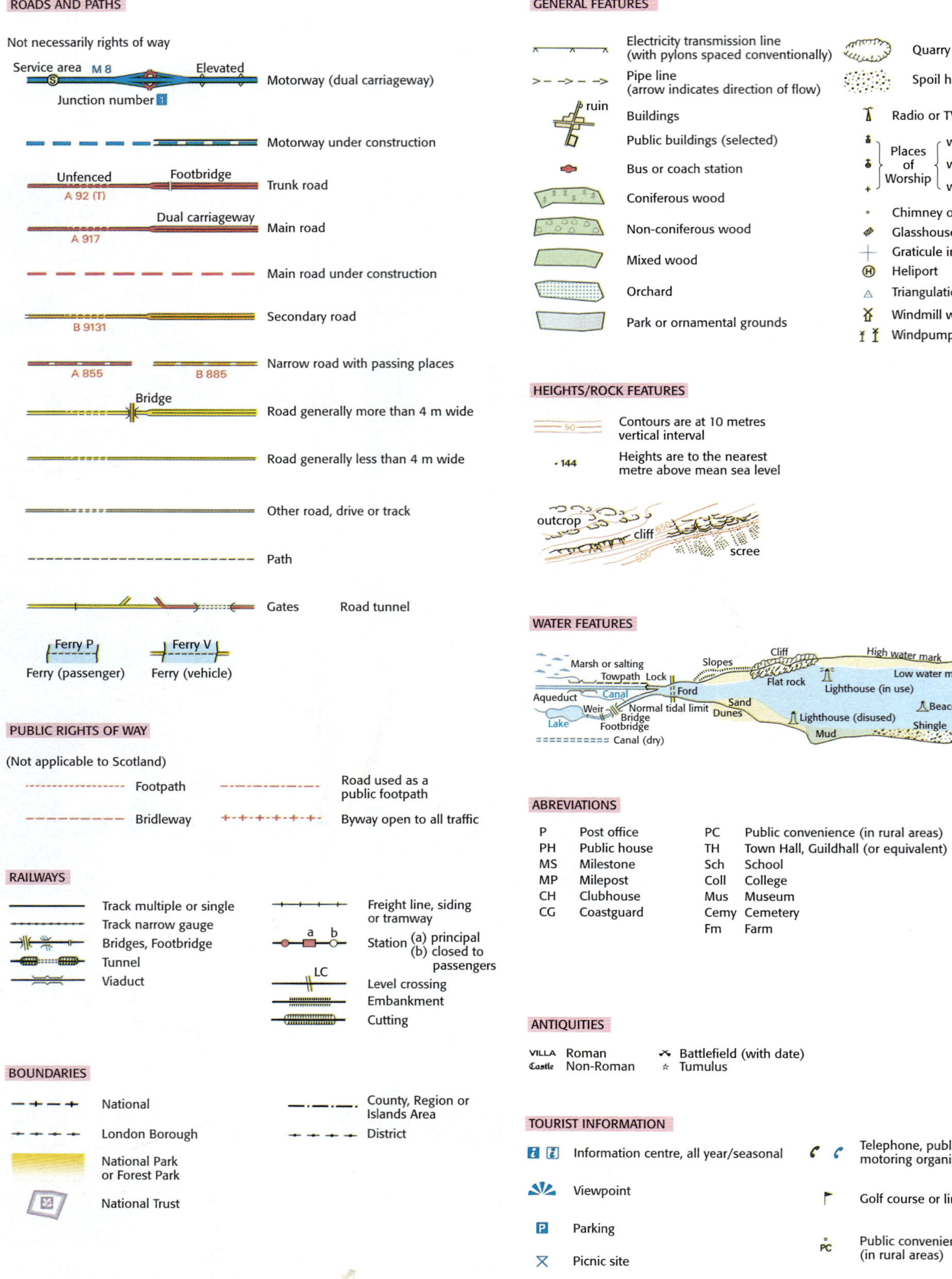

Map of the British Isles

Arctic Ocean
RUSSIA (RUSSIAN FEDERATION)
Moscow
FINLAND
Helsinki
Tallinn
ESTONIA
Riga
LATVIA
Vilnius
LITHUANIA
Minsk
BELARUS
Kiev
UKRAINE
MOLDOVA
Chişnău
Baltic Sea
Stockholm
SWEDEN
NORWAY
Oslo
Copenhagen
DENMARK
Warsaw
POLAND
Berlin
GERMANY
Amsterdam
NETHERLANDS
Brussels
BELGIUM
London
UNITED KINGDOM
Dublin
REPUBLIC OF IRELAND
North Sea
Paris
FRANCE
LUXEMBOURG
Prague
CZECH REPUBLIC
Vienna
AUSTRIA
LIECHTENSTEIN
Bern
SWITZERLAND
Berne
Ljubljana
SLOVENIA
Zagreb
CROATIA
SLOVAKIA
Bratislava
Budapest
HUNGARY
ROMANIA
Bucharest
Belgrade
YUGOSLAVIA
BOSNIA-HERZEGOVINA
Sarajevo
SAN MARINO
ITALY
Rome
MONACO
ANDORRA
SPAIN
Madrid
PORTUGAL
Lisbon
MALTA
BULGARIA
Sofia
Skopje
FYROM
Tiranë
ALBANIA
GREECE
Athens
Mediterranean Sea
Black Sea
Ankara
TURKEY
GEORGIA
Tbilisi
Nicosia
CYPRUS
(Part of Russia)
Atlantic Ocean
ICELAND
Reykjavik
N
Countries named in red are members of the European Union
Scale 1 : 25 000 000

Map of Ghana
BURKINA FASO
Scale 1 : 3 000 000
One centimetre on the map represents 30 kilometres on the ground.
0   30   60   90 km
Bolgatanga
Wa
White Volta
Black Volta
Tamale
IVORY COAST
GHANA
TOGO
BENIN
Lake Volta
Sunyani
Kumasi
Ho
Volta
Koforidua
Accra
N
Cape Coast
Sekondi
ATLANTIC OCEAN
Key
Land height
measured in metres above sea level
more than 1000 m
600 - 1000 m
300 - 600 m
150 - 300 m
less than 150 m
Settlement and transport
capital city
main cities/towns
railways
major roads
Resources
cocoa
oil palm
gold
diamonds
bauxite
manganese

international boundary
capital city
abbreviations
BELG. BELGIUM
B.-H. BOSNIA-HERZEGOVINA
C. CROATIA
CENT. AF. REP. CENTRAL AFRICAN REPUBLIC
CZ. CZECH REPUBLIC
F. FYROM
(Former Yugoslav Republic of Macedonia)
L. LIECHTENSTEIN
LITH. LITHUANIA
LUX. LUXEMBOURG
NETH. NETHERLANDS
S. SLOVENIA
SL. SLOVAKIA
SWITZ. SWITZERLAND
U.A.E. UNITED ARAB EMIRATES
U.S.A. UNITED STATES OF AMERICA
Y. YUGOSLAVIA
Equatorial Scale 1: 95 000 000
Map of the world
Did you know?
The Earth is 4600 million years old.
It weighs 6000 million million million tonnes.
GREENLAND
(Den.)
Nuuk
(Godthåb)
Reyk
Alaska
(U.S.A.)
C A N A D A
Ottawa
U. S. A.
Washington
D.C.
Azores
(Port.)
Bermuda
(U.K.)
Tropic of Cancer
M E X I C O
México
Hawaiian Is.
(U.S.A.)
Havana
Nassau
THE BAHAMAS
CUBA
JAMAICA
Kingston
HAITI
DOMINICAN REPUBLIC
Puerto
Rico
(U.S.A.)
ST. KITTS-NEVIS
ANTIGUA & BARBUDA
DOMINICA
ST. LUCIA
BARBADOS
GRENADA
ST. VINCENT & THE GRENADINES
CAPE VERDE IS.
Belmopan
BELIZE
GUATEMALA
Guatemala
San Salvador
EL SALVADOR
HONDURAS
Tegucigalpa
Managua
NICARAGUA
San José
COSTA RICA
Panamá
PANAMA
Caracas
VENEZUELA
TRINIDAD AND TOBAGO
Georgetown
GUYANA
Paramaribo
SURINAME
Cayenne
FRENCH GUIANA (Fr.)
Bogotá
COLOMBIA
Equator
Galapagos
Is. (Ec.)
Quito
ECUADOR
Tokelau Is.
(N.Z.)
American Samoa
(U.S.A.)
SAMOA
French Polynesia
(Fr.)
P E R U
Lima
B R A Z I L
Brasília
La Paz
BOLIVIA
TONGA
Niue
(N.Z.)
Cook Is.
(N.Z.)
Tropic of Capricorn
Pitcairn Is.
(U.K.)
PARAGUAY
Asunción
A R G E N T I N A
C H I L E
URUGUAY
Santiago
Buenos
Aires
Montevideo
Falkland Is. (U.K.)
Stanley
South Georgia
(U.K.)
North
America
NORTH
ATLANTIC
OCEAN
Europe
Asia
PACIFIC
OCEAN
PACIFIC
OCEAN
Africa
South
America
SOUTH
ATLANTIC
OCEAN
INDIAN
OCEAN
Oceania
SOUTHERN OCEAN
Antarctica
The continents and oceans

124

Amazing – but true!

◆ Nearly 70% of the Earth is covered by saltwater.
◆ Nearly 1/3 is covered by the Pacific Ocean.
◆ 10% of the land is covered by glaciers.
◆ 20% of the land is covered by deserts.

World champions

◆ Largest continent – Asia
◆ Longest river – The Nile, Egypt
◆ Highest mountain – Everest, Nepal
◆ Largest desert – Sahara, North Africa
◆ Largest ocean – Pacific

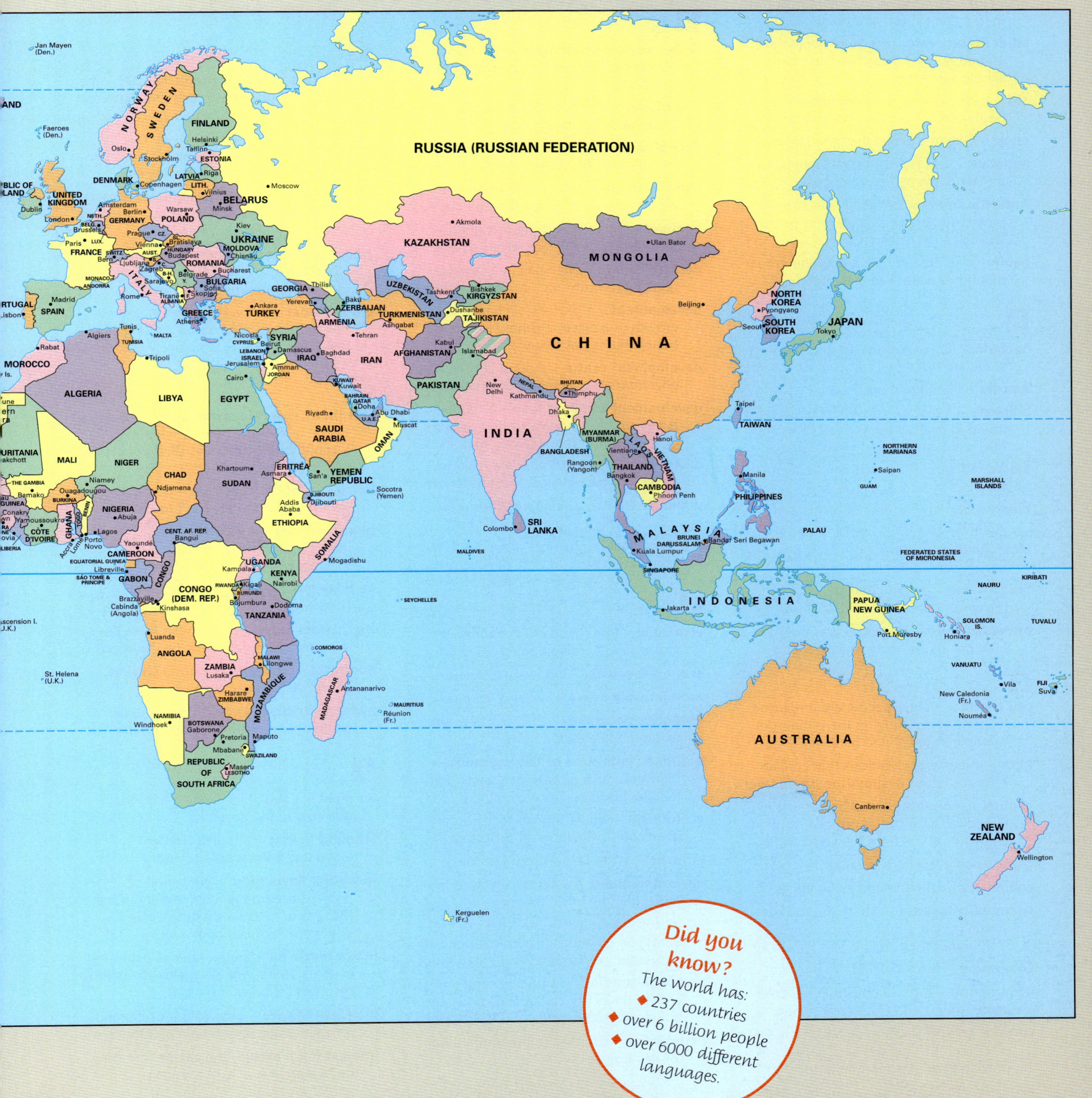

Glossary

A

absolute poverty – so poor that you don't have enough of the basic resources, for example food or clean water

acid rain – rain with acidic gases dissolved in it; it can kill fish and plants

adult literacy rate – the % of people aged 15 and over who can read and write a simple sentence

aid – help given by richer countries to poorer countries; see also *tied aid*

algae – very tiny plants that grow in rivers

annotate – add notes (not just labels) to a map, diagram, text or photo

Antarctic Treaty – the treaty that aims to protect Antarctica as a place of peace and scientific research

aquifer – an area of rock below the ground, that holds water like a sponge

B

bacteria – tiny organisms, each just one cell; some are harmless, some cause disease

bauxite – aluminium ore

bilharzia – a disease caused by tiny worms found in river water; you get fever and may suffer kidney and brain damage

biodegradeable – bacteria can break it down

biodiversity – the variety of plants and animals in a place

biotechnology – making products by using bacteria and other living organisms

brand name – a name that shoppers recognize (like McDonalds)

brownfield site – a site that was already built on, and is being redeveloped

C

call centre – where people are employed to work all day long on the phone (for example in telephone banking)

CFCs – a family of chemicals that contain chlorine, which destroys the ozone layer

cholera – a disease caused by bacteria in dirty drinking water (diarrhoea, vomiting, and you can die from dehydration)

climate – the 'average' weather in a place

colliery – a coal mine and its buildings

community tourism – where the tourists stay in people's homes and villages to learn about their culture and way of life

congestion – overcrowding; traffic jams

conurbation – a continuous built-up area where towns and cities have joined

corridor growth – where development takes place along a line, it makes it easier to provide good transport links

costs and benefits – pros and cons; everything we do has costs and benefits; listing them helps you decide whether an activity is sustainable

D

daily calorie consumption – the average number of calories consumed per person per day

day tripper – a person visiting a place for a day, and not staying over

decentralise – to spread out an industry so that it's not all concentrated in one area

delta – flat area of deposited material at the mouth of a river, where it enters the sea

demand – the total amount of a good or service that people are willing to buy

desertification – when soil in a savanna region gets worn out, dusty and useless

development – a process of change and growth in a place; it should be for the better (but is not always)

development centre – a place chosen (by government) as a focus for development

development compass rose – a framework based on the compass to help you ask questions about people and their lives

development indicators – data used to compare how developed countries are

domestic tourist – being a tourist in the country where you live

drainage basin – the land around a river, from which water drains into the river

E

economic – to do with the economy, money and earning a living

economic activity – work you get paid for

economically active – working for pay

economic geography – is about how and where people earn a living

economic indicators of development – indicators such as GDP per capita that tell you how wealthy a country is

ecotourism – where tourists focus on the plants and animals in an ecosystem

effluent – waste liquid (from factories)

environmentalist – a person involved in protecting the environment

EU (European Union) – the 'club' of European countries that co-operate with each other about trade and other issues

exchange (trading) – a trading centre where commodities like coffee and cocoa are bought and sold on the world market

excursionist – another (more formal) word for day tripper

F

fair trade – where the producer of the goods gets a fair share of the profits

fertilisers – substances put on soil to help crops grow (mostly made in factories)

G

GDP – gross domestic product (GDP) – the total value of all the goods and services produced in a country in a year

GDP per capita – the GDP divided by the population: it gives you an idea of how wealthy the people are, on average

globalisation – the way companies, ideas and lifestyles are spreading round the world with increasing ease

global warming – temperatures around the world are rising, (because of carbon dioxide from burning fossil fuels)

groundwater – rainwater that has soaked down through the ground and filled up the cracks in the rock below

H

HDI (human development index) – a 'score' to indicate how developed a country is; it combines GDP per capita with some social indicators

heavily indebted countries – poor countries with large loans they can't repay

heavy industry – traditional 'bulky' industries such as coal mining, steel making, and ship building

Le Hexagon – France gets called this (because it is shaped like a hexagon)

High Street banks – banks with branches in many towns and cities (eg NatWest)

honeypot – a place that attracts swarms of tourists and day trippers

hydroelectricity – electricity generated when running water spins a turbine

I

ice shelf – a very thick floating ice sheet attached to the coast

inbound tourist – a tourist visiting a country, from another country

Industrial Revolution – the period of history (around the 18th century) when many new machines were invented and many factories built

infant mortality – the number of babies out of every 1000 born alive, who die before their first birthday

interdependence – how countries depend on each other, eg for trade and tourism

interest (on a loan) – the charge for taking out a loan; it is a % of the loan

International tourist – a tourist from another country

L

leakage – how the money tourists pay 'leaks away' from the destination country

LEDC – less economically developed country (one of the poorer countries)

life expectancy – how many years a new baby can expect to live, on average

local actions, global effects – how actions we take can affect people and places in other countries (for better or worse)

M

MEDC – more economically developed country (one of the richer countries)

meteorologist – weather scientist

migrate – to move from one area or country to another (perhaps for work)

millet – a type of cereal crop

N

National Park – a large area protected by law for the benefit of everybody

natural increase – the birth rate minus the death rate, for a place

natural resources – resources that occur naturally, such as oil wells, fertile soil

net donor – the country pays out more than it receives

net migration – the number of people moving into an area minus the number moving out

net recipient – the country receives more than it pays out

NICs (newly industralised countries) – formerly poor countries where the economy is now growing fast

node – a place chosen as a focus or centre (for example for redevelopment)

southern hemisphere – the half of the world south of the equator

O

outbound tourist – a person going off to be a tourist in another country

ozone layer – the layer of ozone gas in the atmosphere that protects us

P

package holiday – where you pay in advance for travel and accommodation

poor south – a term sometimes used for poorer countries (since many are in the southern hemisphere)

population density – the average number of people per square kilometre

population pyramid – a bar graph showing the population divided into males and females of different age groups

porous – has tiny holes that lets water through; gritstone is a porous rock

primary sector (of the economy) – where people are employed in collecting things from the earth (farming, fishing, mining)

processing – converting a material from one form to another (for example cotton to denim or milk to cheese)

profit – left when you subtract the cost of something from what you sold it for

PV cell – cell that converts sunlight straight into electricity; it provides solar power

Q

quaternary sector (of the economy) – involved in hi-tech research

R

raw material – material that has not yet been processed; for example cotton before it is woven into cloth

real GDP per capita – GDP per capita adjusted to allow for different prices (of things like food) in different countries

redevelop – to change or improve a site that has already been in use

redundant – having lost a job

relative poverty – when you are poor compared with most people in your country (but have the basics to survive)

revenue – money you take in from selling goods and services

rich north – a term sometimes used for the richer countries (since most are in the northern hemisphere)

rural – to do with the countryside and small villages

rural depopulation – when the population of a rural area falls (usually because people move away to find work)

S

secondary sector (of the economy) – where people are employed in manufacturing

service sector – see *tertiary sector*

Silicon Glen – the area of Scotland that is home to many hi-tech companies

slave trade – the buying and selling of people to work as slaves (without pay)

social – to do with the way people live

socio-economic – to do with how people live and earn their living (from *social* and *economic*)

solar power – uses energy obtained directly from sunlight; see *PV cell*

southern hemisphere – the half of the world south of the equator

stereotypes – ideas about other races and cultures (or the opposite sex) that we accept as true without thinking

supply – the total amount that's produced, of a good or service

sustainable – can be continued without harm

sustainable development – development that will not lower our quality of life or harm the environment

sustainable tourism – tourism that benefits local people and does as little harm as possible to the environment

sweatshop – a place where people are forced to work long hours for low pay

T

taxes – money we pay to the government; income tax is a % of our income

tertiary sector (of the economy) – where people are employed in providing services (like medical care and transport)

'tied' aid – when one country gets help from another, but has to promise something in return (eg to buy its goods)

Third World – a name sometimes used for the world's poorer countries

Third World debt – the money owed by the poorer countries to the richer ones

TNC (transnational corporation) – company with branches in many countries

tourism – everything to do with tourists, including the activities they take part in and the services that support them

tourist – a person who stays for more than a day in a place that is not his or her usual environment, for any purpose

town planner – a person who helps to plan development in a town; for example where to put new roads and estates

toxic – poisonous

typhoid – a disease you can get from dirty drinking water; you suffer fever and pains in your abdomen, and may die

V

vicious circle – a cycle of events that makes a situation worse and worse

vulcanologist – a volcano scientist

W

web designer – designs websites

weathering – the breaking down of rock; it is caused mainly by the weather

welfare state – a country where the government supports people to keep them out of poverty

World Bank – a joint bank owned by governments of over 180 countries, set up to provide loans for development

WTO (World Trade Organisation) – a body set up to help trade between countries; over 140 countries belong to it

Index

A

absolute poverty 29
aid 22
Akosombo dam (Ghana) 24
algae 86
aluminium 24
Antarctica 98–103
Antarctic polar front 99
Antarctic treaty 101
aquifer 111
Ashfield (Nottinghamshire) 38–39

B

bauxite 24
Benidorm 110–111
biodegradeable 86
biotechnology 40

C

call centres 40
Captain Cook 100
Castleton (Peak District) 94–95
CFCs 102
citizen 116
City of Paris 54
coal industry 36–37
cocoa 21
coffee 76–81
collieries 36
colonised 18
community tourism 114
conflicts (land use) 96
conurbation 54
costs and benefits 97

D

day tripper 104
debt (Third World) 22
decentralise 49
desertification 21
development centres 49
development compass rose 4
development gap 18
development indicators 14
development 12–19
Disneyland Paris 57
drainage basin 84

E

economic activity 32
economic geography 48
ecotourism 15
effluent 86
employment structure 51
EU (European Union) 60–61
Exchange (trading) 78
excursionist 104

F

Fair trade 80
France 42–59

G

Gambia 112–113
GDP (gross domestic product) 14
GDP per capita 14
Ghana 8-11,14–15, 20–21, 24–27
globalisation 65, 72–75
Gold Coast 20
gritstone 92, 93

H

HDI (human development index) 15
heavily indebted countries 23
honeypot 94
hydroelectricity 24, 85
hydrologist 119

I

ICPR (International Commission for
    the Protection of the Rhine) 88
IMF (International Monetary fund)
    22
Industrial Revolution 34, 86
interest (on a loan) 23

L

Lake Constance 85
leakage (in tourism) 113
LECD (less economically developed
    country) 9
Lake Volta 24
life expectancy 14
limestone 92, 93
local actions, global effects 83, 116

M

Marne-la-Vallée 56–57
MEDC 16
meteorologist 119
migration 51
mouth (of river) 84

N

National Park 90
National Park Authority 90, 96
NICs (newly industralised
    countries) 17
Nike 64–67

O

Oxford (on OS map) 32
ozone layer 102

P

package holiday 110
Paris 44–45
Peak District National Park 92–97
phytoplankton 102
poor south 16

porous 93
poverty 10–11, 28–29
primary (economic sector) 34

R

real GDP per capita 16
relative poverty 29
rich north 16
River Rhine 84–89
River Seine 54
River Tajo 111
River Volta 24
Rotterdam 85
rural depopulation 52

S

salmon 88
Sandoz 88
secondary (economic sector) 34
service sector 34
shale 92, 93
Silicon Glen (Scotland) 40
slave trade 18, 20
social indicator of development 14
socio- economic 18
source (of river) 84
St Ives 108–109
stereotypes 43
sustainable (development) 30
sustainable tourism 114–115
sweatshops 68

T

Taff Bargoed Community
    Park 30–31
taxes 28
tertiary (economic sector) 34
Third World 16
Third World debt 22–23
TNC (transnational company) 65
tourism 104–114
tourist 104
town planner 119

V

vulcanologist 119

W

WaterAid 24
welfare state 28
World Bank 22
WTO (World Trade Organisation) 73